CULTURE**SHOCK!**

A Survival Guide to Customs and Etiquette

CZECH REPUBLIC

Tim Nollen

Marshall Cavendish
Editions

Photo Credits:
All photos from the author. ▪ Cover photo: Haga Photo Library.

All illustrations by TRIGG

First published in 1997
Copyright © 2005 Marshall Cavendish International (Asia) Private Limited

This edition published in 2006 by:
Marshall Cavendish Limited
119 Wardour Street
London W1F 0UW
E-mail: enquiries@marshallcavendish.co.uk

Other Marshall Cavendish Offices:
Marshall Cavendish International (Asia) Private Limited. 1 New Industrial Road, Singapore 536196 ▪ Marshall Cavendish Corporation. 99 White Plains Road, Tarrytown NY 10591-9001, USA ▪ Marshall Cavendish Beijing. D31A, Huatingjiayuan, No. 6, Beisihuanzhonglu, Chaoyang District, Beijing, The People's Republic of China, 100029 ▪ Marshall Cavendish International (Thailand) Co Ltd. 253 Asoke, 12th Flr, Sukhumvit 21 Road, Klongtoey Nua, Wattana, Bangkok 10110, Thailand ▪ Marshall Cavendish (Malaysia) Sdn Bhd, Times Subang, Lot 46, Subang Hi-Tech Industrial Park, Batu Tiga, 40000 Shah Alam, Selangor Darul Ehsan, Malaysia

Marshall Cavendish is a trademark of Times Publishing Limited

ISBN : 0-462-00804-5

Printed in Singapore by Times Graphics Pte Ltd

ABOUT THE SERIES

Culture shock is a state of disorientation that can come over anyone who has been thrust into unknown surroundings, away from one's comfort zone. *CultureShock!* is a series of trusted and reputed guides which has, for decades, been helping expatriates and long-term visitors to cushion the impact of culture shock whenever they move to a new country.

Written by people who have lived in the country and experienced culture shock themselves, the authors share all the information necessary for anyone to cope with these feelings of disorientation more effectively. The guides are written in a style that is easy to read and covers a range of topics that will arm readers with enough advice, hints and tips to make their lives as normal as possible again.

Each book is structured in the same manner. It begins with the first impressions that visitors will have of that city or country. To understand a culture, one must first understand the people—where they came from, who they are, the values and traditions they live by, as well as their customs and etiquette. This is covered in the first half of the book

Then on with the practical aspects—how to settle in with the greatest of ease. Authors walk readers through how to find accommodation, get the utilities and telecommunications up and running, enrol the children in school and keep in the pink of health. But that's not all. Once the essentials are out of the way, venture out and try the food, enjoy more of the culture and travel to other areas. Then be immersed in the language of the country before discovering more about the business side of things.

To round off, snippets of basic information are offered before readers are 'tested' on customs and etiquette of the country. Useful words and phrases, a comprehensive resource guide and list of books for further research are also included for easy reference.

CONTENTS

FOREWORD

Czechs are relatively unknown outside their own country, so most people coming to the Czech Republic for the first time have little or no idea what to expect. As a small nation located in the heart of central Europe, the Czech lands have experienced an extraordinarily rich cultural development—and a tumultuous political history, particularly in the 20th century. Forty-one years of Communism came abruptly to an end with the November 1989 'Velvet Revolution,' and since then the Czech lands have enjoyed an exuberant, refreshing, and often complicated independence on the path to membership in the European Union. The transformation to a democratic, market-based society has brought about fundamental change to the people, yet through it all the Czechs retain a unique pride and a humble, quirky zest for life.

Getting to know the Czechs and their culture can be an enriching, if at times trying experience. The purpose of this book is to help you anticipate the differences you will encounter, and ultimately help you not only appreciate these–be they joys or difficulties–but come to love them. You'll probably find, as most long-term foreign residents do, that when the time comes to leave you won't want to go.

A disclaimer must be made: the perspective taken here is an American one. That said, I have tried to take as Czech a perspective on things as possible, and I would note that my American viewpoint may be tempered somewhat after having lived in England and Belgium in stages of my life prior to living in the Czech Republic and having since been married to a wonderful Czech woman for many years. The commentary provided in this book is the result of personal observations, interviews with Czech and foreign nationals on the general topic, and interpretations of published sociological research. I have tried throughout to maintain as balanced a perspective as possible, though at times this may come forth as either overexuberant or overly critical. Certainly, my own cultural background and personal opinions show through at times. While generalising, these comments do attempt to capture common traits and mannerisms of the Czech people; it helps that the country is quite small and homogeneous.

While certain of these do not apply to all people in all situations, I hope you'll find this to be a useful guide to understanding both common foreign perceptions of Czechs, and general Czech perceptions of themselves and others.

The Czech Republic I came to know in the early 1990s was vibrant and welcoming, especially to Americans such as myself—but times and attitudes have shifted somewhat since, and the eagerness with which foreigners (especially Americans) were received has become more a weariness. Let's face it: western, particularly American, culture and lifestyles have saturated the Czech Republic, and many Czechs are frankly tired of it all by now. All the more imperative to assimilate and respect the culture you are about to learn—and all the more opportunity to make real friends and have real professional progress by really sinking in. Most importantly, remember that your experience in the Czech Republic will only be what you make of it.

Organisation of the Book

This book is about living in the Czech Republic, as opposed to travelling here, and the focus is more on life in Prague, which is where more expatriates in the country are located. The perspective applies to Czechs in general and I have made every effort to incorporate insights from other regions as well, gleaned from family and friends living in smaller towns throughout the country.

The emphasis is on the people themselves: after providing a historical background, we dive right into the heart and soul of the Czech character and temperament. Using this as a basis, we proceed to describe social organisation and family life. As most people coming to the country are involved in business, we give a thorough account of standard business practices–and how these can differ from what you may be used to. The rest of the book is concerned with practical matters of communicating, socialising, experiencing Czech culture (including entertainment, food and drink) and dealing with all the nuts and bolts of settling in, from finding a home to setting up a bank account. It's not always easy, but we hope that through this insider's introduction to the people, you'll gain an insight to the intriguing and beguiling world of the Czechs.

What Is Culture Shock?

The most exciting thing about spending any period of time in a foreign country is getting to know the people—and this indeed is the culture shock: the adaptation to foreign customs, mannerisms and traditions. Living in the Czech Republic can be thrilling, beautiful and enriching beyond anything you could imagine—but it can also be frustrating, grey and difficult if you don't approach it with an eager and open mind.

Because the task of relocating can be so logistically complicated and, at times, emotionally overwhelming, it is important to be aware of the culture to which you are moving; that's why this book came into being. The name, culture shock, is a real emotional state that one goes through when adjusting to a different culture.

Perhaps 'shock' is not quite the right word for it, because what you experience in fact is less shock than dulled confusion. This can be a very sensitive thing—sometimes you don't realise why you get frustrated all of a sudden, or why you find yourself blatantly criticising those around you. What's shocking about it is that it can be so subtle, and you'll have a hard time recognising the symptoms.

The stages of culture shock are usually described as going from euphoria in the first month or two, to a rather sudden low period during the third to sixth month or so, to a gradual reawakening to your new country, with a stronger sense of confidence and energy. These time periods can vary considerably, and they can even recur during the stay.

The initial excitement of moving to a foreign country is what brings about the euphoria--and especially in a city like Prague, you'll undoubtedly find yourself walking on clouds. Everything is so new to you that you see every day as a new adventure.

By the time your daily routine is established, you've become more familiar with the difficulties of communicating in a strange language, of not being able to get your favorite coffee, and of being away from your friends at home. There will be times when you find yourself criticising little things, blaming them on your host people, and not understanding why you're so down all the time. If you arrive in the Czech Republic in the fall, this can be particularly hazardous, as winters here are long.

There is a useful and important defense against this blackness: don't start questioning yourself, and don't start lashing out at these strange customs and mannerisms. Just realize that this is a common, cyclical experience that everyone goes through in one form or another—and therefore don't let yourself get too down when the going gets tough. Continue to approach with an open and eager mind: to progress in learning about the culture, in language study and in new friendships as much as possible. Try not to spend too much time with other expatriates complaining about the differences, even though this is easy to do and can help in letting off steam. This down phase can be very deceptive: it's not really a depression or a shock, it's a frustration and a confusion, which can take any form of mildness or severity. This is the hardest time, but it will pass. Those who give up during the low period and go home often regret it later.

By the sixth to ninth month or so, you've lived through the hard times and you'll 'suddenly' realise that you can speak some Czech, that you have some good friends and colleagues, and that you know something about the culture—and this is really what the experience of living abroad is about. Most people find that by the end of the first year, they feel they are finally beginning to really know the culture; deeper understanding then takes place during the second year and beyond.

GOING HOME— CULTURE SHOCK IN REVERSE

Strange as it seems, going back home after living abroad is often much more difficult than moving abroad in the first place. You expect things to be different and confusing when you go elsewhere, but coming home should be so easy and natural, right? Wrong.

While you've been away, you've had experiences which could never have happened at home—and you've grown immeasurably from them. Meanwhile, your friends and colleagues have gone through changes of their own, which you haven't been a part of. It takes time to get back into the swing of things, and you're apt to find that once you do so, it lacks the day-to-day excitement of living in a different culture. Having got to know a different part of the world, and hence expanded your horizons, home will feel smaller and more restricting—not quite like the home it used to be.

So just as you go through periods of depression and frustration when you live abroad, you unwittingly do the same upon your return, and it's even more 'shocking' because you feel a stranger in your own home. Again, let things unwind on their own, think positively about all you've learned while you were away, and realise that reverse culture shock—re-adapting to home life—is just as natural as adjusting to a foreign culture in the first place.

ACKNOWLEDGEMENTS

Like so many other foreigners I've met in the Czech Republic, my first taste of the land and the people in 1991 was thrilling and intriguing. Something in the people resonated wonderfully well with me—although I have no Czech ancestry, I nevertheless found myself drawn naturally into the culture and society. Having originally come for a short stay, I lived in Prague for over five years. Although I am now back in my native United States, I had the great fortune to meet my future wife in Prague, and I return frequently to my adopted home.

Living in the Czech Republic was not all rosy at it seems in retrospect, of course—culture shock for me took on many guises of frustration and boredom, yet as I worked on this book I was able to see clearly why I love this country: it is simply a beautiful, rich, and endearing place. Being away from the country for several years now has helped crystallise some of my observations, and on numerous return trips I've revisited these thoroughly. As the country has been through some immensely difficult periods since the first edition of this book appeared in 1997—through a deep and lengthy economic recession and towards EU membership, through bouts of political malaise, and the through the social changes that have accompanied these—I have rewritten large portions of the text to capture the variations.

Many thanks are due to everyone who has helped me and this book along the way: in roughly chronological order this includes: the staffs at SFC and at SPUSA who helped me get my feet on the ground; Aleš Kaňka, Jarmila Kotůlková, Aleš Bílek, Ludmila Šímková and the Holeňa family; Iva Slámová; Honza Jančar and family; Luboš Ziegler and Bobo; Karel and Eva Pulkrabovi; everyone at PRS, especially Michele Van Saun and Joe Toul, David Biskup, Jiří Flaks; Pat Hertel; Jiří Navrátil; Kelly Joyce; those who aided in the research of this book: Jonathan Griffiths for the original contact and assistance, Ng Li-San and Natalie Thompson for the update; Steve Setian, Chris DesForges, Ekko Kisjes and Janny, Hans-Peter Grimm, Martin Stanley, Odile Cisneros, David deVries, Guillaume Bastard, Leandro Palazolo, Anděla Malá and family; and Mom, Dad and 'Tine.

MAP OF CZECH REPUBLIC

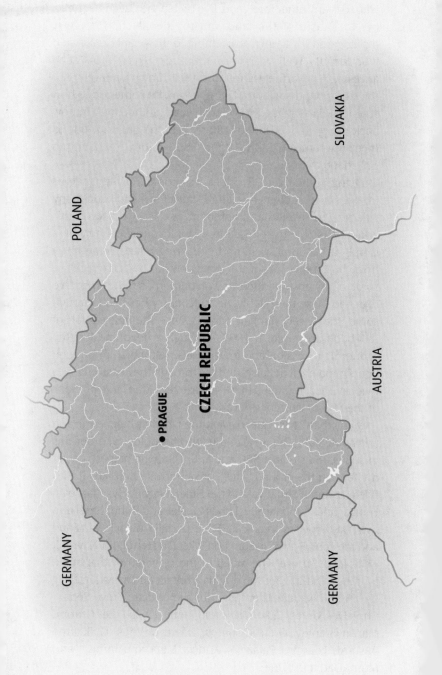

FIRST IMPRESSIONS

CHAPTER 1

'Prague seemed—it still seems, after many rival cities—
not only one of the most beautiful places in the world,
but one of the strangest. Fear, piety, zeal, strife and pride,
tempered in the end by the milder impulses of munificence
and learning and *douceur de vivre*, had flung up an unusual
array of grand and unenigmatic monuments... Prague, of
all my halts including Vienna itself, was the place which the
word *Mitteleuropa*, and all that it implies, fitted most aptly.'
—Patrick Leigh Fermor, *A Time of Gifts*

"YOU'RE GOING TO THE CZECH REPUBLIC? Oh, I've heard Prague is beautiful!" Rare is the person who has not heard this comment, and for good reason. Prague is one of the most visually stunning cities in Europe, if not the world, and your first impression upon arrival in Prague will undoubtedly be of its sheer gorgeous beauty. The castle high above the river, the quaint medieval streets and alleyways, the imposing Gothic churches and Baroque halls, the cafés and pubs and galleries beckoning—all unite to stir the senses. And this sentiment will remain with you throughout your stay, whether it is for a day or for a lifetime.

In such a setting is an air of infinite possibility, which exudes not only from the physical presence, but through something intangible as well. It is the sense of being in a new place, among a people with a deep-rooted sense of self and a laid-back—indeed 'bohemian'—manner, yet a people for whom socio-economic life has been, and continues to be, transformed rapidly. Being part of this evolving culture imparts a real feeling of connection.

NEW DISCOVERIES

Most visitors to the Czech Republic know very little about the history or culture before they go, or indeed about anything other than Charles Bridge and perhaps the good beer. Soon after arrival, those who enter with openness and eagerness often find it ripe for new discoveries, which can be both

Prague Castle Gardens—the lion is on the Czech national seal.

invigorating and rejuvenating. This can come in the form of a sudden appreciation of architecture or of pastoral, rural landscapes within easy reach of the capital, or a recognition of the business opportunities available in a market that is still rapidly changing.

Other sentiments and moods filter in too, and not all of them necessarily positive. Architectural beauty spurns a huge tourist industry, so you'll hardly be alone admiring the views. And the natives? You may find it hard to meet Czechs, unless you have an inside angle, such as through friends, work or study. On the streets, few Czechs seem to take the time to stroll and enjoy life. Many are in such a hurry to make that next meeting or get home to fix dinner for the kids. On the buses, trams and underground, Czechs seem to be invariably withdrawn and glum, especially in winter, and attitudes in shops and office settings can often be short and gruff. In pubs, small groups of friends sit, self-absorbed, around half-litres of beer. In addition, Prague is not all glory and glamour: outside the central districts and a few choice suburbs are sprawling stretches of drab brown or grey housing blocks; should you find yourself holed up here for work or cheaper accommodation, you will find the contrast quite striking.

Outside of Prague it can be a little simpler. While so many people laud the majesty of Prague, so few make it outside the capital, and this is a real loss for them. The Czech countryside is subtly and wonderfully appealing, with rolling hills, quaintly preserved towns and oftentimes more approachable and amiable inhabitants. Just travelling through the Czech countryside awakens the senses to the simple splendour of a largely unspoilt place. Everything is as it should be: a castle pokes up atop a distant hill, a stream meanders through a shady glen, and a walk through the forest ends at a local pub.

A flip side to this, of course, is a sense of provincialism among the people, just as you would find in any other country—local ways tend to be constrained by custom, and you as a foreigner may meet some initial resistance, not for anything you've done, but simply because you are not one of them.

Stay just a little longer, and you will begin to sense a few more traits. Modesty and humility are noticeable in everything, from the quiet tones of most conversations to the shyness you may encounter when in the presence of Czechs for the first time. Accompanying this is a certain folkiness, a down-to-earth simplicity and easy-going approach toward life, which, combined with the straightforward sense of place that most Czechs possess, produces a genuine likeability. Czechs are generally well-educated, with an eagerness to learn and a quick wit to boot—this can serve both you and them well in initial conversations or business transactions.

This modesty can, of course, take another form, which I speak about further in the chapter entitled 'Czech Characteristics': humility can manifest itself as a sense of littleness or insignificance, and this can make it difficult to get things done when your Czech colleagues or acquaintances feel incapable of moving forward. This is also contrasted at times by a brashness among some, particularly the young and those with experience in international business or other affairs, who seem to purposely disregard more traditional habits and adopt a careless, even reckless approach to life. These can, at times, be your more progressive business partners, but at other times they can also exhibit naiveté and hastiness.

A SHIFT IN IDENTITY?

Finally, like it or not, the Czech Republic is rapidly becoming very similar on the surface in many ways to its EU neighbours such as Germany and Austria, and the infusion of American influences is as widespread here now as just about anywhere. Proximity and the easing of border controls has led to rapid commercialisation, and this often means standardisation of goods and services. This has both its positive and negative sides: while economic progress surely is good for society as a whole, life has become much more competitive and therefore difficult for some, and at the same time, the world is becoming more monotone: certain parts of Prague, such as the upscale shops on Na příkopě may be indistinguishable from similar shopping districts in Paris or Vienna, and

Czechs throughout the country aspire to many of the same comforts and conveniences as do people anywhere else in the world.

I confess many of my first impressions from my first visit in 1991 are deeply ingrained in my psyche, and yet these may not quite be the reality of things anymore. I have photos taken in Old Town Square in Prague on a warm afternoon in the middle of August, 1991 with only a few souls wandering around and not a café table to be seen; now, it's almost hard to walk through the square at all for the hordes of tourists and the amenities to serve them. I had no problem at all meeting Czechs in the early 1990s, as I was such as novelty at the time; now, I'm just another annoying American to them, even in small towns in the countryside. Where I used to struggle to find products such as deodorant and fresh orange juice in shops, I now have practically the same choice in Prague

Likely Immediate Impressions

- **Beauty**—both of the cities and the countryside
- **Folkiness**—in the laid-back attitudes and deep sense of self-identity among the Czechs
- **A sense of possibility**—novelty and mystery conspire to produce an eagerness to explore the cultural as well as the commercial opportunities
- **Difficulty in approaching the locals**—modesty and provincialism can make it hard to get to know the Czechs. In the worst cases, this can mean a sense of impossibility at getting things done; you may soon be drawing on your reserves of patience.
- **Increasing feeling of convergence of Czech ways with European standards**—the rapid exposure to so many influences since 1989 has brought a familiarity and commonality to some material and social things.

as I have in Manhattan (and that's becoming less and less of an exaggeration).

Despite the enormous changes since 1989, fundamental character traits do remain largely intact, and Czechs retain a beguiling, sometimes quirky and generally appealing personality that you will likely want to get to know better. And the beauty of the country is untouchable: for this alone, Prague will remain an eminently attractive city to visit and live, and the Czech countryside will likewise continue to be a beautiful place to relax and explore. Your first impressions will be true, and with an inquisitive spirit you'll find yourself drawn in, hoping to learn more and gain a deeper perspective on all things Czech.

HISTORY, POLITICS, ECONOMICS AND RELIGION

CHAPTER 2

'The Czechs' propensity to 'bend' before
superior force was not necessarily a weakness.
Rather, their metaphysical view of life encouraged
them to look on acts of force as ephemera.'
—Bruce Chatwin, *Utz*

WHO ARE THE CZECHS?

The words 'Bohemia' and 'Czech' both come down to us from the first ancient settlers of the land. 'Bohemia' is a derivation from the Boii tribe, a group of Celts who inhabited the western region of what is today the Czech Republic as early as 300 BC. Czechs themselves do not use the term though; they call the region Čechy, the word coming from the legend of a man named Čech who led his early Slavic followers Moses-like to the top of Říp Hill in north Bohemia.

As the words Bohemia and Czech both refer to the western part of the country, they should, in their strictest sense, only be associated with the inhabitants of this region. In the Czech language, it is a misnomer to call the entire country Čechy: the eastern region (approximately the eastern third) is known as Moravia (Morava) and its inhabitants as Moravians. The language is the same, but Moravians claim a slightly different culture pointing to their short-lived kingdom known as the Great Moravian Empire, which ruled the area from the years AD 830–907. Moravia is geographically separated (loosely as it is) by the Bohemian–Moravian highlands and Moravians cling a bit more strongly to their folk traditions. Moravians also claim to speak a more refined, polished and textbook-precise Czech. The differences between Bohemians and Moravians are in fact so slight that you'll hardly notice them at first, though if you do have Moravian friends or colleagues, you'll impress them by being conscious of the distinction.

It's geographically and ethnically correct to refer to Prague as a Czech city and Brno as a Moravian one, but for practical purposes, it's all just called Czech.

Along the northern border with Poland lies the small area known as Silesia (Slezsko), again with a slightly different cultural heritage. Silesia and the Silesian people are a vague concept though, as there never was a Silesian state. The people are historically a mix of Poles, Germans, Czechs and Moravians, inhabiting the region which runs along the border and into southern Poland.

The very name of the country that is now the Czech Republic has changed several times over the course of its political development, and is still a source of confusion to some. This book occasionally uses the term 'the Czech lands' to represent the lands that the Czechs inhabit, that is, Bohemia, Moravia and Silesia. Through most of the 20th century, the state of Czechoslovakia was a union of what are now the Czech and Slovak Republics; the two split amicably in 1993. This split was so peaceful, in fact, that it came to be known as the 'Velvet Divorce,' which is probably why many people outside the country still call it by its old name. Incidentally, when the separation occurred, there was some debate in the new government over what in fact the country should be named. The word Czech is an adjective, so it needed a substantive—Czechomoravia would have been a convenient and fair name, but then that would have left Silesia out, so they opted for the simplest solution.

East Versus West

Czechs don't like to be referred to as eastern Europeans. Since the end of the Cold War, this division of Europe into two parts has become outdated.

Historically, the Czech lands have always been a key player in central Europe, literally a crossroads between the east and west, and this geographical position has always been an important factor in its own economic and cultural development. The 'west' is often referred to casually as western Europe and North America, though the changes going on now throughout the Czech Republic will soon render it nearly as western as any of the western EU countries that it has now officially joined—certainly much more so than most of its neighbours further to the east. So while 'eastern Europe' is an easy tag word to use, the sense of it is becoming less and less defined.

The population of the Czech Republic is approximately 10.2 million, though there are several hundred thousand Czech nationals living in the United States, Canada and western Europe, countries to which Czechs emigrated throughout the 19th century, and to which they escaped during the Nazi and Soviet occupations. Pockets of Czech culture have held together in US cities such as Chicago and New York; rural communities in eastern Iowa, Nebraska and central Texas (not to mention a newer wave of Czechs in more fun areas such as Colorado and south Florida); parts of Canada and Australia; and even towards the east in Ukraine and Kazakhstan.

A HISTORICAL BACKGROUND

We really have to go all the way back to the beginning of the Czech nation to properly understand the culture. Czechs hold a strong identity with their early ancestors, who ruled over long periods of peace and prosperity before and throughout the Middle Ages. The political story of the Czech lands from the 1500s to 1989 was almost exclusively one of non-independence, so today's Czechs take special pride in their past glory, and in their more recent successes at breaking the hold of foreign domination.

Ancient and Medieval Times

Czechs are a Slavic people, descendants of agrarian tribes who migrated to the region from the east around the 6th century B.C, when Celts were dispersed throughout central Europe. The early Slavs lived a peaceful existence, farming and living in close-knit communities, and initially adhering to pagan religious practices. For centuries, the Slavs intermingled with the Franks, a Germanic tribe with whom they alternately warred and traded. In fact, most Czech towns that were founded between the 10th and 13th centuries had large numbers of German burghers;

some cities, such as České Budějovice (Budweis), were almost entirely German.

The first formal state ruled by Slavs emerged in the form of the Great Moravian Empire in AD 830, under the leadership of Mojmír. This extended throughout much of central Europe, encompassing parts of present-day Poland, Germany, Austria and Hungary. The Great Moravian Empire held a tense balance of power in the area, though only for a matter of several decades, cautiously holding the fort against Frankish and Magyar advances. One long-term effect of the empire proved significant though: in 863 Mojmír's successor, Rastislav, invited the mission of Cyril and Methodius from the Byzantine Empire. They created a new alphabet (Cyrillic), used today (in Russian, Serbian and Bulgarian), and spread the Christian gospel in local tongues. But after Methodius' death, subsequent rulers moved closer to the Roman Catholic Church and the Latin script came to replace Cyrillic.

Loket Castle is a prime example of the stern Gothic style which can be seen in the castles throughout the country.

By 907 the Magyars, predecessors to today's Hungarians, had made successful advances into neighbouring Slovakia and effectively dismantled the Moravian Empire. This event had a lasting effect on the history of the Czech and Slovak nations: for the next millennium the Slovaks were heavily influenced, indeed controlled by Hungarians, while Bohemia edged to the west.

As the Great Moravian Empire was falling, the Přemyslid dynasty was rising in Bohemia, where Czech princes and warriors were baptised in 845. Their power was consolidated by Prince Bořivoj, who Christianised a still-pagan people. Bořivoj's grandson Václav (Wenceslas in English) is the first Czech national hero, an intelligent, enlightened leader whose status was further heightened to martyrdom and sainthood after being assassinated by his brother Boleslav the Cruel in 929 (or 935, according to which source you use). Boleslav concentrated power by annexing Moravia and Silesia and establishing a bishopric at the church of St Vitus, which Václav had founded. By the end of the 10th century, the Přemysls had consolidated power, and the position of Prague and the Czech lands was strengthened through the course of the 11th and 12th centuries.

In 1198, Přemysl Otakar I gained permanent hereditary royal status for the Přemyslid dynasty, as recognised by both the Holy Roman Emperor and the Pope, and subsequent Czech kings became important participants in the affairs of the Roman Empire. The economy was powerful at this time, especially during the reign of Otakar II (1253–1278) as evidenced in the establishment of many towns and cities, the building of castles, and the spread of Christianity. By the late 1200s, however, the kingdom had become unstable due to weaker leadership, and the dynasty collapsed in 1306 with the murder of King Václav III, the dynasty's last male member, in the city of Olomouc.

The kingdom was taken over by John of Luxembourg, leader of the House of Luxembourg, who became king through marriage with Václav III's daughter; this effectively held back an early Hapsburg attempt at the throne. John's reign was both grand and ineffective. A truly cosmopolitan king, he forged political ties throughout central and western Europe, winning sympathisers as far off as England. Meanwhile, however, he did not comprehend the political situation in Bohemia, and the country experienced a steady economic slide as he focused almost exclusively on international affairs. These affairs included military excursions to other states—which ultimately let to his death in battle at Crécy in France in 1346. Through the wealth of political and cultural exchange, however, John planted the seeds for the humanist tradition that set the stage for Bohemia's greatest monarch of the entire era.

King Charles IV: The Golden Age

The kingdom came to such bad shape under John that the nobility invited his son Charles (Karel) from France in 1333 to manage the state, and it soon recovered considerably. In 1346, Charles was elected Holy Roman Emperor (from this point on he was known as Charles IV), and moved the Imperial Court to Prague. His reign is considered the Golden Age in Czech history, with territorial consolidation (the kingdom came to be known as the Lands of the Czech Crown, which existed until 1918), a cultural boom, and great economic prosperity due in part to the mining and minting of silver in the town of Kutná Hora. This led to the development of Prague into a great architectural city, with the expansion of St Vitus Cathedral, the building of Charles Bridge and Nové město (New Town) and the establishment of Charles University. Not only was Charles successful in the Czech lands: through smart diplomacy, he kept a relative peace throughout the entire Roman empire.

Charles's act was hard to follow. His oldest son, Václav IV, was a controversial personality, not concerned with his royal duties, and subject to drinking

Europe's Hardships

Europe meanwhile was suffering through universal crises. The papacy was torn asunder by the Great Schism, when a rival pope established himself in Avignon, raising cries for religious reform. Furthermore, a horrible epidemic of the plague passed through Europe in 1380, decimating the population and prompting the emerging religious reformers to declare this as punishment for the sins of the age. These crises had a particularly devastating impact in Bohemia, as they came after decades of order and wealth.

bouts and fits of rage. The state of Bohemia declined in the late 14th century, due to internal conflicts and economic depression, to such a point that Václav IV was ultimately removed from the throne and imprisoned by the nobility.

Jan Hus and the Hussite Wars: Religious Turmoil

Charles University became a centre of the growing movement for church reform, which was essentially at the heart of all social and political matters. Preacher and educator Jan Hus (often written as John Huss in English) became a powerful figure as a passionate speaker on religious reform, crying out that the church ought to be rid of its material possessions and return to its spiritual mission, that of observing the Bible. His work was influenced by English thinker John Wycliffe, and he in turn influenced the work of Martin Luther; the three together are considered the fathers of the Protestant faith. Hus was rector of Charles University under the blessing of Václav IV, and he used this educational platform to set the rules for the spelling of the Czech language that are still followed today. He extended this work into a belief that university courses and church services should be conducted in the native tongue, as opposed to the formal Latin that the Church used. This among other political squabbles caused practically all the foreign professors and students to leave, which brought down the intellectual and cosmopolitan character of the university. All this of course did not ingratiate him well with the authorities in Rome, and Hus was summoned before the Council of Constance, accused of heresy, and ultimately burned at the stake in 1415 for refusing to recant.

The execution of Jan Hus was felt as an outrageous insult to Czech religious reformers, and it served to deepen the split between the reformers and the Church, with the reformers taking the stance that they were a chosen people whose mission was to liberate Europe from its current evils. A few years after Hus's execution, a nationwide crusade run by his followers, the Hussites, rampaged throughout the country. Two factions of this movement soon emerged: the Utraquists, who founded their belief in his teachings, and the more radical Taborites, who took his message to the extreme and became a powerful military force. The Utraquists took their name from *utra que unum*, 'in one kind,' where the bread and the wine were both to be taken at the communion by all members of the congregation, rather than the established Catholic practice of reserving the wine for the priests. Taborites took their name from the town of Tábor, south of Prague, which they set up as a base camp for their communal lifestyle. Re-strengthening of Catholicism in Prague, together with growing religious persecution of the Hussites, however, soon sent them on the warpath.

On 30 July 1419, a mob of Hussite radicals led by Jan Želivský stormed the New Town Hall in Prague's Karlovo náměstí, tossing resident Catholic councillors out of the windows onto waiting spikes of the masses below; this came to be known as the first defenestration (literally, 'from the window') of Prague. Hussite military leader Jan Žižka marauded his troops across the land, destroying all signs of Catholicism they could lay their hands on, demolishing many of Prague's churches and halls, burning books and paintings and attacking homes of the wealthy. Meanwhile the rift between the Taborites and the Utraquists (and many other factions in the reform camp) grew, though they did come together to form alliances against what they perceived as the same enemy—the Roman Catholic Church. However the Utraquists came to a compromise with Rome at the Council of Basel in 1433. The next year, the Utraquists defeated the Taborites at Lipany, with the aid of Catholic forces. Overall it was a period of 14 years of appalling destruction, bloodshed and terror, which detracted from economic development. Eventually, Zikmund, the Holy Roman Emperor, was recognised King of Bohemia by the reluctant Czechs, but the years after his death in 1437 were a time of conflict over the throne, with the Hapsburgs and the Polish Jagellonian dynasty jostling for position.

The chaos was solved by the election of Jiří z Poděbrad (George of Poděbrady), who became the nation's one and only Hussite king. Elected in 1458 at Prague's Old Town Hall, he was the accepted leader of Hussites and Catholics alike, preaching religious tolerance and pacifism and presiding over a period of relative calm and prosperity. 'Rather prudence and discretion than weaponry' was his motto, words that guided his progressive reign until 1471. Jiří's early death again brought chaos to Bohemia, as no clear successor to the throne emerged. Power struggles left the country in a void as the Jagellonians of Poland ruled in absentia, until Ferdinand I of Hapsburg was elected king in 1526 by the nobility. Ferdinand won with an offer to pay off half the royal debt and a promise to respect the privileges of the Czech nobility, both of which he abandoned soon after taking over as ruler of the soon-to-be most powerful dynasty in Europe.

The Hapsburg Era

This began a long period of Hapsburg presence in Bohemia and Moravia. Ferdinand re-strengthened the position of the Catholic church, though his efforts met with much opposition from the Czech Estates, who had considerable power as the ruling nobility, and from the growing Protestant faith. Most of the 16th century was therefore vacuous, with decisions from Vienna meeting little approval with the Czech Estates, whose power was, however, diminishing. The Czech defensive position was symbolised by Protestant leader and educator Jan Amos Komenský (known to English speakers as Comenius), leader of the Czech Brethren who was forced into exile for much of his life.

The late 1500s and early 1600s belonged to Rudolf II, an eccentric figure who moved the Imperial Court from Vienna back to Prague, though he was more concerned with satisfying his own quirky interests than in the administration and justification of either church or state. Rudolf brought to Prague a host of astronomers and alchemists, and was a great patron of the arts, engaging some of Europe's greatest architects and sculptors and buying up a fine collection of paintings. Leaving the actual governing up to trusted advisors, Rudolf's delving into witchcraft was impetus enough to take attention away from matters at hand, and his reversal of the policy of religions tolerance and support of the Catholic

Counter-Reformation opened the way for Protestants to re-form rebellious sentiments.

Tensions peaked in 1618 with the city's second defenestration: two imperial governors were thrown out of a window in Prague Castle. As with the first defenestration of 1419, this event was the radical push needed to start a religious war. The 1618 defenestration was the culmination of the frustration of the Protestant Estates (both Czech and German), and it effectively kicked off the Thirty Years' War, a battle between Catholics and Protestants which spread over much of northern and central Europe.

The civil uprising in Prague was short-lived. The Czechs didn't stand much of a chance, and though they attempted to organise an army with soldiers hired from their allies, they were routed at the Battle of Bílá Hora (Battle of White Mountain) just outside Prague, on 8 November 1620. A furious Ferdinand II underlined his power by publicly executing 27 Bílá Hora rebel leaders at Prague's Old Town Square on 21 June 1621; the spot is marked today by white stone crosses. In a single day the fate of the nation was sealed until 1918.

Hapsburg general Albrecht von Wallenstein (known as Waldstein in English and Valdštejn in Czech) continued on, leading aggressive fronts against the allied French, British, Dutch and Swedish forces until he was assassinated in Cheb in 1634, on orders of the Hapsburg emperor who feared a takeover. The war rampaged through northern and western Europe over the next two decades before returning to the Czech lands in 1645. The Swedes attacked cities and towns in Bohemia and Moravia for several years, though they were resisted in Prague in 1648 as the Treaty of Westphalia was signed.

Under the terms of the treaty, Bohemia was entrenched within the Hapsburg imperial system. The Hapsburgs retained power, which they held until the end of World War I. Catholicism was firmly reinstated as the counter-Reformation swept across much of Europe, German became the official language of most business endeavours, and all politics was dominated by decrees from Vienna (or from Hapsburg emperors living in Prague or elsewhere). The Hapsburg rule was not necessarily an oppressive one, especially as the Treaty of Westphalia finally guaranteed the separation of church and state and tolerance of Protestantism, tenets the Czechs had long before adopted as natural human rights. Much of the Czech Protestant intelligentsia went into personal exile however, and Czech culture began to disappear with them.

The Baroque became the dominant cultural feature of the next two centuries. The style of art and architecture brought out richness and glory in a flamboyant presentation which came to fill churches and halls, in contrast to the sober Protestantism of northern Europe. The Baroque period is heavily associated with Catholicism, which was generally accepted again by the Czech people, and with the Enlightenment. Beyond the worlds of art and religion, though, the Baroque was a time of absolute centralised (and non-Czech) government. This is why the political history of the Czech lands is quiet until the mid-19th century, at which the spirit of nationalism was reawakened.

The 19th Century: National Revival

It was in fact the arts that brought about this reawakening. Nationalist sentiment had been closed up and found little room for expression until the shifting breezes of Romanticism breathed some life back into the people. The Czech identity found a sympathetic root in the countryside among the peasants. Meanwhile large communities of Czech workers began to develop in the newly-industrializing urban centers, and writers, artists, architects, and composers began to bring out this new-found source through their works. Educators and thinkers such as Josef Jungmann wrote important histories of Czech language and literature, and František Palacký produced a seminal history of the Czech nation which encompassed his work as a parliamentarian and proponent of the emerging pan-Slavic movement. Poets and writers contributed to the development of Czech literature—Karel Hynek Mácha's poem *Máj (May)* is now recognised as the classic Czech Romantic work, and Božena Němcová's book *Babička (Grandmother)* has lodged her as the mother of Czech prose. Composers like Bedřich Smetana and sculptors such as J.V. Myslbek used Czech folk themes in their work. In Prague, the National Theatre and the National Museum were constructed, raising the consciousness of the people. And in the 1890s, Tomáš Garrigue Masaryk emerged to become a critical political figure in the shake-up that was beginning to happen.

Czechoslovakia

Tension in the Balkans led to the assassination in 1914 in Sarajevo of the Austrian Archduke Franz Ferdinand (who incidentally lived in Konopiště Castle not far from Prague), next-in-line in the Hapsburg dynasty, an event that sparked World War I. Masaryk and his compatriot Edvard Beneš, both in exile in London and Paris, respectively, during the war were by now actively pursuing plans for the independence of the Czech lands, through a union with Slovakia. Their lobbying effort was strongly supported by the tens of thousands of Czech soldiers that defected from the Austrian army, forming the Czechoslovak Legions in Russia, France and other sympathetic countries. With the imminent Austro-Hungarian collapse, the consolidation of German power and the chaos of the Russian Revolution forming pressure from all sides, the joint defense of the Czech and Slovak states was a timely and bold idea, that won the support of US President Woodrow Wilson.

On 28 October 1918, the independent state of Czechoslovakia was announced from the now-renamed náměstí Republiky (Republic Square) in Prague. The Prague National Council, made up of Czech and Slovak members from all political groups, elected Masaryk president of the new republic. Masaryk's First Republic, as it is now called in perspective, was a mighty economic force; in fact, the state ranked eighth in the world in GDP per capita, largely due to German capital which made up three-fifths of the whole. The industrial and agricultural sectors were solid, and the country came to be famous especially for its engineering, automotive works, and military output.

Nazi Occupation and World War II

All this was short-lived however. President Masaryk died in 1937, just before Hitler's Third Reich began to expand through central Europe. Hitler exploited the heavy German presence in the region known as Sudetenland, ringing the border to the north and west of Bohemia, and in the historic Munich Accords of September 1938, British prime minister Neville Chamberlain agreed to 'cede' a section of the country 'about whom we know nothing.' The Czechoslovak government, now headed by Edvard Beneš, felt powerless to resist it; Beneš resigned and exiled himself to London as the Nazis began their inevitable advance on the rest of the country. On 15 March 1939, Hitler declared all of the Czech lands German territory in the cynically-named Protectorate of Bohemia and Moravia, while enthusiastic Slovaks established their own fascist state.

The Protectorate had its own domestic government, led by the Nazi Reinhard Heydrich. A resistance movement was at work, though, in the form of Czechoslovak agents under the endorsement of President Beneš who organised an assassination attempt on Heydrich. The SS commander's car was sabotaged, and Heydrich died a few days later of injuries sustained, prompting revenge from Hitler in the form of a vicious levelling of two Czech villages, Lidice and Ležáky. All male inhabitants were executed and the women and children (except those deemed sufficiently Aryan to be placed with Nazi families) were sent to the concentration camp at Terezín (Theresienstadt).

The Nazis held tight in Prague until the bitter end. American troops, as agreed in the Yalta accords, halted their advance in Plzeň, while the Red Army marched on Prague. On 5 May 1945, the citizens finally rose up to drive out the oppressors. Key nerve centres such as the radio and railway stations were besieged, and barricades were erected throughout the city to halt reinforcements from entering. The uprising had just about succeeded in its task when the Soviet Red Army arrived on 9 May and 'liberated' the city, expelling the last Nazis from an occupied European country, and thereby ending the war in Europe. Despite the six-year occupation, Prague remained miraculously unscathed, while cities such as Berlin, Dresden, and Warsaw had been demolished.

Communism

For three years after the war Czechoslovakia was again independent under President Beneš, but with the Cold War getting underway, the country found itself on the wrong side of the fence. Beneš was unable to quell the rising voice of the Communists, and, unable to form a coalition government, he instructed parliament to settle the matter on its own. Beneš resigned in 1948. Communist party members, who had been voted into office in 1946, thus won control of the government, and their leader, Klement Gottwald, became president. The irony of it all is that the Communists were in fact freely elected.

German Expulsion

By this time nearly all ethnic Germans living in the republic —about 3.5 million—were forced to move back to Germany, even though their ancestors had lived in the Czech lands for generations. The forced expulsion of Germans from Sudetenland is the source of an ongoing controversy in political ethics and legal proceedings here.

The period from 1948 to 1989 was essentially a political blank. Most private property, from land to private enterprise, was nationalised and individual freedoms of travel and expression were cut off. The politics of fear played by Communism had a dangerous effect on people's mentalities, and instilled certain transitory mannerisms which will be discussed in subsequent parts of this book.

The Prague Spring uprising of 1968 was the lone hopeful event during this dark era, prompted by Party leader Alexander Dubček's calls for 'socialism with a human face.' Summer-long protests rallied behind Dubček's proposed reforms, though they ultimately resulted in a summons to Moscow, from whence Dubček returned a broken man. Soviet tanks supported by Warsaw Pact allies rolled through the city in late August, and the rebellion was dismantled. Dubček was replaced by Gustav Husák who led the country into the 1980s.

The spirit went underground, however, and a movement known as Charter 77 emerged to monitor political events. Its members, including the charismatic philosopher and playwright Václav Havel, became political prisoners themselves for their 'subversive' activities.

The Velvet Revolution of 1989 and the Velvet Divorce of 1993

The November-December 1989 revolution (termed the 'Velvet Revolution' for its remarkable lack of violence) was the pinnacle in a long buildup of frustrations, sparked into manifestation by the fall of the Berlin Wall in October. Occasional demonstrations had in fact taken place in Prague from 1987, and a growing sense of revolution became tangible. Information was provided by the Voice of America and Radio Free Europe, whose very purpose was to let people behind the iron curtain know what was going on. The year 1989 was critical, as larger demonstrations picked up on the fever in Poland, Hungary and East Germany; meanwhile the Czechoslovak hardliners remained among the most resistant, even censoring news from the Soviet Union, whose own period of *glasnost* precipitated all these gyrations.

On 17 November 1989, a relatively calm student march in Prague commemorating a 1939 anti-Nazi demonstration had strong revolutionary undertones, and suddenly became a full-blown protest. Students were attacked by waiting security police, and the so-called *masakr* (although nobody died) rallied the people into widespread civil disobedience.

This memorial marks the scene of the 1989 Czechoslovak Revolution - often called the 'Velvet Revolution' for its lack of violent protest

General strikes brought the operation of the country to a halt, and the quickly-organised Občanské Forum (Civic Forum) led by Havel met with the hardliners and their leaders to push for possible new governmental configurations. Finally, on 10 December a provisional government was announced in which the Communists were a minority party, and presidential elections were scheduled for 29 December. Havel was the unanimous choice of the federal assembly and he took office that day.

Three years later the Slovak parliament elected to secede from the Czechoslovak federation; this too was a peaceful event, and was hence dubbed the 'Velvet Divorce.' Since 1 January 1993, the Czech Republic has been a small independent state with sights set firmly on integration with the European Union, an event that finally came to pass in May 2004.

GOVERNMENT
For a nation that has had such a tumultuous political history, Czechs are surprisingly loathe to talk politics. Perhaps it's a hangover trait from Communism, when one was forbidden to debate or question the almighty Party directive. Perhaps it's because Czechs don't worry too much about anything beyond their personal comfort and contentedness. Or perhaps it's because most Czechs are so disillusioned by a limping government and a feeling that the common person has no power in the political process, that any political discussion will only lead to a rolling of the eyes or indifference to current events.

Czech politics today functions under a parliamentary democracy. Two hundred regional representatives are elected to the parliament, and the majority party elects its own leader, who serves as prime minister. There are currently some 20 political parties, of which four or five are legitimate contenders, including a surprisingly strong Communist party.

The parliament is bicameral, consisting of a Chamber of Deputies and the Senate. The Chamber of Deputies is composed of numerous ministries, such as those of agriculture, industry, finance, internal affairs, and justice, and numerous committees. General elections are held every four years for all legislative branch positions. Apart from the Chamber of Deputies stands the Senate, not formed until later in the game, in 1996. As a larger legislative body, its role is to provide more local representation, although the general feeling among Czechs is it simply augments the bureaucracy and provides cosy positions of power for local bigwigs.

One reason for the Czech Republic's impressive economic success in the early years of the post-Communist era was its line of what at the time was considered strong, clever politicians. As events unfolded, however, political and economic interests were revealed to be a bit too intertwined, and this ultimately led to the collapse of the government in 1997, followed by an era of political fumbling and bumbling that has hung around since.

Václav Klaus, as head of the conservative Civic Democratic Party (ODS), became prime minister in 1992; before this he had served as minister of finance, and due to a keen grasp of some important measures needed to transform a socialist economy to a market-based system, he produced generally laudable accomplishments that won him praises both at home and abroad. Klaus' seemingly firm position was shaken, however, with the surprise results of the 1996 elections. Rural and lower income voters, tired of living in a strange new world of competition, inflation, and high taxation, turned out in hope of slowing down the private-enterprise machine when it affected issues such as the cost of housing and transportation. Klaus's right wing ODS party still won the most votes, but was blindsided by much stronger competition from the left wing Social Democrats (ČSSD), who finished a close second and effectively fragmented the government. Klaus did manage to form a coalition with other parties and retain control over the ministries, but the suddenly popular Miloš Zeman, leader of the Social Democrats, became chairman of the parliament, a position that effectively diluted Klaus' ability to govern.

This shaky arrangement did not last long. The country was heading into economic recession in 1997, caused in large part by widespread failures in the banking system (see next section, The Economy). Overly cosy relations among banks, companies and investment funds were eventually revealed to have been overlooked by the government, or worse, encouraged by Klaus and other politicians who may have had personal interests at stake. The resulting scandal forced Klaus from office and brought in an intermediate government headed by the central bank governer, Josef Tošovský, until new elections could be arranged. These events also heralded a new era of political instability and general voter apathy.

In 1998, perhaps not surprisingly, Zeman and ČSSD won the general election over Klaus (who maintained his position as the head of ODS) and the Communist party, which finished a strong third. For all Zeman's foibles (he was widely regarded as a slouch and a boozer), he in fact oversaw some laudable accomplishments over the next four years, including the cleaning up and privatisation of the banking sector and the firm positioning of the Czech Republic on the road to EU admission. The Czech Republic joined NATO in 1999 and finally joined the EU in 2004.

Communism Today

Despite the turmoil it hasn't been quite as volatile as in neighbouring countries such as Hungary, Poland and Slovakia, all of whom have elected former Communist officials back into power. The Czech Communist and extreme right wing parties have made gains, particularly among the disaffected, and as unemployment grows there remains the worrisome possibility that they will continue to gain influence. In any case today's Communists are of course not the iron-fisted Communists of old, and it is generally thought that enough disgust remains from the pre-1989 age that any serious threat of a Communist victory would bring more forward-minded voters back to the polls.

Despite these advances, politics at home has continued to flounder, not least due to the existence of five viable parties with a tendency to disagree on just about everything. This has hampered reforms on important initiatives including fiscal reform (such as tax, social and healthcare systems) and strengthening of the legal framework. It has also deepened the sense of complacency amongst the Czech populace, who place very little faith in their government.

The 2002 elections hence brought about another ČSSD victory, but the tally was again close: ČSSD won 30 per cent, ODS 24 per cent and the Communist party 18 per cent. Upon Zeman's retirement in 2002, ČSSD's new leader became Vladimír Špidla, who while generally perceived as a clean-cut, straight-laced person, was hampered by a fractious parliament. ČSSD was initially unable to form a coalition to govern, but finally did, with the cooperation of the KDU-ČSL (Christian Democratic Union-Czech People's Party) and Union Svobody (Freedom Union). At one point the idea of a shared government of ČSSD-ODS was even floated.

Špidla's position was tenuous to begin with, and as the government drew into gridlock his popularity plummeted. Recognising his weakness, Špidla resigned in 2004 and was replaced by Stanislav Gross, who at only age 34 had risen through several high-ranking positions in ČSSD. Gross' tenure was short-lived, however: less than a year later he too was forced to resign in the midst of a scandal involving shady origins of funds he used to buy a luxury flat. Gross was replaced by Jiří Paroubek, a ČSSD deputy and former Prague city official. It is thought that ČSSD has lost so much support since 2002 that the next general election, in 2006, will catapult ODS back to the top.

The Role of the President
Standing aside from the parliament is the president, who is voted into power by the parliament rather than the general public. His job is largely symbolic and as figurehead of the nation, he usually represents the Czech Republic at international functions. The real job of running the country, however, lies in the hands of the prime minister.

Václav Havel served as president of Czechoslovakia from the Christmas 1989 elections until 1992, when he stepped down in protest of the forthcoming secession of Slovakia, claiming he didn't want to preside over the breakup of a state. He was then elected president of the Czech Republic in 1993, a position he held until 2003 when he retired in poor health.

Havel has been noted by some as being the incarnation of the Greek's 'philosopher king,' a label which he has humbly denied, especially as he had little executive power anyway. Nevertheless, it is tempting to see him in the light of great Czech leaders, from the Přemysls to King Charles IV to Masaryk. Much of the admiration for Havel comes from abroad; there is a faction of Czechs who did not quite identify with his high-minded intellect, feeling that he did not represent the common person.

Havel's retirement in 2003 brought on some political disturbance in its own right, as parliament found it hard to agree on a worthy successor. It took three rounds and several weeks of haggling until a surprising victor emerged: Václav Klaus. Rising from the political graveyard, Klaus used some cunning to position himself to finally win the third ballot by one vote. The result is surprising given Klaus' notoriously self-assured and uncompromising style and ODS's minority ranking in parliament, plus the irony of the quite open distate that he has for his predecessor, Havel.

Despite the rather unusual and shaky political arrangements, the government has succeeded in charting a forward course. Over the next several years the country will continue to face enormous change, even as (or some may argue, especially as) a member of the EU. President Klaus, a notorious Euro-sceptic, doesn't exactly lend stability to the government in this regard. The top issue on many agendas is of course strengthening the economy and bringing Czech economic standards up to a European level, and many Czechs are oblivious to all else.

THE ECONOMY

The Czechs have historically been a wealthy nation; in fact, it was only during the Communist era that the country fell behind western Europe, and the goal in some ways now is to regain the level of prosperity the state enjoyed up to the time of the Communist takeover. The socially-planned economy ruined all market orientations, and the Czech Republic has slogged uphill since 1989, re-establishing capitalist economic, financial, and legal systems in line with those of the European Union.

HISTORIC ECONOMIC LEVEL→

Industrial strength has long been based in heavy industry such as machinery, transportation equipment, electricity, and chemicals, as well as light industry such as food production. The past decade or so has seen an uptick in foreign direct investment in technology, with major western and Asian companies outsourcing the manufacturing of products such as auto parts, electronics, and pharmaceuticals. Since the early 1990s, the service industry has also boomed, with tourism a huge source of revenues (tourism is now a 125 billion Kč (US$4.5 billion) industry, second only to auto production). Chief agricultural products include potatoes, wheat, barley, hops and sugar beets, as well as livestock.

The Communist Legacy

Immediately after the Communist takeover in 1948, most private property and privately-owned companies were nationalised. What this essentially meant was that private citizens lost ownership of their homes and businesses, and job descriptions changed as everything was ruled from the top down. Market-economy fundamentals of supply and demand were suddenly irrelevant, as farms and factories were geared for production to meet lofty Soviet goals, with little relation to consumerism. And to propound the pride of the working class, the central authority forced drastic measures, such as employing certain intellectuals as window washers and food canners.

There was no need for specialisation, and therefore machinery works turned out the same models year after year, with the intention only of meeting quotas. Shops had all the basic goods, but there was little choice involved in purchasing them: you took what was offered. Prices and salaries remained almost unchanged for decades.

The concept of service was damaged as well. Where the individual was merely a functioning cell in the organism, and few were satisfied with their menial jobs, life became a monotonous existence. The service industry was reduced to its bare bones—this is why it has taken years for hotels, restaurants, and government offices to improve the attitudes of inattentive and surly employees.

Yet the Czech Republic retained many of the essential ingredients for success even under this regime; indeed, the Communists recognised the Czechs' clear comparative advantages in manufacturing, rendering it an industrial bulwark of the Eastern Bloc. While investment declined relative to western European standards, the country was still in fairly good position to pick itself up in 1989.

Post-1989: The Transformation to a Market Economy

Extraordinary changes have taken place since 1989. The fundamental shift to a market economy was undertaken in 1991, after more than a year of preparation, and after a difficult first year in 1992, GDP grew impressively through the mid-1990s. A recession in 1997–1999 helped expose some of the remaining adjustments needed, most notably in the banking sector, and weeded out some of the elements dragging on the economy. The global recession of 2001–2002 kept the Czech economy down, but as things improved in 2003, and as the Czech Republic worked hard to prepare itself for EU entry, in 2004 the future again looks brighter.

A system of restitution was established whereby persons who owned property previous to 1948 were eligible to reclaim it, though this has encountered predictable squabbles over ownership rights: Germans who had been kicked out in 1946 often laid claim to real estate subsequently taken over by Czechs, and Jews had claims of their own dating back to pre-Nazi 1938. Now, as the Czechs find themselves in the political and legal framework of the EU, they find that some of these issues are indeed not yet settled, with Sudeten Germans trying again to regain ancestral property.

Assets that were not subject to restitution were sold through a unique system of privatisation vouchers. All Czech citizens over age 18 were allotted a book of vouchers which they could use to invest in whatever company they chose on the market, with the goal of promoting widespread public ownership of assets. The Prague Stock Exchange reopened in 1994. By 1996 over 90 per cent of formerly state-owned firms were in private hands.

Enormous amounts of foreign investment money greatly aided the transformation. Foreign direct investment rose quickly up until the 1997 downturn, as foreign companies sought to expand their operations not only in the Czech Republic, but to use the country as a base for their central and eastern European operations. (Who, indeed, would choose to live in Warsaw if the business can be managed in Prague?).

Shock Therapy

The term 'shock therapy' was applied often and aptly to the new economic policies undertaken post-1989. The most important step taken in 1991 was that of privatisation of property owned by the government. Property that had been nationalised, from factories to farms to businesses to homes, was privatised either through restitution or selling of assets, and the process was long and complicated.

Inflation during this time declined from 100 per cent in 1990 to the single digits by 1994. Amazingly, unemployment remained very low as well, in the low single-digits through the mid-1990s, as the economy grew. In retrospect though, part of the reason for the low unemployment was that companies were slow to adopt productivity measures that might indicate the need to lay off workers. The unemployment figure in Prague remained below 1 per cent throughout most of the 1990s, making the city a world of opportunity for those seeking work and advancement.

Of course, 'shock therapy' also meant shock to the people, who suddenly faced unprecedented uncertainty. The government tried to monitor the transformation by continuing to pay generous subsidies to essential enterprises such as transportation, housing, and health care. Yet salaries did not keep pace with the rising cost of living: the national average net wage in 1995 was approximately US$350 a month—enough for subsistence living, but precious little else. By 2000, the average wage had only risen to about US$400 per month, as a result of a slowing economy and depreciation of the Czech koruna. It is hoped that EU membership will help cause the tide to rise.

Rich Versus Poor

Disparities were and have remained dramatic: many Czechs involved in private business were soon earning US$2,000 a month and more, placing them in the highest tax bracket, and rendering a 50 cent beer laughably cheap. This of course began to create a new stratification of society which was practically unknown prior to 1989, which has brought with it new social tensions.

The Late 1990s: Recession and Shakeout

GDP growth slowed in 1996 before turning negative in 1997. The underlying factor in the economic downturn of the late 1990s was inefficiencies in the financial sector, which impeded efforts to structural reform in many industries. What had appeared to be a successful privatisation effort in the early part of the decade turned out to be flawed by ongoing government control and mismanagement of the banking industry, and it wasn't until the late 1990s that these flaws became evident.

Voucher privatisation did not pan out quite as designed. Rather than investing directly in companies, most Czech citizens—who were understandably inexperienced in stock market transactions—sold their vouchers to investment funds that promised diversification and many-fold returns. Many of these investment funds were established by banks, which were in turn still owned or at least controlled by the state. Banks under the centrally-planned economy tended to have long-term relations with companies, and often provided their client companies with relatively easy access to credit (not unlike the order of things in Japan). One implicit complication of this scheme therefore was that since the banks were not privatised, and since banks indirectly became the largest shareholders in privatised companies through an unexpectedly concentrated investment fund operation, the entire mechanism was too intertwined. With continued easy access to credit, companies had little incentive to improve corporate governance or operational efficiency, and therefore were not effectively restructured to compete in the new market economy. When firms failed to properly restructure, they did not function as efficiently as competing firms, such as those from the neighbouring EU. Czech companies were overlevered and lacked cash, so were unable to service their debt.

Other investment funds were blatant scams, preying on investors' lack of experience and controlled by uncouth managers operating their own grey market. The most notorious of these, Viktor Kožený, ran an investment company called Harvard, which effectively made off with millions as he escaped to offshore havens in the Carribean; his exploits may have finally caught up to him, however, as the US Securities and Exchanges Commission has joined the Czechs in investigating some of his actions.

At the same time, Czech trade policy was to reduce tariffs in line with WTO regulations, which the country adhered to upon joining in 1995. As foreign competitors moved in, Czech firms found they could not compete, sales fell, and this led to an external imbalance: Czech imports overwhelmed exports, and the resulting trade deficit left the economy vulnerable. Speculative pressure then increased on the Czech koruna, and the Czech National Bank was forced in 1997 to devalue the currency by approximately 10 per cent; following this devaluation, the koruna subsequently fell by as much as 60 per cent over the next few years, to more than 40 Kč to the US dollar. The central bank also abandoned the currency peg (the koruna had been pegged to the US dollar and Deutsche Mark), and since this time the koruna has floated on currency markets, with only occasional government intervention.

All these fluctuations in the economy created further difficult social consequences: inflation rose to over 10 per cent in 1998, and unemployment, which had remained low for several years post-1989, hit 9 per cent in 1999.

2000 and Beyond

By the end of 1999 the economy had pulled out of recession, as exports grew and the government began a concerted effort to privatise banks, which has resulted in more effective reforms (all major Czech banks are now owned by western European congolmerates). Czech consumer spending remains fragile, however, as real wages continue to lag behind consumer price inflation. Expendable income thus remains low relative to that of EU countries, and savings are also relatively thin: total GDP in 2000 was equal to about $5,000 per capita in current US dollars, or nearly $10,000 in terms of purchasing power parity. This amounts to real consumer purchasing power of only some 20 per cent of the EU average, or approximately 45 per cent in purchasing power terms. The large difference reflects the comparative price differential between many imported and domestically-produced goods. Average monthly net salaries in 2004 were about 17,500 Kč (US$700); meanwhile unemployment had risen to over 10 per cent in 2004.

The Czech Republic is increasingly converging with EU standards, and EU trade is particularly vital: trade with the EU has risen from 32 per cent of the total in 1989 to about 70 per cent today, and total trade volumes with the EU have increased more than five-fold since 1989. The local workforce has always been highly skilled, and labour costs are still much lower than in neighbouring western European countries (about 40 per cent of the EU average); this has led to a resurgence in foreign direct investment after the recession, and a number of investments by firms such as Volkswagen, Intel, Philips and DHL have begun to solidify the country's position as a major technologically capable producer. The government has actively sought such investment through the establishment of CzechInvest, an organisation that promotes foreign direct investment. The agricultural sector meanwhile has struggled with the removal of tariffs and slow pace of reforms, yet again cheap labour and land costs render the country capable of extensive production and export.

The Czech Republic looks toward incremental improvements as a member of the EU in the coming years, although the state of progress will likely not be as dramatic as the build up to accession, as most of the institutional changes were already made in preparation. Outstanding issues as the country joined the EU included strengthening the legal system, easing the tax burden and dealing with corruption. Meanwhile, as a member of the EU, the Czech Republic faces economic issues common to most member states: a strict focus on inflation (which stood at only 0.1 per cent in 2003 but was back in the low single digits in 2005), serves as a tradeoff to unemployment, which remained above 10 per cent in 2004. The Czechs (along with the more vocal Poles) still face some restrictions on EU employment, which limits their membership status somewhat, at least in the interim period.

RELIGION

Czechs overall are not a religious people, which is surprising considering the country's large number of churches and its proximity to such heavily Catholic countries such as Poland and Slovakia. Perhaps again this can be traced back through history.

The early Slavs were pagan, though the Přemysls Christianised them with help from the Byzantine missionaries Cyril and Methodius starting in 863. Catholicism reigned throughout Europe during the Middle Ages, but by the beginning of the 15th century, voices in Bohemia led the cry for reform. The work of Jan Hus was instrumental in the development of Protestantism: a few decades after his execution Martin Luther emerged to organise the first true Protestant faith in Europe. Although the strong winds of the counter-Reformation blew through the Czech lands with especial force, the people were reluctant to re-adopt Catholicism. Under Communism, religion was effectively

Art Nouveau in Prague's Jewish Quarter.

banned. Priests and monks were forcibly removed from office, and churchgoers worshipped at their own risk.

Judaism was firmly established as early at the 10th century, and Prague especially was home to a large Jewish population up until the Nazi invasion. The Josefov district of Prague's Old Town was inhabited by several thousand Jews until the end of the last century, when the ghetto was demolished for urban renewal. Jews suffered the same persecutions in the Czech lands as everywhere, and by the end of World War II, nearly 80,000 Czech Jews had been exterminated in Nazi concentration camps. Only a handful remain today.

Those Czechs that do worship today are predominantly Catholic, but the number of active believers is remarkably low. In fact, the numbers of Czech priests are so low that in some regions priests are actually brought in from Poland and Slovakia. Most churches have less than full capacity services, and the majority of worshippers are the elderly. Why?

Czechs are somewhat agnostic, preferring independent thought and their own folk traditions, the latter perhaps a vestige of the ancient pagan ways. Most people will quite openly and without hesitation state, for example, that there is no God, and when we die, we simply lie underground, end of story. Czechs are in this sense true skeptics, not only in religious matters but in their general social outlook. Given their history of religious and political oppression, one can admire the wit and clarity of the response to any institutionalisation or organisation. Bitter and pessimistic they are not; straightforward, upbeat and well-rooted in their normal life, they are a sensible people.

The changing times have brought forth a cautious renewal of interest in religion among a few younger Czechs, particularly in more 'exotic' faiths such as Buddhism; interest in Judaism is in fact something of a minor fashion in Prague. And as is witnessed in countries undergoing changing times, some have returned to churches as a means of comfort.

FALLOUT FROM COMMUNISM

The damage done by Communism, both economic and psychological, has already been mentioned. Through these comments, and those in subsequent parts of this book, it should become clear that Communism was a real leech from which Czechs are still working to disengage; this is a long term, ongoing project.

It is impossible for any of us who did not live under this system to really imagine what it was like. Controls were extremely tight—speech and expression were censored, professionals risked their careers (and in extreme cases, their children's too) if they didn't join the Party, and these measures had remarkable effects on people's ways of thinking. Almost everybody detested (but silently accepted) the system they were in, though with such oppressive societal monitoring, the effect was of the beaten dog who simply gives in and endures the whipping. The weight of it all pressed down and produced a lifeless person. In a system that successfully stamped out individuality, people lost their sense of social purpose and importance, and hence, incentive. This contributes no doubt to the introverted, self-supported nature of Czechs: in its simplest form, this mindset espouses the view that we are alone in this world and there is little we can do to influence things beyond ourselves. Hence the ambivalence toward government and societal matters, and the focus on individual, personal interests such as family and free time.

There is another side to this experience, however, that manifests itself in unusual twists in today's society. Many have found the transformation difficult. One irony in current Czech society (and there are indeed many) is that a lot of people actually have fond memories of the Communist era, thinking of it as a time of almost a perverse innocence, where life was provided for, goods and services were cheap, and work and living were largely free of the stresses that come with a competitive market economy. Oddly enough, because basic social services were provided by the state, and everyone had a job and a home, one did not have to worry about things like job security or the price of eggs, and everyone could afford ski vacations in the Krkonoše. For those without career motivations, extensive material needs, political concerns, or passions to see the world, this was a time of simple living, where everything was predictable, most things were affordable, and as long as you kept to yourself, it was easy to slip into an almost carefree comfort zone. Many, therefore, long for a simpler life that is harder and harder to have today.

The experience certainly helped concentrate the Czechs' wicked sense of sarcasm as well: indeed several popular films produced since 1989 (such as *Pelíšky*, *Báječná léta pod psa*, *Kolya* and *Pupendo*) bring forth themes of mischievous abandon as characters take a laissez-faire approach to life, contenting themselves by withdrawing into their own interests, playing harmless pranks on the authorities, and generally taking a morbid fascination to life by making fun of the predicament they are in. The positive aspect to this is that people maintained a healthy sense of humour to get them through tough times; the downside is that this also reinforced a feeling of helplessness and insecurity, which sometimes plays out today in people's lack of initiative.

I cannot give a first-hand account of real life under this system, I can only relay the effects and changes since then. Virtually everything that is covered in this book has been touched in negative ways by Communism, which I've tried to work in where appropriate, so please be aware that many of the social and business traits discussed below have been tainted by the system, from which it will still take years to completely disentangle—yet changes are taking place at a remarkable rate, such that in time many of these comments will become obsolete.

For a better idea of what life was like here under this regime, refer directly to contemporary writers such as Václav Havel, Bohumil Hrabal, Ivan Klíma and Josef Škvorecký, whose works are mentioned at the back of this book.

CZECH
CHARACTERISTICS

CHAPTER 3

'Dad was thoroughly Czech. He always did
his duty consciensciously while thinking the
opposite of what he was supposed to think.'
—Josef Škvorecký, *The Engineer of Human Souls*

THE CZECH IDENTITY

One tends to generalise about a people when one becomes familiar with them. While it is senseless and even dangerous to group people into categories, it's inevitable, and for our purposes, it is important to understand character traits and mannerisms. Recognising these is a step towards better cultural awareness, which means better appreciation of the time spent in that society. The Czechs are a very small and homogenous nation, and anyone who has spent any amount of time amongst them can quite easily come up with a few constituent features. Some of these will hit you in the face; some are more subtle and it takes quite a bit of probing to start to discern patterns.

Digging into the source of these traits is a revealing exercise. Robert B. Pynsent's excellent book, *Questions of Identity: Czech and Slovak Ideas of Nationality and Personality*, serves as a source and support for many of the following observations. In it he speaks of the 'question' of identity being the study of a nation's history, language and cultural development. Czechs have a very definite identity, based in their own ethnic roots and historical mingling with other nations—it is thus a curious blend of cultures and ideologies. The years under Communism had an additional lasting (and destructive) effect on the character of the people—so many of the traits discussed below are in effect transitive, and difficult to pinpoint. It's amazing, in fact, to see how influential politics can be on society in this regard.

So let's speak of some of these, with full respect to the fact that what follows is a broad scope of generalisations, certainly not to be applied to all Czechs in all situations, and that the negative aspects will only bother you if you let them.

Czechs as Slavic, Czechs as Germanic

While Czechs ethnically are Slavs, we can see from the very dawn of their nationhood that the course of events through their entire history is intrinsically interwoven with Germans and German-speaking Austrians. A well respected Czech intellectual of the early 20th century, Josef Pekař, observes that both Czechs and Germans have a legitimate home in Bohemia, and he even goes so far as to say that the Czechs' economic and cultural success is a direct result of German education. If one considers that the Hapsburgs ruled the Czech lands from the age of the late Renaissance through the Baroque and Romantic eras into the 20th century, it can be seen that huge cultural advances were made during this long era, even though it was not particularly within a Czech framework. This, indeed, is Pekař's point: that cultural development in the Czech lands was a cosmopolitan, European endeavour.

Most agree that Czechs are much less 'Slavic' than their neighbours—the simple fact of geography certainly contributes to this idea (the Czech Republic is the westernmost Slavic country, bordering Germany and Austria, and Prague is actually further west than Vienna). Czechs themselves, meanwhile, hold a strong aversion to anything German (no doubt due to WWII, but also due to centuries of being considered second-class citizens), and the very idea of insinuating their 'Germanness' is taken as quite an insult.

The Bridge Metaphor

Czechs seem to believe that they occupy a special place in the world, or at least they occupy a central role in Europe, and the latter is a valid precept. They feel themselves to be a sort of bridge between east and west: the east, which happens to be emerging from Communism, and incidentally is predominantly Slavic; and the west, which has long been more culturally open and economically 'free', and is at least in part Germanic. But, it must be noted, a bridge connects points A and B without really belonging to either; Czechs in this way defy classification.

The Quiet Nature

Your first impression of Czechs will likely be that they are a cold and reserved people, and this could well be your single greatest barrier in adjusting to the culture. Outwardly, this is not an exuberant nation: Czechs aren't given to emotional displays, and interactions with strangers—in shops, on the underground—are generally kept to impersonal comments and curt replies, if anything at all. Part of this attitude may stem from the simple fact that they live in a climate which is cold and dark for half the year.

City vs Countryside

There are, of course, vast differences between the attitudes of those living in the city and those in the countryside. Prague can feel like a nasty city at times, especially in the heart of winter when nobody's happy; meanwhile you'll find residents of small towns and villages more friendly and open.

The Czech sense of community and friendship is a little more protected and sheltered than that of many countries. Czechs have a strong sense of privacy, and of the closeness of the family unit. They tend to stay at home, and don't really venture out except to go to the pub or the cottage; life on the street, as practiced in most Asian and Mediterranean countries, for example, does not take place here.

Another factor in this behaviour is quite likely the lingering effects of Communist societal monitoring. A sense of insecurity and distrust was implanted in the citizens, who lived in dull fear of being observed or judged. Václav Havel, in his essay 'Article 202' from the collection *Open Letters*, writes of this 'power that is happiest when people don't socialise too much with each other (that is, unless the authorities organise and control it themselves), when they don't go out very often and, when they do go out, always behave with proper humility. It's a power that finds it convenient when people keep an eye on each other, watch each other, are afraid of each other, a power that sees society as an obedient herd whose duty is to be permanently grateful that it has what it has.' In such a herd mentality, where the individual has no responsibility to himself or others, he accepts impersonality. This likely reinforced the Czech tendency to self-sufficiency and as a defence mechanism, they have learned how to take care of themselves.

Surprisingly, they don't put too much effort into getting to know one another. I lived for nearly three years in a flat in Prague and only very rarely saw my neighbours, never once exchanging anything more than a quiet *dobrý den* (hello). If this happens to you, and it probably will, don't take it as a snub: it's just how it is. It is interesting to note, meanwhile, that Czechs think of themselves as naturally warm and friendly, though it does take time to dig into this deep-rooted layer of hospitality.

Czechs are often shy and quiet when meeting people for the first time. They may, for example, not look newcomers in the eye, with almost a childish shyness. It is, in fact, not uncommon to not be properly introduced to people, and I have often been ignored as a newcomer in a group of people. Naturally I have perceived it as being strangely rude, and it has taken me time to recognise that this is more a type of shyness and insecurity at meeting outsiders than of overt distaste. Not to defend this behaviour—it still represents a certain tactlessness or baseness, but at least I think it helps to understand where it comes from. In such a situation, it never hurts to go ahead and introduce yourself, and any ability to speak Czech quickly goes a long way to break the ice.

Neighbours

Don't expect, upon moving into your new home, to be welcomed by your neighbours, or even to be greeted in a friendly way the first few times they see you. In fact, don't expect to get to know your neighbours at all. Most flats in Prague and around the country have been lived in by the same families for years, and they start to get suspicious when there is some sort of change.

Though they are firm in their beliefs and they do enjoy a good conversation, they are sometimes wary of speaking out. Czechs in their day to day lives are simply a calm and reserved people, and they admire modesty and humility in all situations. If you keep a low profile and approach Czechs with a minimum of crassness and vanity, you'll make a positive impression.

The tone of voice used in conversations is always level, rarely raising into a shout (except perhaps in the local pubs). In fact, Czechs complain about Germans and Americans especially for speaking so loudly, confidently and forcefully.

You could go so far as to say that Czechs are a passive people. It seems they focus on what they are doing with their own lives, and they try to ignore any perceived disturbances therein. Problematic situations often end up in embarrassed silences and looks of "Oh, I just wish this would go away." A friend of mine, who is American, relates the story of how she once fell as she was boarding a bus; her bags went flying and she ended up on her knees. Nobody made any effort to help—her fellow passengers just watched, or turned away, embarrassed. So she bravely got up and announced, in Czech, "Thanks, it's OK, I'm fine!" The humour was lost on them.

Don't let this intimidate you though, and don't make the mistake of making negative generalisations about your host people. It's easy to have something like this happen and instantly criticise Czechs for being so this-and-that, but this is just a symptom of the down period of culture shock. You're just as likely to witness the encouraging sight of a passenger giving up his seat to a senior citizen.

Judging from the glum faces you see on the underground, and the grey clothes and withdrawn mannerisms you first encounter, your first image may be of a certain detachedness on the part of Czechs, even of non-interest in the world around them. It does take an effort to get beyond this. While it is very easy to grumble about the rude service at the newsagents, the gruff attitude of the waiter and the seemingly non-responsiveness of Czechs to events around them, a little probing into their casual lifestyle reveals a wealth of spirit and life.

For Czechs, socialising and drinking often go hand in hand.

Merriness and Drinking

Czech merriness is a dearly held trait, though it is usually experienced in private, after a bond of friendship and trust has been established. Social gatherings often quickly turn into light-hearted joking, aided in part by the national passion for drink.

Most drinking is done in the pub in the evenings, though there is always an excuse to lubricate. Birthdays and *svátky* (name-days) often turn into noontime office parties, and friendship is celebrated in many different guises over a beer or three.

I recall one evening when I was teaching English in Prague, I was suffering from a cold, so the students in my English class volunteered to end the lesson early. I was on very friendly terms with them, and one of them invited me up to his flat next door for 'a drink'—home-made *slivovice* (plum brandy), supposedly the best cure for minor ailments. One drink of course became several and each time I looked at my glass it was full. I ended up stumbling home three hours later. At the next lesson the culprit looked at me with a sly grin: "So the sore throat is gone? But you woke up with a headache."

No, they are not a nation of alcoholics. Czechs drink in a very sociable way, for camaraderie, for fun, and they do moderate,

For the Love of Beer

Surveys show that Czechs are far and away the world's greatest consumers of beer—an average of 162 litres per capita per year—well above fellow European guzzlers in Ireland, Germany and Belgium. If we dissect this figure a bit, and eliminate say 25 per cent of the population (those under age 18), then it's more like 200-225 litres per person. If we further eliminate non-beer drinkers (say another 25 per cent), then call it roughly 300 litres per person per year, and we're getting close to a litre per day—or roughly two large beers per beer drinker per day. Assuming not all beer drinkers actually drink every day, then you've got several days in the week where lots of people are consuming large quantities of the stuff.

though their levels of moderation are significantly higher than most cultures.

When questioned about their love and capacity for drink, Czechs always put it into perspective. Reports from places such as Russia indicate a wild abandon in many circles, excesses that Czechs look down upon. Drinking is a social event, one with its own standards of refinement. Plus beer is 'soft' right? But this doesn't even account for the vast quantities of wine and hard alcohol that Czechs also down.

Czechs abstain in formal situations—at business lunches they often order just mineral water, a soft drink or coffee, and if they are driving they strictly avoid alcohol. Drinking is reserved for certain situations, but when those times come up, they like to let loose.

Czech Folk

Czechs retain a strong folk element. All Czech homes are decorated with lace curtains and handicrafts, and they treasure their record and photo collections, books on art and culture and family heirlooms. Markets around the country, even in the touristy areas of Prague, are full of trinkets such as wooden toys and Bohemian crystal. Moravians, especially, take a very casual approach to life, and folk music and craft festivals abound in the summer. Czechs love the simple life found in nature, and they escape whenever possible to their cottages in the country.

The love of nature is a deeply-rooted trait. Slavs have traditionally been farmers, and therefore have developed a strong appreciation of and love for nature. Pynsent notes the work of Johann Gottfried von Herder, a German writer of the last century who speaks of Slavs historically occupying unclaimed land, often wasteland, tilling it and building functioning communities. Furthermore, they have rarely fought over land, achieving peaceful settlements through diplomatic means.

A Czech Proverb

There is a Czech saying which goes: "Every man must build a house, plant a tree and raise children." A friend of mine's father took the proverb to heart: he built a country cottage entirely on his own, even refusing offers of help from friends and family, and this for him was a humble, though significant, expression of freedom (a particularly meaningful one under the former regime). The work doesn't stop there though; he, like so many Czechs, takes pride in the upkeep of the cottage, and he and his wife maintain a large garden producing apples, pears, garlic and carrots.

Every weekend during the summer is spent out in the countryside, and should you be lucky enough to become well acquainted with a Czech friend, you'll find a visit to their cottage one of the most rewarding experiences of your stay. Czechs take their country escapes very seriously, finding peace and relaxation in returning to the woods. Evenings are often spent in front of a campfire, where family and friends gather for conversation, song and beer.

Czech Non-Conformity

Perhaps it is an escape mentality which plays in here. Czech lore is filled with the nonconformist, escape-minded mentality which exhibits itself in such weekend activity. To call Czechs nonconformist is not to say rebellious or temperamental, however; it is a quietly defensive trait developed through history. While the nation bristled under foreign occupation for so many centuries, the people found comfort in their country roots.

Czechs take an intellectual pride in their informed separatism. Jan Hus set the ball rolling with his challenge to the Church, and Czechs were reluctant members of the Hapsburg Empire for nearly four hundred years. Novelist Jaroslav Hašek made his mark on the Czech literary world by introducing the playfully deviant personage of Soldier Schweik (in Czech, Švejk) in his World War I-era book *The Good Soldier Schweik*. The Schweik character is an embodiment of a particular element in the Czech spirit, which Czechs today freely admit as a valid stereotype. Schweik is an unwilling Czech soldier in the Austrian army, a happy-go-lucky swiller of good beer with an uncanny ability to make a hash of any situation, and emerge the unwitting victor. Society all around is restrictive, controlling, pressing, yet nothing seems to faze Schweik. His light-hearted approach to resolving sticky situations is a characteristic that endears him to the reader and demonstrates a particular Czech tendency to make light of difficulty and to find a way around it. More recent incarnations of Schweik are evident in characters such as those in 1960s-1980s novels by writers like Bohumil Hrabal, and figures such as František Louka in the 1997 film *Kolya* (*Kolja* in Czech) or Bedřich Mára in the 2003 film *Pupendo*.

Pohoda: The Life of Ease

Czechs pride themselves on knowing the priorities in life—family, wellbeing and an appreciation of the simple things in life. There is a very descriptive word, *pohoda*, which means something like comfort, ease or wellbeing; its root is similar to that of the words for value, worth or goodness, and it is used in many situations to say that everything is as it should be.

The Well Rounded Czech

As they say, *Češi umí*—Czechs know how. It's that simple. You will soon realise in almost any conversation with a Czech that they are well educated and appreciative of culture; in fact this is an excellent topic of conversation in virtually any situation, and you may well find yourself and your country the subject of a lively discussion. While Czechs are quite a homogenous people, they have cosmopolitan interests.

Czech primary and secondary schools are excellent, and students seem to retain much of what they are taught. Their position in the heart of Europe undoubtedly instills an awareness of the world around—not only do Czechs know every last detail of their own country, they are surprisingly knowledgeable of many aspects of European culture in general. In fact, one common perception that Czechs have about Americans is that they are not educated, that they are ignorant of foreign languages and the arts, which of course are an essential component of European life.

Czechs essentially try to enjoy all that life has to offer. This generally includes active participation in sports (such as soccer, skiing and ice-skating) and interests in things such as cooking, conversing (particularly in foreign languages), music and dance.

The Musical Inclination

Co Čech, to musikant (He who is Czech is a musician): Czechs are well-acquainted with music, everything from classical to folk songs to the latest tunes on the radio.

Folk songs, especially *trempink* (tramping) songs are known and loved by all. American country and bluegrass music is surprisingly popular (well-known songs include *Country Roads* and *Good Hearted Woman,* sung in Czech!), and folk songs from around the world gain a receptive ear. Evenings in local pubs may witness an accordion player striking up a tune, and soon the table of beer-toting old ladies and grizzly men start to mumble out the classic old lines, covering themes such as laying out in a tent under the stars, or running off to the woods with your best friend's girl. The tempo picks up with a few more drinks, and soon the whole room is misty-eyed and laughing along with it all.

Summertime sees a plethora of music festivals, and even the young, while raised on rock and pop music, are wont to pull out guitars and sing the old traditionals. While there is a strong homegrown folk music scene, a good portion of it is drawn from American roots (which itself is often drawn from English, Irish, German and indeed various Slavic roots). Artists such as Bob Dylan, Bill

Musical Culture

Czech children all are encouraged to pick up an instrument; it's considered part of the development of the mind. Similarly, children are all taught how to dance properly. As winter balls are an important event in the social calendar, it is important to know how to waltz and polka.

Dixieland in December: Jazz musicians in Prague's Old Town Square.

Monroe and Joan Baez have an active following through Czech bands and singers such as Druhá tráva, Cop and Věra Martinová.

Music has a special power to inspire, and under Communism the influences of American and British rock music played an instrumental role in the development of political awareness. The Beatles were an especial source of inspiration, and the John Lennon Wall in Prague was a gathering place for Czech youth's quiet counter-culture. Somehow the wall survived the final decade of Communist rule intact, via numerous midnight repaintings. In the 1970s, an underground Prague band called Plastic People of the Universe was censored by the authorities; this act was the first in a series of protests by Charter 77, a political watchdog which was formed to monitor human rights violations under the auspices of the Helsinki Accords. One of the band's biggest fans was Václav Havel, who was jailed for helping form Charter 77. Havel's determination through the 1970s and 1980s ultimately led him to help bring down Communism, and he indirectly credits Lou Reed and Frank Zappa for his rise to the presidency!

Linguistic Sensibility

Again, Czechs have a fitting expression: *Kolik jazyků znáš, tolikrát jsi člověkem*. (You are as many people as the number of languages you know.)

Most educated Czechs speak two or three languages; those who do not speak English or German are working at it now. Of course, under the entire Hapsburg reign, many Czechs spoke German out of necessity. Older Czechs especially speak German: it was in their lifetime that the country was ruled by German-speakers, whether Hapsburg or Nazi, but some young Czechs are studying it as well, given the proximity. Under Communism, all schoolchildren were forced to learn Russian, which everyone by now has done their honest best to forget. The sophistiqué speak French, and it's interesting to note the haute-culture affinities that the French and Czechs have for one another, such as the proliferance of Art-Nouveau architecture and the intellectual café culture.

English, however, is now clearly the language of preference. Just after the 1989 revolution, language schools were flooded with students, and by now almost anyone in university or business speaks at least some English. With so many multinational companies now active in the Czech Republic, and with a huge tourist industry helping support the Czech economy, English is practically a second language in the business world.

Love of the Czech language was a key to the National Revival of the nineteenth century. Writers such as František Palacký and Josef Jungmann contributed enormously to national sensitivity through their works on the questions of Czech identity and history. Reverence is paid to Jan Hus, who, as rector of the Charles University, developed a precise system of spelling and pronunciation

Making A Linguistic Effort

Czechs express a sincere appreciation for foreigners who learn to speak their language. While acknowledging that it is extremely difficult to master, and that it is insignificant outside their tiny country, they revel in its beauty, and have deep respect for anyone who is 'sympathetic' enough to learn it. You will score big points by even learning a few select words and phrases and being able to pronounce them correctly. Please refer to the language section in Chapter 8 which tries to lay the groundwork.

which is still followed today. The very name of the Přemyslid dynasty implies a certain incisiveness: the word is almost identical to the Czech verb *přemýšlet* (to think about).

Human Diplomacy

Such intellectual versatility, as one Slovak philosopher calls it, certainly contributes to a universal love for peace and democracy. The medieval kingdoms functioned on a basis of international trade and relative economic freedom. Bohemia has always been made up of cohabiting Czechs and Germans, and Jews maintained a strong presence from the 10th century straight through until World War II. Masaryk's achievement of an independent Czechoslovakia in 1918 was a great triumph, in which the long sought dream of an independent, democratic state for the Czech people was finally attained.

It's interesting to note that the Velvet Revolution of 1989 was conducted purely on the basis of civil disobedience, with a complete lack of violence on the part of the protesters. And

when the Czech Republic and Slovakia split in 1993, the event was simply a political decision, in which the citizens raised only a curious voice. Compare these two peaceful events with much more violent happenings in Romania and the former Yugoslavia, respectively.

Several commentators note that this peaceful nature hasn't always worked to the Czechs' benefit. In fact, at times it may have contributed to their undoing. Not that they didn't fight when called upon to do so: the Hussites were ferocious warriors against Catholicism; Czech soldiers fought bravely, but were simply overpowered in the Battle of Bílá Hora; and the number of plaques you see on buildings in Prague commemorating the victims of the Prague Uprising of May 1945 attest to the will of the people to destroy Nazism. Yet Czech pride and nationalism is kept within an intellectual sphere. They may distrust and disapprove and be disdainful of outsiders, but their peaceful nature precludes confrontation: they would often just prefer to look away and ignore a trouble spot, even taking on a self-defeating 'there's nothing I can do' attitude.

Motionlessness

Herder comments on what he calls the Czechs' submissiveness and obedience. Arnošt Procházka, a Czech contemporary of his, even goes so far as to declare: 'We are shallow and flabby. We love feebleness; we take pleasure in torpor; we protect and tend our feebleness and torpor like flowers in a greenhouse.' And as this passage indicates, Czechs are quite good at complaining. They seem comfortable sympathising with how difficult things are—it just comes naturally to shake the head in disgust and mutter, "Oh it's terrible." One Czech friend concurs with the trait, that so many people spend so much time complaining about 'problems' without offering any solutions, and accepting the notion that this is their lot. Yet she falls into her own trap, shaking her head and turning up her nose: "It was terrible! And now we don't know what to do about it."

Normal Problems

You come across the words 'problem' and 'normal' a lot.
Anything which is not quite within the realm of 'normality'
is difficult to grasp, and therefore creates a 'problem'.
The irony, though, is that not only are they accustomed to
saying that something is a problem, they seem to have little
initiative to change it. "Why make something easy?" They are
apt to joke. Meanwhile, they are sometimes content to just
let things happen as they will—perhaps this is a reasonable
acceptance of life as it is.

Communism seems to have exacerbated the tendency
to mope. In one of his first speeches after taking over
the presidency in December 1989, Václav Havel warned
about the learned incapacity to think, which Communism
instilled and which Czechs are now trying to shake. Many
of the 'negative' traits spoken of here are instantly and
categorically put down by Czechs as a result of the mindset
of Communism.

Scepticism and Complaining

Not only do they sit on their heels, however; comments like
this demonstrate that Czechs are world-class complainers,
with a finely-tuned sense of scepticism. Complaining about
injustices is almost a national sport: there always seems to
be something wrong with something or somebody, and it
comes with the turf to simply refuse to believe just about
anything one is told.

Czechs are quick-witted, and easily able to turn a negative
into a joke: you will soon determine a very wry sense of
humour that in its own way neutralises any complicated
or difficult situation. Much of this is almost second-nature,
and therefore shouldn't be taken too seriously. The negative
side to this, though, is that there is an almost latent drag
placed on progress at times: such constant complaining
can be self-destructive, and certainly can put a damper on
things. The optimism and enthusiasm that many in the west
are accustomed to (especially in the US) is not necessarily

the order of the day here, and expressions of ideas or goals in business or personal life are often met with a sense of impossibility among listeners. I almost find it difficult to be too forward-thinking or optimistic among Czechs sometimes, as dreamy thoughts or exuberant goals can be met with smirks and guffaws.

Self Pity

The Czechs have spent many centuries under foreign rule, so it's understandable that they would adopt an attitude of self-pity. Many observers refer to the defeat at the Battle of Bílá Hora as the 'fall' of the Czech nation. Similarly, the internationally known novelist Milan Kundera laments 'the Czech lot' in one of his works.

Perhaps this attitude helps explain the abundance of martyrs in Czech history, through which Czechs may form a self identification. First and foremost among these is sv. Václav (St Wenceslas), the patron saint of the nation. Václav was a Přemyslid prince who founded the first cathedral at Prague Castle, and who was murdered by his own brother, Boleslav the Cruel. With equally great aplomb, Jan Hus's martyrdom was a rallying cry for his followers, who still exist today, at least in the name of the Hussite church. And in more recent times, Jan Palach was an 18-year-old student who set himself on fire in protest at the Soviet invasion of 1968. Each of these occupies a special point of reverence in the Czech pyche.

Jealousy

Another unfortunate outcropping of the Communist era is the expansion of feelings of jealousy. Perhaps it is natural that as society begins to stratify, feelings of jealousy emerge. Indeed, this is not really any different from the situation in countries where the working classes, often in run-down areas, resent the more educated and upwardly mobile elements of society. There is often a suspicion of successful people that easily slips into resentment, as if those who have gained wealth must have done so through dishonest means. Some of this is in fact well-placed—who had easier access to assets after 1989 than the former Communist party bosses?

Jealousy can in fact take active form in its worst cases. One business acquaintance of mine for example, an American, complains that he actually has trouble advancing at work because his colleagues don't want to see him succeed, and he at times worries about back-stabbing; this may well be exacerbated by the fact that as an American he probably makes more money than his Czech colleagues, plus he can always just pack up and move on if he wants to, which the locals may not.

Pragmatism

Nonetheless, Czechs are a practical people. Once you get past the vagaries of certain business practices and stagnant personalities, they are inherently logical, practical and efficient. Perhaps this is related to the very technical nature of the Czech language, which may instil a technical, ordered mindset in the people.

Czechs have an inbuilt sense of order and classification: almost every aspect of life is placed in neat little cubes. They generally live in small flats, they follow a daily pattern of work, rest and sleep, and the life cycle is remarkable for its predictability. They also organise their thought process and world view into compact functional units and they tend to draw up focused ideas and opinions.

Conversations with most Czechs will reveal an endearing simplicity and an uncluttered worldview. This certainly reflects most Czechs' approach to life, and I've found myself learning important lessons from my Czech friends and colleagues about how to keep things simple. For example, one friend of mine could probably make more money running his own company, rather than doing the same work for someone else, and for much less money. But he doesn't even consider the possibility, as this would be too complicated for him; he would rather just take home his salary and have his evenings and weekends free to work in his garden and go cycling.

There is of course a forward-thinking, professional element ingrained in many people as well, and lots of Czechs are working harder than ever these days. Hard work means material reward, and this is the goal of virtually every Czech you are bound to meet—indeed, this allows the life of ease that everyone wants.

It is remarkable how quickly many Czechs have adapted to western life—there is a real thirst for novelty, action, and inclusion. Technology has skipped many generations here: so many people have gone, for example, from living without a land-line phone for much of their lives to using the latest colour screen mobile phones, or from their old army jackets to Gore-tex. In business, many Czechs are fully at ease with European business practices and the latest internet applications, and again this is a function of utility: the better things work, the more efficient you will be.

Humour

You will eventually begin to notice a deep-rooted sarcasm, perhaps a necessary outgrowth of any small nation's pride. Czechs have a subtle and dry sense of humour, and they seem to take everything life throws at them with a grain of salt. One joke that emerged from the Communist era is very telling: regarding the exhortations to work, to build a socialist society, Czechs retorted, "We pretend to work and they pretend to pay us." I once saw a statue erected during the Communist era, decorated with the hammer and sickle and 'Dedicated to the victims of war and oppression, 1914–1918 and 1938–1945.' Underneath, someone had added a plaque with the telling dates '1948–1989.' Of course, the humour isn't limited to the oppressors from the East: with so many Americans in Prague now, the locals have adopted a sort of 'Oh, you again' attitude. A cartoon in a Czech newspaper thus referred to the 1995 space hook-up of American and Russian astronauts, with a woman querying her husband, "The Americans and Russians together in space? Finally! Does that mean all of them?"

THE SUM OF IT ALL: CZECH PRIDE

Through all these generalisations, one can see a strong, deeply rooted national pride. Having lived through several centuries of foreign occupation, Czechs are stubbornly, almost defensively proud, and yet they approach the world today with an admirably fresh, youthful face. Perhaps it's fitting that the symbol on the national seal is the lion.

One simple event sums it up for me. During an English course for intermediate level adults, I posed one student the conversation topic question, "Of what are you proud?" I expected an answer relating to his entrepreneurial success, or the fact that his son is a university student, but he just shrugged his shoulders and looked at me as if it were a silly question: "I am proud that I am Czech."

SOCIALISING

CHAPTER 4

'Slavs are 'well behaved, gentle; they love peace,
the laws of the community, national customs and,
particularly, providing hospitality and free passage to
well-intentioned guests; they are immensely considerate'.'
—Johann Gottfried von Herder, as quoted in
Robert B Pynsent, *Questions of Identity:
Czech and Slovak Ideas of Nationality and Personality.*

MEETING AND BEING MET

Czechs tend to stick with the groups of people they know and feel comfortable with. They are generally eager to let more people into their social circle (particularly if they are foreign), but it often takes a certain catalyst to open the doors of friendship. Relationships springing from within offices, schools, or friends of friends are the easiest to form, as one feels more comfortable as part of this larger organisation. Within such social organisations, Czechs are open, friendly, and accommodating, and, assuming you have such a network at hand, you'll find Czechs to be a cordial and amicable bunch. Meeting people at random, however, is much more intimidating, so use the resources you have.

You may have a certain advantage simply in being foreign, although on the other hand, some Czechs, particularly in Prague, are getting tired of the foreign invasion. It may take a little more effort to get through to them, and you may have to prove yourself as being appropriately down-to-earth. Again, efforts to demonstrate cultural or linguistic awareness are met with appreciation and respect.

CONVERSATION

The very fact of your being in the Czech Republic is probably going to be your greatest conversation piece as you get to know someone, especially if you are living outside of Prague. Conversation in any social setting will likely revolve around cultural issues. Talking about your own interests, your national customs and traditions and your family will always meet an attentive audience.

Where Czechs are innately curious about foreign things, they also take great pride and become wonderfully open to you when they see you taking an interest in their culture. Thus, your best inroads into winning one's affections are to express an interest and excitement in them. This can also be an excellent opportunity to find out more about the country's history, art and social customs. This means a lot of question asking in the beginning, but later, when you start to know a few things about Czech culture, your friends and the people you meet will be delighted at your knowledge of their little country.

Politics is generally avoided as a conversation topic, as most Czechs simply aren't interested in it. Perhaps it's the built-in distrust and sarcasm on the part of most Czechs that precludes political debate of any kind; certainly today it is a reflection of disgust at the perceived ineptitude of many politicians. Whatever the reason though, they pay little attention to local or international politics, so the conversation would soon die in its tracks. Try to steer clear of any discussion of the Communist era, despite the interest that you may have in it. Czechs are fighting as hard as they can to forget about it. They may bring it up themselves, though only in the context of today's changes. Likewise, unless your audience is economically or politically inclined, most Czechs won't have too much to say about current political events; they'd rather talk about their upcoming ski vacation or a recent film.

> ## Respect Your Hosts
>
> A well advised suggestion can be made here when conversing with Czechs on any level: do not patronise. Many westerners make the mistake of coming in and trying to impose values on Czechs, and Czechs often complain that some foreigners come in with a 'you monkeys' attitude. Once again, this is a well educated and a self conscious nation, proud of its achievements and its identity, and any showing of disrespect or superiority on your part will backfire immediately.

Those Czechs that are interested in politics and economics, however, will be eager to use you as a sounding board. The educated classes are indeed very well-read and eager to learn more, and therefore to engage foreigners in conversation. They may well have their opinions, for example, on the potential merits and pitfalls of EU membership, and they may be interested in seeing if your non-Czech viewpoint corresponds with their local perspective.

CZECH IMPRESSIONS OF OTHERS

Czechs overall are extremely curious about foreign culture, and it's surprising what they are apt to know. Yet some still have had relatively little direct contact with other nationalities, so there can be misunderstandings. Czechs are always curious about other nationalities, and wherever you're from, if you can present yourself as a respectable human being, you'll likely meet an inquisitive audience.

Americans were held in high regard here in the years following the revolution, undoubtedly because they were the supposed 'enemy' for so many years. But the degree of penetration of American culture has started to meet some pretty stiff resistance from many Czechs, who quite simply want their own country back. Americans therefore hold a sort of dual distinction here.

Germans

If you're German, you may continue to be the object of a light scorn for all the damage your country did to the Czechs during World War II. Germans have an image of being loud and demanding—which disturbs the local peace. Again, approach the locals with humility and a desire to know and understand them.

On the one hand, American business practices and attitudes are generally well respected, and Czechs remain insatiably curious about many American cultural exports such as pop music, film, cars, clothes and the multi-tasking lifestyle—some of this is based more on images than on reality or experience. Americans are seen as being strong and productive, direct, knowing what they want and being able to achieve it. On the other hand, though, American confidence and the smiley all-is-well mentality is seen as superficial. Many of those who have encountered Americans personally or have visited the US may have their reservations, and as a whole, Americans are seen, as in much of Europe, as the economic and cultural invaders from the west. Americans are thought of as a bit uncultured when it comes to European history and society, so it makes a great impression if you are an American and direct your behaviour towards humility and a genuine interest in the local people.

Other European nationals are held in fairly high regard. The British are generally seen as being friendly, excepting the hordes of young Brits who have started to invade Prague's pubs and brothels on weekend jaunts via the low-cost airlines. Italians and Spaniards seem to have taken a particular liking to the Czech Republic in recent years, and Czechs generally remain interested in the usual Italian traits of fashion-consciousness and enthusiasm for life. The French are generally respected as being highly cultivated.

Neighbours from bordering states such as Poland and Hungary are generally looked upon with neutrality, given the quite similar histories of these countries. Russians, however, are almost universally disliked as a people—this stems of course from the dark ages before 1989 but also from the presence of Russian mafiosi, as well as arrogant hordes of Russian visitors that descend upon Prague and the spas in Karlovy Vary.

Asian or African nationals may meet an initial cold shoulder. This is pure naiveté on the part of those who choose to remain closed and unaware, particularly with regards to Arabs who are often regarded these days with some suspicion. There's nothing particularly wrong about an Asian or African in the eyes of a Czech, but because he knows so little about them he has a built-in fear and misunderstanding of them. It just takes a bit of conversation to break down the walls.

"He Was Normal"

One acquaintance of mine from a small town in the country told me the story of how he was shocked to come across a black pharmacist in the local pharmacy (evidently a foreign exchange student from Africa who had graduated and stayed on to work). Amazement was soon alleviated, "but then he asked me what I needed so I told him, and he helped me—he was completely normal!"

Racism

A vestige of non-thinking hungover from Communism is the inherent suspicion amongst many Czechs toward anything or anybody different. There is an undertone of latent racism and sexism in many Czechs, more due to naiveté than any real malice, although there are factions of skinheads, particularly in the poorer areas of northern Bohemia and northern Moravia. There hasn't yet been much cultural exchange here other than the historical shoulder-rubbing with Germany, Austria, Slovakia, Poland, and more recently, Russia, all of whom are incidentally white peoples.

The Communists did organise student and worker exchanges—African nationals, especially those of Communist-sympathetic countries such as Angola, came to study at Czech universities and technical schools, and some Vietnamese came to work in commercial fields. Many of these choose to stay of their own accord, as conditions and opportunities are often better here than at home. The numbers are small, so whereas there are large numbers of African or Asian nationals in countries such as the US, Britain or France, Czechs are much less accustomed to seeing dark faces around town.

Not Quite

Once personal contact is established, you will encounter respect, but you will start to get a funny feeling that you're just not Czech and therefore you have unfortunately missed something somewhere.

It is extremely rare to have an openly racist incident. Sentiments, while frank, remain beneath the surface, and general attitudes are non-confrontational. The natural reaction of many Czechs to anyone not white is avoidance. There is something different about a dark-skinned person, which the average Czech would simply rather not know anything about. Think of it as simply an additional (and unfortunate) barrier to breaking the ice, but when you do get through, you will be equally respected as a person.

The Gypsies

Much of the misunderstanding, or non-understanding, is due to the long-held distaste for 'gypsies' in Eastern Europe. The

Roma (their proper name) have lived a nomadic existence—both physical and cultural—in the Czech lands for centuries, have not assimilated into society, and thus remain outcasts. Romanies are in fact descendents of the lowest caste of people in India, who migrated across the Eurasian continent from about the 10th century. Unlike other immigrant groups, it is unknown why they left their homelands, other than perhaps to escape the inhumane conditions of the 'untouchable' caste, and they have indeed preferred to remain in their own tight social and family structures and maintain their own culture. While very few actually are nomadic today, most Romanies live in virtual shanty-towns on the edge of villages, or cluster in certain neighbourhoods of cities, such as Žižkov and Smíchov in Prague.

Many Czechs dislike Romanies, claiming they are lazy, they don't work, they steal, they destroy property and they basically drain the welfare state. Many are indignant about the fact that Romanies receive the same social benefits as all Czechs, including unemployment pay and child support, which some Czechs feel simply encourages them to remain unemployed and have lots of kids in order to gain higher monthly government stipends. Society in general here has acknowledged them as permanent outsiders, and has attached a negative stigma which has naively been applied to all similarly dark-skinned peoples. While a productive dialogue appears to have begun, cultural differences and long-entrenched mindsets will not be overcome overnight.

SOCIAL ORGANISATION
City Life Versus Country Life
The perspective taken in most of this book is one centred on life in Prague, which is where most expatriates in the country are located. Prague is by far the largest city in the country, with 1.2 million inhabitants; the second-largest city, Brno, numbers only 400,000. Many of the progressive attitudes and the positive economic changes spoken of here are indicative of the advances being made thoughout the country, though with a particular emphasis on the capital city. In a city that attracts so much attention from international businesses and

Working in the garden is part of the family's activities at the cottage.

tourists, it is a natural development, while in smaller towns and in the countryside, the changes are coming more slowly. Traditional ways are more adhered to, people are often more reluctant to accept change, and sometimes, you may get the feeling that these are two different worlds. This means, of course, that where Prague is becoming increasingly more cosmopolitan and predictable, small towns retain their typical charm and hospitality.

FAMILY AND LIFE CYCLE
The family is the basic element in the social fabric, and society as a whole is structured around this unit. The homing instinct is powerful here: family is absolutely the core of life, and even when children grow up and move away and start their own families, they come home as often as possible.

Childhood
The state provides a generous maternity leave: new mothers are allowed up to three years of partly paid leave, and they are fully entitled to get their jobs back when they are capable of returning. Many women prefer, however, to raise children themselves, without relying on child support. This again is adherence to traditional ways, and in fact many Czech women look down on the western tendency to continue career advancement while there are young children to raise.

It's not just a matter of mouths to feed, it's a matter of raising children in a close knit and well balanced family.

Where the mother may take several months or years off work to raise a family, and the father is generally expected to provide the income to do so, the development of the family is a wholesome and integrative affair. Both parents assist in all aspects of raising the children, from teaching values, to helping with homework, to taking ski vacations in winter. Czechs are very conscious of being independent and well rounded, and to achieve this, a healthy family dynamic is considered essential. While divorce certainly does occur and indeed is rising, many Czechs are shocked and dismayed at the high rates of it in the west. Families rarely have more than two children, perhaps due to space limitations—nearly all families live in small flats, and it's not unusual for children of the opposite sex to share a bedroom throughout their time living at home.

As parents take a serious and caring approach to the practice of raising children, so children are properly appreciative of them, and hence, obedient. Kids are not usually spoiled, due in part to the fact that many families don't have financial resources to buy expensive toys, although this is starting to change as more and more Czechs are exposed to western commercialism and earn comparable salaries. Indeed, many Czechs have adopted western ways quite effortlessly: kids often spend time after school watching rubbish on TV or playing Play Station, while their parents are at work—or doing the same! More traditionally, though, the family participates in enjoying life together: going to the theatre, visiting the grandparents, and enjoying the outdoors.

Part of the task of rising children, of course, is administering punishment, and Czech parents can discipline with vigour. I've seen the following event unfold several times: a mother is dragging her toddler along the pavement, and the child falls because he can't keep up; his mother then yanks him back up, slaps him (not too hard), the child starts crying, she gets huffy, and off they go again. Destructive behaviour, no? Corporal punishment of this kind is not a social problem, though it does occur. In the same vein of crassness, it is a common amusing/revolting sight to walk past a mother on a busy street or in a park helping her toddler pee into a gutter. Prague's Wenceslas Square—a prime business/shopping/nightlife area—is one of the more popular locales. It's things like this that make you wonder, where is the sense of refinement?

Growing into Adulthood

Until recent years, Czech society was spared many of the pressures running rampant in the west. As times are changing, however, children are becoming more rebellious and starting to feel less obliged to conform. Adolescent rebellion is still held somewhat in check, but the increasing pervasiveness of corruptive influences, including drugs, along with the increasing absence of parents who are now working more, is producing a different set of teenagers than a decade or two ago. Yet family remains paramount, and teens continue to respect their parents and enjoy being with them. Parents are therefore quite good about giving their children freedom as they mature.

A Close-Knit Unit

It is not unusual for children to continue to live with their parents well after age 18. This is due in part to the chronic lack of housing in Prague and throughout the country. Those who do move out visit their parents regularly on the weekends well into their twenties and thirties, to get their weekly dose of home cooking and parental attention.

Children receive state supported education until age 18. The secondary school years are surprisingly specialised: at about age 14 children decide if they want to attend a *gymnázium* (secondary school) or a technical school. Universities are difficult to get into, and most are now introducing tuition costs which Czechs find hard to bear. As evidence of the Czech practical nature, a large percentage of university students opt for technical and business degrees.

Marriage

As tradition dictates in many countries, Czechs often marry at a young age: women are often *vdaná* (literally, 'given') around the ages of 20 to 23, while men are often *ženatý* (the word derives from *žena*—woman) by the age of 26 or so. This is changing rapidly, however, especially in Prague. It is perhaps over-generalisng, and even insulting, to say that couples often get married soon after the woman becomes pregnant, as if this is the motivation they need to tie the knot. Yet one of the first questions typically asked when someone announces they are getting married is, "Do you have to?"—parents and friends actually half-assume that this is the reason. So what might in other countries be considered shameful is almost the way of things here. I know several such cases where the first child was born some three to six months after marriage.

Life Expectancy

The average life expectancy is low in comparison with many western nations. This could arguably be attributed to a less than perfectly healthy lifestyle: Czech cities until very recently suffered from terrible pollution (this is only starting to change in recent years as older cars finally come off the road and homes and commercial buildings use more and more natural gas heating in place of coal), and the traditional Czech diet is rich in fatty meats and starch. Czechs also seem to consider death as a natural part of life, or simply an end to life, and they don't necessarily nurse the elderly with pharmaceuticals to sustain a bedridden existence. The elderly are held in high esteem, such that when they became incapable of taking care of themselves, they often move in with their children rather than heading off to a nursing home. Again, the family is the core of life, and one is expected to care for one's elderly parents just as one was cared for as a child. A person who has lived beyond the age of 70 is considered to have lived a full life, and because of this there are few regrets or grievances for those who pass away at a 'reasonable' age.

Sex

Anyone who has read Kundera, Škvorecký or Hrabal may easily jump to the conclusion that Czechs are highly sensitised to their libidinal instincts. All three contemporary writers speak quite openly and shamelessly of sexual trysts,

Keep An Open Mind

Czechs are easy going and liberal-minded, though the general rules governing romantic and sexual etiquette are the same here as in many other countries.

extramarital affairs and the human instincts behind these. Perhaps because all three wrote within the context of political oppression, sex is used as a theme for personal freedom and individual expression. And though they rarely flaunt it, Czechs do seem to take a relatively loose approach to sexual relations. There always seem to be sly rumours of unfaithful husbands and wives, and foreign men often delight in the beauty and approachability of Czech women.

Homosexuality is still a hush subject, as most Czechs feel uncomfortable discussing it. It's not a religious matter here as it is in some countries. It's more something that is just 'not normal' and therefore disquieting to most. Gays and lesbians remain very much in the closet, and while there is no overt discrimination or animosity toward homosexuals, most Czechs would just prefer not to address the issue, and ultimately would simply prefer it not to even be there at all. Prague does have a fair number of gay clubs and bars, and the media (especially such western publications as *The Prague Post* is opening the floor to awareness and acceptance, but overall, there is little movement or social phenomenon to speak of.

The attitude toward homosexuals in the Czech Republic is similar to their feelings toward any social trend or phenomenon: it's just not really worth talking about. Czechs admire individuality and tend toward privacy, and they don't bother with talking just for the sake of talking; whether someone chooses to wear Levi's, or to smoke, or has a partner of the same sex, it's their own business.

Women

It's the same with the feminist movement. Because men and women already occupy fairly equal positions in society, and because many women are happy enough with their traditional roles, there isn't a strong desire to address any feminist issues. One tenuous advantage to Communism, in fact, was that women were considered equal to men, at least on paper. What this meant was that women were expected and in some case assigned to work in factories alongside male colleagues, though they also worked as doctors, professors, and accountants just as their male counterparts did. Women therefore don't overtly object to discrimination, because it doesn't really exist as a problem in this domain.

This, again, is the situation on paper. In reality, women in the Czech Republic suffer the same subtle prejudices as in any male dominated society. While employment is officially not discriminated upon the basis of sex, men still occupy most of the top positions. Even as the political correctness of the west is trying to soften the traditional male-female roles, men here are still expected to bring home the bacon, and women are still expected to cook it.

If you are sensitive to such a world view, you may be quick to take offence at the still traditional roles that men and women play in the Czech Republic. You will likely object to some of the random comments you are bound to hear, mostly by men, but some also by women, though in fact no harm or seriousness is generally meant by it. In a way, they're just reinforcing their traditional roles with which they feel most comfortable.

You'll find, if invited to a Czech home for example, that the women do all the meal preparation while the men sit and talk. If you make an attempt to help out with chopping the onions, the man of the house may say no, leave it, it's her business. At the same time, though, it is not a gruff action: the woman will see it as her responsibility, and the man will be very gracious, complimenting his wife on how well she cooks.

Men in this way are seen as respecting women and their sexuality. They don't look upon women purely as objects of lust, nor do they simply put them down as incompetent because they are women (at least no more than men in other nations).

BEING INVITED TO SOMEONE'S HOME

Being invited to a visit or for dinner at a Czech person's home is a rare event, and should be jumped at because of it. Because an invitation to a Czech home is such a special occasion, you should carry yourself with appropriate humility and respect, as you will be treated with considerable honour. Try to determine before you go whether this is indeed a dinner invitation or just a get-together, especially if it's planned for late afternoon or late evening, or you may wind up eating pretzels all night. They do invite friends over just for a chat every once in a while.

A token gift is always happily received, though it's not necessarily expected. Do not overdo it. Any offering of something expensive or exceptionally personal will meet with recoil: your host may then feel obliged to reciprocate with something of equal or higher value, and you may well find yourself presented with beautiful books and family heirlooms. It's only a token gesture anyway, so keep it simple. A bottle of wine or liquor is your safest bet, particularly a bottle of something from your home country if possible. If you have any typical trinkets from home, they can be given to symbolise the cultural exchange.

Flowers hold a particularly romantic, even sexual connotation here, so a gift of a bouquet of flowers may be perceived as a bit untoward, unless, of course, that is the point. Just note that Czechs usually don't take flowers out of

the plastic wrap; if you are ever offered flowers you should adhere to the same practice.

Note that Czechs always remove their shoes before entering a home. You should automatically expect to do this as well. Your hosts will probably offer you *bačkory* (slippers) which you should accept.

You will be greeted royally. From the moment you enter the home you will be offered a drink, and from the moment you finish it you will be offered another. Small appetizers, such as chips or nuts, may be served, and during the meal you will be constantly doted upon. Don't offer to help with any aspect of preparation or cleaning up. You are the honoured guest, and your host is expected to properly care for you. Any overly-friendly gestures, such as offering to help clear the dishes, are perceived as a sort of sign of discontent, as if the hosts had overlooked it themselves, and can be quite embarrassing.

When settling down at the table, a simple *dobrou chut'* (enjoy your meal) suffices as a toast; the host will always say it with an honest hope that you will like the food. It is therefore imperative that you praise the meal at some point during eating. This is always a conversation starter anyway, as you may well want to comment on its preparation, while your hosts will invariably want to discuss your personal and national eating habits. It is generally good form to accept a second helping, which will likely be offered, even if you ask for just a little bit. Let yourself be spoiled; when you really can't take any more, say something like, "It's really excellent, but I can't eat any more" (in Czech, *už nemůžu*).

After the meal, you'll probably move back to the living room for conversation and coffee, and perhaps a glass of Becherovka. You should always accept what is offered, or if you'd prefer not to have it, suggest a glass of water instead—they will always feel obliged to serve you something, so to say, "Oh, no, I don't want to trouble you" is beside the point. More conversation will follow, and you'll probably go through photo albums and listen to music. *Chlebíčky* (small open-faced sandwiches) are often presented in a nice display on a platter after the meal as well.

INVITING CZECHS TO YOUR HOME

Pay special attention to returning the favour with an invitation of your own. It is indeed a friendly gesture, though note the socio-economic differences between your culture and your hosts, if such a disparity does exits. Keep in mind that most Czechs still live in small, humble flats and their salaries may be lower than your own. If you live in a big house or flat paid for on company money, you'll likely only instill a sense of embarrassment if you invite Czech friends over. Czechs are therefore more likely to invite you back again, to avoid what they may sense as a potentially uncomfortable situation.

Nevertheless, they are innately curious, and if you do feel comfortable enough to invite a Czech friend over, try to prepare a meal typical of your own country. If you are, say, Brazilian or Japanese, this is a marvellous opportunity to turn them on to something completely different; if you're American, this is a good chance to prove that American food is more than just pizza and hamburgers, or if you're British, that there's more to life than fish and chips. They will undoubtedly want to see photos of your family and country, and learn of your hobbies; again, cultural relations are at the forefront.

DINING ETIQUETTE

One must always precede the first bite of a meal with a proper incantation to the life giving qualities of food. Just as the French say *bon appetít*, Czechs make sure to say *dobrou chut'* as a form of blessing. The expression doesn't quite translate into English, though we don't have one of our own anyway, a fact that Czechs find almost barbaric. The literal meaning is 'good taste,' and it's sometimes preceded with *přeju Vám* … ('I wish you …'). Be sure to respect this formality, and when your host or dinner guest bestows it upon you, respond with the same, or use the French *bon appetít*; it's widely understood. Your non-fluent host may try to be clever and proclaim in English, "good taste!"

Czechs rarely offer a speech-like toast. The proper action is to raise the glass and pronounce "*Na zdraví!*", ('to health') at the first drink. (A common linguistic confusion amongst foreigners lies in the similarity of the words *na zdraví* and *nádraži*, which means 'train station;' you'll get an appreciative laugh by purposely mixing them up.) Czechs often simply clink the glasses and say *"Ahoj"* or *"Čau"* ('hi')—this serves as an acknowledgement of friendship, and is said with a sparkle in the eye and a satisfied smile.

Czechs usually eat with the fork in the left hand and knife in the right; it's practical. Most Czech dishes come with a sauce; the proper way to eat is to pick up pieces of food with your fork in the left hand, and slather the sauce onto your meat or potato or dumpling using your knife in the right hand. Those who attempt to cut and feed the mouth all in one fork motion are seen as rather classless.

The napkin remains neatly folded on the table, not on the lap. There is no apparent reason for this though, especially as many pub and restaurant napkins are merely a cheap piece of almost non-absorbent paper. When you've finished eating, it's considered good form to lay the knife and fork parallel on the plate and to scrunch up the napkin and place it on the table (or on the plate itself, if it's a paper napkin). In more formal settings, it's acceptable to place your napkin on your lap during the meal and leave it on the table when they clear the plate.

WEDDING TRADITIONS

Czech weddings encapsulate closely-held values and traditions, and attending such an event can afford a wonderful insight to the rich customs of this country.

Czech weddings are generally smallish affairs, reflecting the modest means of most; a wedding celebration with more than 50 or so family and friends is considered rather large. The smallish size of the wedding reception is also intended to emphasise the importance of the closest friends and family members. Civil ceremonies are very common, given the Czechs' non-religious bent; these often occur at town halls or at a castle or chateau in the countryside—a marvellous setting. A smaller, more select group then receives an additional card inviting them to the reception afterward; make sure if you receive a wedding announcement that there is a separate card inviting you to the reception, or you may unwittingly crash the party! Gift-giving is only really expected if you actually attend the wedding; common gifts include items for the home, such as vases, dishes and so on.

Order Of The Day

Wedding ceremonies often begin in the late morning or early afternoon. Attendees congregate outside the chapel, and then a procession into the chapel is led by the bride and groom—contrary to traditions in many countries, where the bride enters last. The ceremony itself is not overly long and the proceedings are not much different from those in most other countries in Europe or North America. After the ceremony, the bride and groom then lead the procession out of the church and wait together outside; attendees then line up and one-by-one offer congratulations and best wishes to the happy couple, led by the immediate family members. At the reception site, all attendees congregate outside, where the bride and groom must pass three 'tests'. First is to determine who is the master of the new home: the bride and groom are presented with two small shot glasses, one containing water and the other an identical clear shot of slivovice (plum brandy). Each takes a glass and drinks: the one who gets the slivovice is declared master of the house.

The second test judges how well the couple will work together in their new home: a plate is smashed on the ground, and the groom is supposed to sweep the shards into a dustpan held by the bride—the difficulty with this is that interlopers often complicate matters by kicking the shards in all directions. The third test is a test of strength: the groom must split a block of wood with an axe.

Once inside, the festivities begin with lunch and often continue throughout the afternoon and evening, often culminating with dinner several hours later and drinking and dancing throughout.

Czechs have not quite adopted the practice of using gift registry through a retail outlet, so you're on your own to choose a present. Cards are also expected whether you attend or not; Czech wedding cards often have poems and words of wisdom along with the usual wishes for good health and happiness, and at some point during the reception the bride and groom often open cards and read them aloud, to the alternate sighs and laughs of all attendees.

SETTLING IN

CHAPTER 5

'Lepší třikrat vyhořet, než se jednou stěhovat'
(Better that your house burns down
three times than to have to move once)
—Czech folk saying

HOUSING

Finding housing in Prague is a lot better now than in the 1990s, but it can still be a real game involving lots of searching, negotiating, and compromising. In the rest of the country, the real estate market is not well established and you may have to rely on contacts from work to help secure a place. Either way, you can expect to take lots of time and either spend lots of money or make lots of concessions. In Prague at least, you are fortunate now that supply has finally improved and demand has tailed off somewhat, so the Manhattan or London-type of rental prices that dominated the 1990s have at least subsided. Prices may be entering a period of stabilisation, but you will still be paying something approximating western European or North American rents. Many expatriates living in Prague earn salaries from home that are adequate to cover this, but if you intend to relocate here as a free-lancer or English teacher working on a Czech wage, you may still be hard-pressed to meet these prices. This should give you an idea of the cost of living quandary faced by many Czechs.

If you have a high standard and the means to fund it, you will likely find that Old Town pad or suburban spread, but you may still have to make a sacrifice or two. There is now plenty of good-quality real estate in attractive neighbourhoods, but it does come with a price. If you're on a low budget, it's a matter of luck and quite possibly lowering your standard. Flexibility is your greatest asset. And remember that the extra money you spend on housing can be made up on the cheaper costs of things such as food, entertainment and travel.

This is the Situation

An explanation of the housing situation is necessary here to understand what is a particularly complicated issue. The real estate rental market is still unraveling itself from the former regime, and a two-tiered system is in effect: many Czechs live in state-owned properties and still pay subsidised rents (or have plumped their life's savings into buying such properties from the state as they have become available), while foreigners are usually forced to pay hundreds or thousands of euros per month for their apartment or house of choice. Landlords therefore often try to get foreign tenants, who can usually pay much more than Czechs. Now that real estate is integrating into the market economy, locals seeking housing are subject to the same rent costs as foreigners, though they often don't have the same resources.

Under central planning, the government provided only a bare minimum of adequate housing while stifling private investment in real estate. People were simply assigned housing by the authorities, with respect to family size but not to location. One could not simply decide to move or to rent one's flat out without proper authority, and waiting lists for flats lasted several years. This meant that many people were forced to share flats with family members and acquaintances in the meantime: in many cases students and young adults still lived with their parents, and separated couples even continued to share flats!

Things are improving for Czechs: people are gaining more financial flexibility, the government is actively selling flats to its current tenants, and banks are aggressively offering mortgages to help pay for these investments; this has fueled a boom in housing prices in recent years. But it will still take years for the market to sort itself out.

The massive grey housing projects you see on the outskirts of all Czech cities were built as a quick-fix solution to housing: these *panelák* (prefab) blocks of flats are functional to an extreme: not only are they aesthetically revolting, the flats therein are tiny and uniformly cheap. Yet families live in them just as anywhere—under central planning, whether you were assigned a flat in a *panelák* or in a classy neighbourhood was a matter of pure chance. Because of this, the *sídliště* ('housing estates,' as they euphemistically call them) are nothing like the housing projects of an American inner-city. In fact, there are some advantages to them: heat and hot water generally work well, public transportation to the centre is usually excellent, and there are always shopping centres and schools in the immediate vicinity.

At the same time, many older apartment buildings (including some older *paneláky*) have deteriorated. Utilities occasionally fail, public hallways haven't been painted in years, and there is precious little money for surface or structural improvements. Those fortunate enough to own their property are in a privileged position indeed—if they can do a good reconstruction job, their property becomes part of an exclusive pool of attractive homes. Many relocating foreigners simply cannot bear the lower standard of housing in general, and are thus forced to pay large sums in order to get good standards.

Who Owns Your Flat

There are three types of landlords, or lessors: (1) the city or state; (2) a co-operative, meaning a Czech legal entity that has purchased and invested in a building and whose members include the building's tenants; and (3) a person or company who has either bought a property or regained it through restitution, and is thus the private owner.

If a building is owned by the city or state, and many still are, the tenant who has legal rights to a flat may rent it out with permission from the city or state. The tenant is thus the lessee, and the person to whom he rents it is the subtenant. If you rent a city or state owned flat from a lessee who has not been granted permission to do so, the lease is illegal and both you and your 'landlord' can be evicted from the premises. The likelihood of anyone catching up to you is very low indeed (I 'squatted' in this way myself for two years), but exercise caution, particularly with regard to neighbours, who may harbour jealousies or territoriality issues.

If a co-operative owns the building, the tenants within have a sort of membership status and can basically do what they want with their flat; they do officially need to be granted permission to sublet from the cooperative as a whole, but this is usually a mere formality. The city or state plays no role in this procedure.

If a private individual or a company owns the building, he is the official landlord, and a lease agreement is negotiated directly with him.

A distinct advantage to working with a good agency is that they do all the work for you, which includes finding property

How to Find Housing

You have three options in finding a place to live:

- Check with friends and colleagues. If you are replacing somebody at work, you may want to consider renting his or her flat, or if you have contacts in the city, scour around and see what they may come up with. If you're on a low budget, this is a good way to finagle something.
- Check the classifieds newspaper *Annonce* (it appears in two editions—ask for section A), sold every Monday, Wednesday, and Friday at any newsagent, or available online at http://www.annonce.cz. There are lengthy listings of flats and houses for rent, which you'll need Czech-speaking skills to decipher. Thousands of people rely on *Annonce*, so start early, work the phones immediately, and get out to see places as soon as possible. You may also strike it lucky through listings in *The Prague Post* or a Czech daily newspaper, but these are usually placed by real estate agents.

and scheduling visits, translating an agreement with the landlord, and signing a legally binding contract.

Once the deal is inked, you should be set. Prague landlords seem to have finally learned that once they rent their apartment under contract, they cannot do things like enter at their own free will, or raise the rent without warning. This was a problem in the 1990s, but apparently still seems to be something of an issue in towns other than Prague.

Price

Now the fun begins. The chances of actually finding a home suited to your needs for a price that Czechs themselves would pay are slim to none, so be prepared to spend at least

- Use a real estate agent. For many, this is the only way. Because many landlords want to rent their flats and villas to foreigners (at western European rent levels or higher) they go directly to agents who specialise in such dealings. Many real estate offices in Prague in fact deal almost exclusively with a foreign clientele, and a network has developed amongst agencies, western companies and landlords. Be careful, though, whom you choose. It's no problem to use more than one agency, but be sure to contact one that advertises itself in both English and Czech, and that has experienced agents on staff. Likewise, there is no listings or exclusivity system, so real estate companies often share properties. Most agencies charge commissions to the tenant, usually of one month's rent; many agencies try to take a month from the landlord as well. The generally reputable agents usually place ads in the real estate classifieds of *The Prague Post*; I have listed more in the Resources Guide at the back of this book.

what you are accustomed to spending at home, and quite possibly more. Rent prices are often quoted in euros, due to the perceived greater stability of that currency. Sometimes prices are quoted in Czech crowns (Kč), and payments are usually accepted in crowns.

As of 2005, when this edition was published, for a quality one—or two-bedroom flat in or around the centre of Prague you can expect to pay at least 800 euros per month, or more like 1,500-2,000 euros for a larger, more luxurious place. The Old Town and Malá Strana areas of course command top euro, but there is some good value to be had in areas such as Vinohrady or Letná, a little off-centre though still within easy commuting distance. Single-family homes and rowhouses in the suburbs start around 1,500 euros, but the luxury villas and newer developments in Prague 6 near the international schools often start at about 2,500 euros, going up to as much as 6,000 euros at the top of the line.

If you're really scraping the barrel you may have to settle for a place in a more run-down area such as Žižkov or Smíchov, or even in the *sidlíště*, which can be had for around 300–500 euros.

What to Consider

An interesting phenomenon seems to take place among expatriates relocating in Prague. Those who are accustomed to driving up to an hour to work every day and sending the kids to faraway schools refuse to live the same way in Prague; because the city is so compact, they insist on having a place in or near the centre, or near the international schools, most of which are in Prague 6. Don't be too sold on living in Pragues 1 or 6—these are generally perceived as the glamour districts, though in fact there are plenty of other nice areas, often in cheaper rent categories.

The guide to Prague's districts below should help in deciding where to live. Remember that Prague has an excellent public transit system, so even if you live in an area that feels far away, it's probably not more than 20–30 minutes to the centre.

PRAGUE BY DISTRICT

Prague is divided into ten districts, each of which is loosely subdivided into neighbourhoods. The following is a summary of each district, with positive and negative points on each.

Prague 1 is the central area, which includes the Old Town, Malá Strana (the Little Quarter or Lesser Town) and the castle district. The advantages to living in Prague 1 are obvious—it is beautiful, historical and dead central, but there are certain disadvantages too. Because the city lies in a valley, the air in Prague 1 is about the worst. Parking is very difficult to find, and certain streets can be noisy, particularly at night.

Prague 2 includes the close-in residential neighbourhoods of Vinohrady and Nové město (New Town) along the river. Because of its pleasant surroundings, easy access to shopping and nightlife, and well connected transportation lines, Prague 2 is in high demand.

Prague 3 is an interesting blend of pleasant neighbourhoods and working-class grit, located just off-centre and to the east. Prague 3 borders on Vinohrady to the south, thus includes many of Vinohrady's architectural and residential advantages, though it is largely made up of the historically working-class area known as Žižkov. All of Prague 3 is well served by public transportation, shopping, and nightlife.

Prague 4 is difficult to characterise, as it is spreads over the entire southern sector of the city east of the river. Closer-in areas such as Nusle, bordering Prague 2, have some good blocks of flats and views; further-out areas such as Podolí and Braník contain fine villas at rents lower than in Prague 6—in fact many people overlook Prague 4 in the rush for Prague 6, which is a mistake. Prague 4's disadvantages are mainly that it contains vast tracts of *panelák* buildings, a huge eyesore. The city not too long ago reclassified these further reaches of the city as Pragues 11 and 12. Direct transportation links can be scarce; many trips involve a bus ride to the metro or tram. The new metro line D, which is supposed to be up and running sometime after 2010, should provide much better service through Prague 4.

Prague 5 covers the southwestern suburbs across the river from Prague 4, and contains everything from the dirty section of Smíchov along the river to impressive villas (with great views) high up on the hills of Barrandov to the enormous grey *paneláks* of Jihozapadní město (actually now part of Prague 13). Prague 5 has some fine parks such as Prokopské údolí and relatively clean air in the higher elevations. Transportation is good, though you may need to catch a bus or tram to the metro.

Prague 6 is generally regarded as the city's most prestigious district after Prague 1. The Dejvice and Hanspaulka areas in particular are home to many foreign businesspeople and local politicians. The area has many embassies and fine villas, and is close to the airport and nice parks such as Hvězda and Šárecké údolí. Families often choose to live here for the proximity to the American International School in Nebušice (there is even a subdevelopment adjacent to the school filled exclusively with international families), though prices here are amongst the highest in the city. Most public transportation connections to the centre involve a tram or bus to the metro.

A view of Prague, from above the Vltava River.

Prague 7 includes the commercial/residential Holešovice and Letná areas tucked in the loop of the river Vlatva, plus a piece of land called Troja just north of the river. The fantastic parks Letná and Stromovka take up sizeable chunks of the area, and much of Troja is occupied by the Prague zoo. The inner loop of the river has excellent underground system and tram service.

Prague 8 occupies the northern section of town, and except for the rundown Libeň neighbourhood, which was severely damaged by the 2002 floods but does have a metro line running through, most of the district feels far out and decrepit. The Kobylisy neighbourhood does have a few nice homes up on the hill, however, and the new metro C-line extension brings it a little closer to the centre.

Prague 9 disappears off the map to the northeast and is too far away and/or too unattractive for most. If you happen to work in the area, though, you can probably find a good home for significantly cheaper rent than anywhere else in town.

Prague 10 wedges itself in alongside Pragues 2 and 3, then spreads out into east-southeastern infinity. Close-in Prague 10 offers some fine residential neighbourhoods—Vršovice and parts of Strašnice, for example, are little different from Vinohrady in appearance and are similarly well-connected, and nice blocks of flats, detached homes and row houses exist elsewhere. Much of the district, however, is similar to Prague 9—far away and industrial.

GENERAL STANDARDS

Standards of quality of flats and houses vary widely, and it is important to be certain of what you want and what you can expect.

Flats in older buildings are often spacious, while newer ones can be pretty cramped. Size of flats is always referred to in square metres and in number of rooms (not number of bedrooms), plus a kitchen. Therefore a 3 + 1 flat has three rooms and a separate kitchen; a 3 + kk flat has three rooms, one of which has a 'kitchen corner.' Czechs often live in flats that serve the bare minimum of necessity: a family of four may occupy a small apartment with two bedrooms, a living room, kitchen and one bathroom.

Kitchens normally contain a sink and countertop, cabinet space, stove/oven and refrigerator/freezer, the appliances usually being on the small side. Dishwashers are rare.

Bathrooms normally have a tub, though sometimes only a shower. Tubs for some reason almost never have shower curtains or hooks on the wall for shower heads, though there is always a detachable hose. The hot water boiler often hangs above the tub, and if it's an older model you'll be able to see the flames from the gas boiler. Toilets (WC) are usually in a cubicle separate from the bathroom. Washing machines are quite common, though are small, and are usually located in the bathroom; dryers are rare, and Czechs usually hang laundry up to dry above the bathtub or on the balcony.

Flats are often rented unfurnished, though some, especially in the lower price range, come furnished. Furnished flats and houses should include the following: bed(s), table(s), desk(s), chairs, wardrobe or closet space, chest of drawers, wall units or bookshelves, curtains and basic kitchen appliances. Check about silverware, pots and pans and linens; furnished flats may or may not include these.

If you take a furnished place, you will not need to buy much, if anything else, though old Czech furniture can indeed be quite old. Single beds are generally narrow, while double beds are often in the form of a unit with two single mattresses laid together, not a queen or king-size mattress. As impersonal as this may seem (how unromantic is that?) again it has a practical basis: if one person moves around at night, or goes to bed or rises separately from the other, there is less chance of waking the other person. Sheets and blankets are not normally used, rather a thick duvet called *peřina* wrapped in a sheet is used to cover the bed year round; double beds usually have two duvets, one for each mattress. Pillows are usually very large and fluffy. Most flats have double-paned windows, to help keep out the noise.

Buildings can be old and decrepit, with creaky lifts and peeling walls. Some are in decent condition, and a few have been nicely fixed up. All blocks of flats have a series of bells

with names on the door outside so you can ring up. It is extremely rare to have a building porter or attendant, and tenants usually take turns sweeping or mopping the public areas. Most buildings are kept locked at all times, and every tenant has a key to the front door. Many blocks of flats in commercial areas have shops on the ground floor.

Because of chronic pollution, you may wish to invest in an air purifier. Also, because it is dry in the winter, a humidifier could come in handy.

Lifts

Many apartment buildings have lifts (elevators), but some do not. Many lifts are slow and creaky, making you feel a bit nervous the first time you ride in them. Older lifts operate on a system whereby you push a button to call the lift—but if the red light next to the button is on, the lift is already moving because someone else has called it or is in it. Older lifts don't have any sort of memory here, so you have to wait until the light goes off, then push the button—you might want to stand with your finger poised over the button until the light goes off, to make sure you get to call it ahead of someone else on another floor. Similarly, if people going to different floors get in the lift at the same time, it is important to push the lowest floor number destination first, then when that person gets out, to push the next highest floor. You can avoid disgruntled neighbours by announcing your floors as you get in the lift. Most lifts have doors which must be closed before the lift can move. This is important to note especially when you get out—if you just walk off without closing the door properly, the lift will just sit there, unusable to those on other floors. I have had to walk up five floors to my office on many occasions when someone who wasn't aware of this failed to close the door properly.

Student Accommodation

If you are a student, you will likely be assigned a room in a *kolej* (dormitory) which may be single or shared with a roommate or two. As universities don't have campuses as elsewhere, university dorms are scattered throughout the city. You'll likely have to use public transportation to get to classes every day. Dorm rooms have a bed, desk, lamp, linens, bookshelves, wardrobe, bathroom and toilet (often shared with suite-mates though sometimes in the corridor), and there is a community kitchen on each floor.

Useful Words

byt	flat or apartment
vila or *rodinný dům*	detached or semidetached house. The rather grandiose word *vila* is used to avoid confusion over the word 'house,' (*dům* in Czech) which also means 'building.'
zařízený	furnished
nezařízený	unfurnished
pronajmout	to rent
k pronajmu	for rent
pokoj or *místnost*	room

kuchyň	kitchen
koupelna	bathroom
záchod	toilet
sporák	stove
telefon	telephone
inkaso	utilities
topení	heat
elektřina	electricity
plyn	gas
voda	water
přízemí	ground floor
l. patro (první patro), *2. patro (druhé patro),* etc.	first floor, second floor, etc.
výtah	lift (elevator)
složenka	postal money order

Legalities and Tenant Rights

The same basic tenant rights apply here as elsewhere, assuming you have a legal lease. Lease contracts are usually signed for a period of one, two, or three years, often with an option-to-review clause attached. There are no legal regulations regarding length periods—it's whatever you agree with the landlord. There is an official notice period of three months for both sides if either decides to break the lease with sufficient reason but actually tenants can leave without giving a reason after three months notice. Landlords are bound by a series of regulations outlined in the Czech Civil Code. That said, enforcement of these rules is lax, and should you get stuck with a difficult landlord, you may have trouble going about legal resolution to disputes. Keep in mind too, if you are renting illegally (which is fairly common) you have no tenant rights.

Deposits are rarely demanded, though landlords often request advance payments of two months, sometimes more. Again, there are regulations on this. If your landlord requests two months upon signing the lease, you are usually not expected to pay rent again until the beginning of the third month. Many landlords do request telephone deposits, which are often calculated as the average monthly phone bill, paid two months prior to the end of the lease. Insurance on the premises is the responsibility of the landlord. If you bring or buy your own furniture, you must pay your own insurance for it.

PROPERTY OWNERSHIP

Many Czechs hurried to buy property in the year or two building up to EU entry, in fear that once the country was in the union, the Germans would descend and snatch everything up again, thereby driving up prices as well. This of course drove prices up rapidly on its own.

The rules on foreigners owning property are a little uncertain. Whether a flat or building is for sale to foreigners depends on who is selling. City- or state-owned property is likely not available for sale to foreigners, as the government understandably wants to protect the interests of its citizens. Property owned by co-operatives or individuals may be available for sale to foreigners—it depends on local laws, which vary, and, if a co-operative, the rules of the co-operative.

Real estate agencies as listed in *The Prague Post* often have listings of properties for sale, and the classifieds newspaper *Annonce*, as well as classifieds listings in daily Czech papers, are good places to look as well. *Hypotéka* (mortgages) are becoming quite commonplace, as banks such as Česká spořitelna, ČSOB and Komerční banka are expanding their portfolio of retail offerings.

UTILITIES

Utilities include gas/oil, water, electricity, sewage and waste removal and building charges. One difficulty Czechs have faced in the transformation to a market economy is that utility prices are equivalent to those anywhere else in the world, even on much lower salaries. Imagine your electricity bill suddenly rising by a factor of five or ten, and you can start to understand why Czechs are very careful about leaving the lights on.

If you are paying your own utilities, you will receive the bills in the post and will be expected to pay them in cash at the post office, or through bank transfer. Note that landlords will want to keep the telephone bill separate, even if all other utilities are included in the lease, because of long-distance calls that foreigners are wont to make. *(For information on setting up telephone and internet connections, refer to the Telephones and Internet sections later in this chapter.)*

Utility Bills

Some landlords include utility bills up to a reasonable level, though utilities are usually paid in addition to the rent. This must be worked out on an individual basis.

Electricity

The Czech Republic uses 220 AV and 60 cycles, in line with most of the rest of Europe. Plugs are of the large, round three-prong type. If you are coming from North America, which runs on 110 AV and 50 cycles, you will not be able to use your electrical appliances without an adaptor and transformer, but even these can be touch-and-go. These are easily obtainable at any electronics shop at home, though are difficult to find here, so be sure to stock up. Most appliances such as hairdryers, electric razors and irons are best bought here, but if you're bringing anything that plugs into a wall, be sure to get the proper converters before you come.

Commercial Leasing

The laws regarding leasing of office space are generally similar to those for residential property, although the lease of commercial space falls under a different set of laws. Most of the real estate agencies that list in *The Prague Post* also do commercial leasing.

LEGAL DOCUMENTS FOR LIVING AND WORKING

Work and residence permits need not be obtained before you arrive in the Czech Republic, although you will find the going much easier here if you have things arranged beforehand. If you choose to sort things out after arriving on your tourist visa or stamp, or you are unable to finish the process before you come, note that you may need to visit the foreign police immediately upon arrival. In either case, be forewarned that the process is long and complicated. The bureaucracy here is terrible (but then, so it is in most countries), the reason being that there is very high demand for Czech residency status. The Czech Republic is still an attractive place to live and work for North Americans and western Europeans, as well as for eastern European such as Slovaks and Ukrainians, who find the employment prospects and pay much better here than at home. At the same time, the rising level of unemployment in the Czech Republic prompts the government to limit the numbers of work permits issued.

If you are legally employed or are related to someone who is legally employed, or if you are a student in the Czech Republic, and if you have a legal residence, then you can obtain a long-stay permit which entitles you to all advantages that Czechs have here, such as state-provided health insurance. There are two types of long-stay permits beyond the regular tourist visa or passport stamp: (1) regular long-stay permit called a *Průkaz o povolení k*

Documents Required

Work and Spousal Visas
Note: Be sure to check with the Czech embassy in your home country before moving, and always bring multiple copies of required documents. These may need to be notarised or apostilled.

- Passport
- Official copy of birth certificate
- Official copy of marriage certificate
- University diplomas, trade licenses or other relevant professional qualifications
- Evidence of an offer to work or study in the Czech Republic
- Evidence of financial solvency

pobytu cizince, on which is noted your work and residence status, valid for up to one year with unlimited renewals; and (2) permanent residence permit—only available for reasons of marriage or other permanent relationship to Czech nationals.

You must fill out all forms and provide all notarised and/or apostilled and translated documents exactly as dictated—and the regulations change frequently. Because the rules change so often, the information provided here is a general guide only. Check with the Czech Embassy in your home country before leaving. You may find it useful to employ the services of a good lawyer to help guide you through the maze of paperwork; we have listed a few at the back of this book. If you are arriving as an employee of a foreign or Czech firm, including a language school, they should have some experience with the procedures. If you are a student, your study-abroad programme or the office of international students at your university should be able to help.

In order to obtain a long-stay permit, you must provide a number of documents that include (but may not be limited

Long-Stay Permit

In order to obtain a long-stay permit, you must have the following three documents:

- Proof of a clear criminal record in the Czech Republic and abroad
- Residence permit
- Indication of a reason to stay (i.e. work permit, Czech trade licence, student visa, or relationship to someone with one of the above)

For all of these applications you will need to provide your passport; you should also be sure to bring all relevant marriage certificates, university diplomas and trade licences that you possess.

to) a residence permit; an indication of a reason to stay (i.e. work permit, Czech trade licence, student visa or relationship to someone with one of the above); proof of a clear criminal record in the Czech Republic and abroad; and evidence of financial solvency (which may include notarised credit card statements and/or evidence of sufficient funds in a Czech bank account). For all of these documents you will need to fill out forms and provide your passport and passport photos; you should also be sure to bring official copies of birth certificates, marriage certificates, and relevant university diplomas or trade licenses that you possess to help ease the process.

Obtaining a Residency Permit

To gain legal accommodation you must present an official sworn affidavit (*čestné prohlášení*), provided by the foreign police, which must be signed in front of a notary, and stating that your landlord is renting a living space to you and has the legal right to do so. All family members over the age of six need their own affidavit, so be sure that your landlord signs as many documents as there are family members.

Obtaining a Reason to Stay

Reasons to stay in the Czech Republic include the following:

- Ownership or co-ownership of a company legally established in the Czech Republic. Such a person does not need a work permit, rather he must provide documents such as the articles of association of the established company, trade licenses, and proof that the company is registered in court.
- Sole entrepreneurship, that is, independent work in a practicing trade, not necessarily in connection with any company; this includes freelance work. Sole entrepreneurs come in various trades, which can be broken down into two main groups: (a) Those in regulated fields, such as law, medicine, dentistry, pharmaceuticals, restaurant and catering services, etc. Such persons

who are professionally licensed in regulated trades in their home country must obtain an equivalent qualification in the Czech Republic. (b) Those in special fields which do not have an accepted governing body, such as computer programmers, consultants, freelance writers, etc. Sole entrepreneurs in non-regulated fields must obtain a trade license (*Živnostenský list*), of which there are many kinds.

- Employee status in a Czech legal entity, whether it is a Czech company or a foreign company legally established in the Czech Republic. This person then needs a work permit as his reason to stay. In order to protect Czech workers, the government has a system whereby an employer who wants to hire a foreign worker must first be presented with potential Czech substitutes. The employer must register at the employment office in his municipality indicating that he has a vacancy; the employment office then has a few weeks to send potential employees to the employer. The employer can refuse the offerings with a simple reason, then proceed to approach the work permits office.
- Student enrolled in a school or university in the Czech Republic. Students can and should obtain a student visa before arrival in the Czech Republic, and then upon arrival obtain a long-stay permit if needed. Your institution here will help.
- Permanent relationship to a long-term resident; i.e. a spouse or child over the age of six. Documents of a relationship, such as marriage or birth certificates, are required.

Verifying a Clear Criminal Record

This is a formality which must be done to assure the authorities that you have no outstanding record of criminal behaviour in the Czech Republic. Further inspection may also delve into the Interpol network to verify that you are not a fugitive from elsewhere. Check with the foreign police in Prague (or wherever you plan to live) for details on the procedures.

Once all relevant documents are obtained, proceed to the Foreign Police (*Cizinecká policie)* in your city. Be sure to arrive very early in the morning to get in line, and be sure to have adequate cash on hand to pay the fees. Be prepared for rude service. All going well, you will still have to wait several weeks for them to issue your long-stay permit, affectionately known as a green card.

SCHOOLS

If you have children, you will of course want to find good schools for them in a language they will understand. Only the very youngest children have the innate capacity to pick up languages with enough rapidity that they could attend a Czech school; therefore any children over the age of about five will probably need to attend a private international school. If you do have very young children, and you plan to stay at least a year in the country, you can do your child an enormous favour by sending him or her to a *mateřská škola* (Czech nursery school). Young children are always quick to adapt, and you'll be amazed to hear your kids actually speaking Czech after a few months. One British acquaintance of mine has a daughter who went to a Czech *mateřská škola* for two years: her Czech is near-fluent and her parents learned vocabulary from her!

Nursery schools in general are very good, and after-school day care is usually provided if both parents work.

If you are interested in sending your child to a regular Czech public school, contact the *školský úřad* (office) of the school district in which you live.

International Schools

If your children are over the age of about five, you'll probably have to send them to an international school, of which there are several excellent (if expensive) ones in Prague, accredited by American, British, French, German and other countries' school systems. It is important to contact these schools well ahead of time as applications can be lengthy processes due to high demand. Some embassies also have schools attached to them, primarily to provide education for the children of embassy staff. *(Several international schools are listed in the Resources Guide at the back of this book.)*

PETS

If you are bringing your pet with you, you must have a certificate of health, which you obtain from your veterinarian at home—you must also have an animal passport with its photo!

Czech vets are excellent, inexpensive, and can be found in the Yellow Pages under *Veterináři*. Finding a vet that speaks English, however, may be a different story. Ask your embassy for suggestions.

Be aware that some landlords do not want tenants to have pets, although there is no official regulation about this. Czechs themselves are great dog lovers, and you always see dachshunds, schnauzers and German shepherds in every park and train station. Czechs have an amusing habit of carrying small dogs in bags on the underground—this saves the ticket price for children and animals.

MONEY

Unless and until the Czechs join the European Monetary Union (currently not expected before 2009 or 2010), the currency is the Czech crown (*Koruna česká*), abbreviated as Kč, and broken down into hellers (*haléře*). Crown notes come in denominations of 20, 50, 100, 200, 500, 1,000, 2,000 and 5,000 Kč. Coins come in denominations of 0.50, 1, 2, 5, 10, 20 and 50 Kč.

The crown has been floating on money markets since early 1990 with varying degrees of government control, and has remained relatively stable against the US dollar, British pound and Euro—generally not trading at any further extremes than these currencies do versus one another. Czechs are permitted to exchange any amount of crowns into any other currency, but note that foreigners may be required to provide exchange receipts if they want to change large sums of Czech crowns back into foreign currency.

Czech banks and shops do not honour personal cheques, and there is no system of personal cheque-writing available. Credit cards are gaining wider acceptance; most shops or restaurants that deal with western clients will accept American Express, MasterCard, Visa or Eurocard. Most banks offer cash advances on MasterCard and Visa, and most bank branches throughout the country have ATMs called *bankomat* that honour the above cards as well as Czech-bank issued debit cards.

Banking

As discussed in the History, Politics, Economics and Religion chapter, banks underwent fundamental change beginning in the late 1990s. Crises in the Czech financial sector forced rapid consolidation among commercial banks, and all the major Czech banks have by now been acquired by larger foreign banks. While the transformation was difficult, foreign ownership has brought about better controls and standards, rendering the services and capabilities of most Czech banks comparable to what you might expect anywhere. Savings accounts, wire transfers, commercial loans, mortgages, investment advice and other such services are regular activities. About the only difference you will notice in terms of your day-to-day financial dealings is the lack of personal chequing; transactions are carried out in cash, by credit card (this is still somewhat limited but growing), by wire transfer or direct deposit, or for things such as rent and utility bill payments, through the post office.

Foreign Banks

Foreign banks in the Czech Republic function as representative offices or branches, and they face some limitations on account opening and on lending as their role is more to service their corporate clients and participate in the Czech financial markets. Foreign banks with commercial/retail services include ABN-AMRO, Bank Austria-Creditanstalt, Citibank, Commerzbank, Dresdner Bank, HypoVereinsbank (HVB), GE Capital Bank and ING.

The leading Czech banks are Česká spořitelna (owned by Austria's Erste Bank), Komerční banka (owned by France's Société Générale), Československé obchodní banka (ČSOB) (owned by Belgium's KBC), Investiční a poštovní banka (IPB, owned by ČSOB after a failed privatisation attempt by Japan's Nomura) and Živnostenská banka (owned by Italy's UniCredit). As European banking itself continues to undergo mergers and acquisition activity, it would not be surprising to see some of these ties change.

Personal and Business Accounts

It is not difficult to open a savings account in a Czech bank for personal or business use. For personal accounts you will need your passport, and you may need evidence of residence and visa status. Still, be ready for a few frustrations here and there: it can take several days until your account is functioning properly, and you will probably have to apply separately for an ATM card, which can then takes take several days or even weeks to be issued.

TAXATION

Many people consider taxation a good reason to live abroad, as most do not have to pay taxes at home when not conducting business there. Foreigners living in the Czech Republic are responsible for paying Czech taxes, though, unless working under their embassy.

Whether you work as a freelance entrepreneur or as an employee of a Czech legal entity, you are required to pay income tax, which is graded. All legally employed workers pay income tax, social insurance and health insurance, which can work out to quite a high percentage overall. If you work independently, you must file for and pay taxes yourself—contact an accountant for the help you will certainly need. If you are an employee of a Czech company, your taxes will be automatically deducted from your pay, but check with your company's accounting department nonetheless to make sure you face no further tax payments. Check also on provisions for tax deductions for certain legally-resident foreigners—you may be able to claim some deductions depending on your activity or length of time spent in the country. Corporate taxes are currently quite high; the government plans to reduce this over time to bring it more in line with rates in other neighbouring countries.

VAT

The state value added tax (VAT) is presently 19 per cent on all goods, including food. All prices quoted in shops, restaurants etc. include VAT. Service industries face a tax of 5 per cent.

INSURANCE

As with banks, the insurance sector has undergone fundamental change, and as with banks, the system is improving. The local giant Česká pojišťovna has evolved into the market leader, offering health, life, personal property and liability, industrial, agricultural and international travel insurance. Such services are available to foreigners legally living and working in the Czech Republic, though most expats prefer to arrange personal insurance through their agent at home, or opt for one of the foreign companies operating in Prague. For a list of these, consult with one of the foreign companies listed in the Resources Guide below, whose numbers and services are ever-expanding.

HEALTH

It is a good idea to have a complete physical exam before you come. The long-stay authorities do not have health requirements included in their entrance requirements, but it is always a good idea to check given global public health threats.

The Czech Republic is overall a very healthy country in which to travel and live: standards of cleanliness and hygiene are high, except for the rather poor air quality in many cities which you can't avoid in winter. Health care is quite good and still fairly inexpensive, though this latter fact is a bone of contention in the current political agenda: doctor's salaries are remarkably low, and the heavily subsidised health care industry is burdened by rising costs.

Illnesses and emergencies can often be treated by English-speaking Czech doctors, many of whom have studied and worked in western countries. Please refer to the Resources Guide at the back of this book for lists and descriptions of health care providers. Outside of Prague, you'll have to rely on the local hospital or clinic which are easily located in local directories.

Health Insurance

If you have a long-stay permit, you are covered by state health insurance—you're paying for it out of your monthly or yearly taxes. Doctor's visits require little or no payment, though you must show your health insurance card, which you will be issued after obtaining your long-stay permit. Prescription drugs are also covered, in part. Present your doctor's prescription note at a chemist and you'll be charged pleasantly low amounts for medication.

If you are not on Czech health insurance, you had better obtain an international insurance policy. Your provider at home can help you arrange this, or can at least refer you to other companies that will. For a regular doctor's visit, you are expected to pay the fee as charged (it is usually quite reasonable), then claim reimbursement from your insurance company at home. For more serious (and hence, expensive) medical treatments, you will have to arrange something between your hospital and your insurance company. For such serious problems as surgery, you may feel more comfortable at home.

Many foreigners living in Prague prefer to retain their policies from home and receive treatment from western doctors working here. In some cases this is prudent, though the Czech health care system is generally adequate and in many cases equivalent to most international standards.

Pharmaceuticals

Most any medication you need is available from pharmacies here, though you will not always find the same brand names. Most Czech-made medicines are equally effective, and foreign-made products are usually available. If you have a fondness for particular drugs, bring a supply with you. Similarly, if you are on specific medication, be sure to bring a stock with you, as the exact same product may not be available.

Most medications beyond pain relievers, vitamins and cold medicines require a doctor's prescription, so if you are accustomed to buying antihistamines or sleeping pills over the counter, be forewarned that you probably can't do the same here.

CRIME AND SECURITY

The Czech Republic certainly does not feel like a dangerous place, though statistics throughout the country indicate that rates of theft and violent crime are rising. At least in well-travelled public areas, though, it is quite safe to walk around, even at night, and with the crowds on Prague's public transportation system, it is generally safe enough to take a late metro or tram home.

The most rampant crimes are pickpocketing and car theft. Especially in touristy areas of Prague, and especially in summer, slippery fingers are something to worry about. Keep your bags close to your body, carry money in a secure money belt, or in a wallet in your front pocket or inside jacket pocket, and be especially wary of crowds. It's easy to imagine tourists wowed by the city being an easy target for clever thieves. Groups of gypsies are watched with a particularly keen eye by locals.

The drug trade is picking up force, and marijuana has become quite a popular indulgence among the young. Of course, it's officially illegal to sell or buy any drugs, and the police have succeeded in making some raids on dealers of pot as well as hard drugs such as cocaine and locally produced Pervitín. Still, at certain bars and nightclubs you will see the dealers lurking and possibly get a whiff of smoke.

Be Aware!

Car theft has become a serious issue of late, and most car owners now secure their vehicle with a steering wheel clamp. Flashy Mercedes and BMWs are an obvious target, though the domestically produced Škoda is equally desirable—with close to 75 per cent of the cars on the road being made by Škoda it is quite easy for them to disappear into the crowd.

Prostitution

Prostitution is quite a business here, and in fact Prague has developed something of a reputation throughout Europe as a sleaze capital. Certain streets in the city have become mini-red-light districts, with *bordely* (brothels) hiding behind the façade of legal 'massage parlours' and sex shops, and street walkers are generally tolerated by the police. Wenceslas Square and streets around at night become favourite stomping grounds. Surprisingly, the motorways leading into the country from the German borders also are a prime red-light district of their own, and it's quite a sight: short-skirted women sitting on guard rails in full daylight, who make a living off Germans crossing the border for a couple hours!

SUPPORT GROUPS AND HOME HELP

You will likely find the expatriate community to be an invaluable source of support, both materially and emotionally. It's easy to get together with someone from your own country—colleagues from work or contacts from your children's school—and talk (or complain!) about the differences you are experiencing. This can be a great way to adjust to living in a foreign country, especially in the beginning, and it's easy to make new friends in this way. Try not to limit yourself, though; so many people come here and associate only with their own kind, and they really miss out on the most important part of living abroad, that is, assimilating into the local culture.

Societies and Organisations

Prague has plenty of organisations that serve as social focal points for foreigners. Religious organisations, business societies, cultural centres under the guise of various embassies, and even self-help groups such as Alcoholics Anonymous are active in Prague, and these advertise regularly in *The Prague Post*. These are also a good source of information for help around the home. As services such as babysitting, cleaning and catering are a little more difficult to come by here, use these built-in networks to your advantage.

If you work, you are likely to come into contact with other expatriates, be it colleagues in your own company or business contacts that you're bound to make. Spouses often have difficulty, however, as they don't necessarily have the same network at hand. Many relocating families with children say that schools are the best source of support—there are lots of other parents in the same position, and all the international schools have regular functions such as picnics and ski trips to bring their communities together. Organisations such as parent-teacher associations and after-school programmes also provide spouses the opportunity to do community and charity work. It's easy to mope when you've got little to do, and finding ways to keep yourself busy is the tried-and-true best method of avoiding lethargy and depression.

INFORMATION SOURCES

The Yellow Pages (called *Zlaté stránky*) are provided for all homes and offices, with listings in Czech. If you don't know the Czech word for the category of goods or services you need, turn to the back, where they provide cross references in English and German—very helpful. *The Prague Post*, the weekly English newspaper, is an excellent source of information on just about anything you need. It comes out on Wednesdays. Aside from news, it runs a complete entertainment listing every week, and has a good classifieds section as well. Since its establishment in 1990, *The Prague Post* has maintained the pulse of expat community here.

THE EXPATRIATE COMMUNITY

The expatriate community in Prague merits a special section of its own here. Somehow Prague has been a magnet for backpackers and businesspeople ever since 1990. It was estimated at one point in the mid-1990s that up to 30,000 Americans were living in Prague, and this was easy to believe gauging from the numerous bookstores, restaurants, nightclubs and even laundromats established by and haunted by these visitors from the west. The numbers have probably declined since then as Prague has lost some of its 'bohemian' novelty, but the expat dives still thrive.

To be quite honest, I avoid such establishments as much as possible. Sure, they are a great place to meet people of similar interests and experiences (getting together to harp on culture shock topics is a prime motivator in many people's social lives here), but it becomes a pit that swallows you up—by limiting your contact with Czechs, you miss out on what is one of the most critical factors in experiencing and enjoying your stay abroad. It also becomes that much easier to complain about things here and seek justification and validation for your problems. As the owner of one local expat hang-out told me, "Business is great, but we've created a monster." Several such places did serve a very useful function back in 1992 or so when they first appeared—the city was still very much lost in time, and for those who were used to having burritos, bookstores and fellow patrons speaking a familiar language, it was hard to stay away. This purpose has largely been eliminated in more recent years, as more and more eating, drinking and socialising establishments owned by Czechs have opened up that offer greater variety and quality than what was available before. (I've listed several expatriate gathering points in the back of the book).

So you're quite lucky in that life here is now almost on par with the rest of western Europe in terms of comfort and convenience; though on the other hand, the sense of daring and adventure has been reduced. Back in the early 1990s (oh so long ago), daily life was still a bit of a challenge: everything was grey, standards and variety of goods available was much lower than now, and for many foreigners relocating here, the country was exotic and exciting in many ways. Many (myself included) were charmed by the frozen-in-time feel to the place, kind of a back-to-the-future nostalgia and innocence which is rapidly disappearing.

A MAGNET FOR BACKPACKERS

Many of the first visitors in the country were backpackers who got caught up in the charm (and cheap beer and, for men at least, the beautiful women) of Prague, and ended up spending months hanging out on Charles Bridge, learning Czech, and mingling with the locals. At the same time, businesses jumped in, using Prague as the base not only for their Czech, but in many cases for their entire central or eastern European operations, and western managers came in droves to set up shop and train Czechs. Now that many Czechs are well qualified to operate branch offices of foreign firms (and indeed many multinational corporations are taking advantage of cheaper labour here), some foreign managers are leaving; though with companies continually investing in the country, the numbers of incoming expatriates remains steady.

Still, it seems extraordinary that so many foreigners have chosen to live in Prague. Part of the reason is simple: this is a gorgeous city with a captivating atmosphere, and Czechs are a wonderful people once you get to know them. You'll never tire of walking around the city on a quiet weekend, or going to concerts and pubs, or discovering different parts of the country, and even though it will take a bit of effort, you'll find the Czech people an irresistibly funny and friendly lot. In more practical terms, there are so many opportunities in the Czech Republic, and especially in Prague, that many people find themselves either experiencing success in their current occupation, and therefore wanting to stay for economic reasons, or coming across new and exciting prospects while here.

DAILY NECESSITIES
Shopping

The emergence and evolution of a consumer culture in the Czech Republic since 1989 has been astounding to observe. Visitors returning after a long absence are always amazed at how things have changed (though keeping in mind this is building from a minimal level). While you'll hardly be knocked out by the variety of goods on offer, you will not find yourself wanting for much, and in many cases you'll be pleasantly surprised by the high standards and general availability of most items. True, you will still have to know where to look, and this can take time. You will have to adapt and modify your expectations to a degree. But once you've identified your needs and where to fulfill them, you'll probably find you can get just about anything you want, plus some local goods that you hadn't even known or appreciated before.

Indeed the retail sector has developed by leaps and bounds. Large, multinational department stores and supermarkets such as Tesco, Carrefour and Delvita are by now well established even in the smaller cities, and at the same time, the economy supports a satisfying array of boutique shops, speciality shops and local products. Prague in particular is replete with large department stores and an almost galling array of new shopping centres, sporting such tenants as Marks & Spencer, Benetton and IKEA. The outskirts of most cities throughout the country now have large supermarkets or 'hypermarkets,' which are immensely popular for their low bulk prices and greater selection. Speciality shops selling hip clothing, imported wines, exotic fruits and vegetables, art and music supplies and English-language books are also popping up throughout the country, and are particularly plentiful in Prague.

All this is a great advance over the Communist years, when shopping in the Czech Republic was a torturous rigamarole to be avoided if not absolutely necessary. It's not that there weren't any goods or that there weren't enough of them, it's that obtaining them was a Herculean endeavor and the selection was unpredictable. The grocery shop that carried your favourite biscuits one day didn't have them the next; the selection of trousers offered by the department stores was uniformly cheap; the service anywhere you went was almost purposefully savage. In a society not kind to materialism, you were supposed to be grateful for what you got.

Part of the change is due to foreign incursion, but a good portion of the credit is also due to a Czech entrepreneurial culture that has spawned a creative array of new shopping opportunities. The increasingly competitive market has forced local manufacturers to improve their products, and they have often done this while keeping retail prices lower than the imports, so the act of shopping becomes more and more interesting.

Not Exactly A Shopper's Paradise

The Czech Republic is not a place one would think of to come to on a shopping spree and it probably never will be. While the variety is adequate, it cannot compare with that in major commercial centres elsewhere in Europe, and prices of imported goods are at least as high here as anywhere else.

The distinguishing factor is the availability of specifically Czech products, and you will have fun poking into craft shops and through Christmas stalls, where traditional Czech things such as world-famous Bohemian crystal, wooden puppets and lace are widely available. These can be quite inexpensive by international standards, and make great gifts and home decorations. If you've got time to kill, there are also some great bargain opportunities at antique shops and flea markets, where again you'll be struck by how cheap some items can be.

For your standard, day-to-day shopping needs, you'll likely build a memory bank of a few places that consistently have what you're looking for, and return to these places whenever it is necessary.

FOOD SHOPPING
Grocery shops

Food shopping is often done at small, local grocery shops called *potraviny*, and at a burgeoning supply of supermarkets, usually called a *supermarket*. Czechs often pick up the daily essentials at the *potraviny* around the corner, rather than in a weeks-worth trip to the supermarket, though changing work patterns—as well as the relative price advantages offered by the large chain stores—are having an impact on this custom.

Potraviny are generally quite small and crowded, and stock the essentials: frozen meat and vegetables, canned goods, dairy products, fresh bread and rolls, bottled and boxed drinks, sweets, soup mixes, spices, alcohol and often a mini-delicatessen with pickled salads and fresh cold cuts and cheese. Most also have a bottle-return counter—be sure to save all glass bottles and return them for a 3-5 Kč refund of your deposit. Supermarkets are often located on the edge of town, though many large central department stores have supermarkets in the basement. In Prague, these include Tesco, Kotva and Carrefour.

Potraviny and supermarkets stock both domestic and imported brands, though you may have no choice in the matter. You will recognise many brands such as Coca-Cola,

Heinz, Knorr and Nestlé next to the local equivalent (and usually at a higher price). Don't be afraid to go local—quality is generally as good, and sometimes better. Many international brands are now manufactured in the Czech Republic, making them competitively priced against the humbler local products.

One custom to be aware of in most grocery shops is that you must have a shopping cart or basket to enter the shop, even if you're just picking up a chocolate bar from the check-out counter. Shopping carts sometimes require a deposit of a 5 Kč or 10 Kč coin, which you insert into the slot on the cart and then turn the attached key. When you return the cart, turn the key back and your coin pops out. The practical reason for this is to keep all the carts in one neat place at the entrance, as well as to limit the numbers of shoppers (and potential shoplifters) in shops. During busy hours there are sometimes lines in front of the check-out counter of people waiting to get baskets and carts from paying customers, just to get into the shop! Some small, local *potraviny* (also called *lahůdky* or *koloniál*) employ a highly-inefficient system of keeping all groceries behind the counter—you have to just wait in line and have the shop assistant get everything for you.

Plastic bags are rarely offered—you must ask for one specifically and will probably have to pay a few crowns or so for it. Most people bring their own bags with them. You are expected to bag your own groceries, so a time-saving trick is to start bagging while the check-out person is ringing up the tab.

Late-Night and Weekend Grocery Shopping

Most grocery shops close between 6:00 pm and 8:00 pm daily, and have limited hours on weekends, but most city neighbourhoods have a *večerka*, or late-night shop, which may stay open until 9:00 pm or midnight, or sometimes even 24 hours a day, as well as at weekends. These usually have a fairly limited supply of goods—the basics—and seem targeted toward late night revellers or insomniacs who need another bottle of booze, a sausage fix or a replacement tube of toothpaste. Prices may be slightly higher than normal grocery shops, but you'll probably be glad to have this option.

In addition, many petrol stations sell a surprisingly extensive array of groceries. You should at least be able to get an emergency supply of bread, cheese, canned plums and toilet paper, plus of course that extra bottle of beer or wine.

Fruits and Vegetables (Ovoce a Zelenina)

Potraviny don't normally carry much in the way of fresh fruits and vegetables, though they do have shelves and shelves of items such as stewed fruit, pickles, pickled carrots, pickled peppers and pickled cabbage.

For a better selection, find an *ovoce-zelenina* shop (greengrocer's) or an outdoor fruit and vegetable stand. Hardy local fruits and vegetables, such as apples, pears, potatoes, carrots, cauliflower and cabbage are always available; others such as tomatoes, bell peppers and broccoli are usually available as well, though as anywhere, are cheapest and best in-season. A lot of fresh produce is now imported and you can almost always get oranges, bananas and the like at most produce vendors. Even 'exotic' produce such as pineapples and mangoes is sometimes available.

Fruit	
jablko	apple
pomeranč	orange
banán	banana
hruška	pear
švestka	plum
broskve	peach
meruňka	apricot
mandarinka	mandarin
hroznové víno	grapes

Fruit

třešně or *višně*	cherries
citron	lemon
grep	grapefruit
jahody	strawberries
borůvky	blueberries
maliny	raspberries
angrešt	gooseberries
brusinky	cranberries
rybíz	currants
meloun	watermelon
ananas	pineapple

Vegetables

brambory	potatoes
mrkev	carrot
paprika	bell pepper (in summer these are light green and hot)
cibule	onion
rajčata	tomatoes
zelí	cabbage/sauerkraut
květák	cauliflower
houby or *žampióny*	mushrooms
hrášek	peas
ředkvičky	radishes
kedlubna	kolrabi
hlávkový salát	lettuce
brokolice	broccoli
lilek	eggplant/aubergine
cuketa	zucchini/courgette
špenát	spinach
pórek	leek

While it's common to ask for, say, two bananas, or five onions, most fresh produce is purchased by weight. If you're unfamiliar with the metric system, this is a good opportunity to learn it; some guidelines are provided below, under Weights and Measures.

Meat (Maso), Poultry (Drůbež) and Fish (Ryby)

While *potraviny* always have a decent selection of meats, whether fresh-packaged or frozen, the best fresh meats are to be found at a *řeznictví* (butcher's shop). These usually have signs outside saying simply *maso-uzeniny* ('meat-smoked meat'), and generally stick to beef and pork products, as well as chicken. You can order special cuts of meat and sausage by weight (it is normally requested in decigrammes or in half or whole kilogramme quantities).

Note that the methods of butchering meat are somewhat different from what you may be used to. Ground beef is rarely out on the shelves, but can be requested (ask for *mleté hovězí*). Hams and salamis are also quite common, packaged or sliced at the deli. There is actually a broad variety of excellent salamis worth sampling.

Czechs eat a lot of beef and pork, and therefore fish and poultry are less common. Fish is usually bought frozen at grocery shops, though there are a few shops around selling fresh fish. Note also that the growing expansion of a supermarket society means the quality and selection available at supermarkets is often as good as, if not better than, the speciality butchers.

hovězí	beef
vepřové	pork
kuře	chicken
kachna	duck
husa	goose
játra	liver
šunka	ham

turistický, lovecký, uherský and *poličan*	different types of salamis
párek and *klobása*	types of sausages
zvěřina	game (most commonly venison or boar)
pstruh	trout
kapr	carp

Dairy (Mléčné výrobky)

Cheeses are available in wide variety at *potraviny*, though many butchers offer good selections as well. Aside from the soft, spreadable cheese called *tavenný sýr* so popular here, hard cheeses are common, whether packaged on the shelf or cut for you at the counter. Yoghurts are creamy and very good. Note that low-fat dairy products are still not very common, though they are catching on.

mléko	milk
smetana	cream
máslo	butter
zakysaná smetana	sour cream
tvaroh	curd
jogurt	yoghurt
uzený sýr	smoked cheese
eidam	a Czech variety of eidam cheese
gouda	a Czech variety of gouda cheese
hermelín	a cheap version of camembert
zlato	soft, mildly pungent yellow-white cheese
niva	blue cheese

Spices (Koření) and Nuts (Ořechy)

Czech cooking makes liberal usage of basic spices such as salt, pepper, garlic, marjoram and caraway seeds. Paprika, dill, bay leaf and celery root are also used in a variety of sauces and soups. In baking, Czechs use common ingredients such as vanilla, chocolate and cinnamon, and they use a lot of nuts and poppy seeds as well. Most grocery shops have a full array of these basic ingredients.

Spices for Cooking	
sůl	salt
pepř	pepper
česnek	garlic
kmín	caraway seeds
majoránka	marjoram
bobkový list	bay leaf
paprika	paprika
kopr	dill
petržel	parsley
pažitka	chives
celer	celery root

Spices for Baking	
cukr	sugar
vanilka	vanilla
skořice	cinnamon
mák	poppy seeds
hřebíček	cloves
vlašské ořechy	walnuts
lískové ořechy	hazelnuts
hrozinky	raisins
zázvor	ginger
muškát	nutmeg

Bread (Chléb) and Pastries (Pečivo)

The best place to buy fresh bread is at a *pekařství* (bakery). The most commonly seen grains are *chléb* (always spoken of as *chleba*), a thick heavy rye variety of loaf, which you can buy whole, halved or quartered; and *rohlíky* and *housky*, tasty white rolls of mini-baguette and braided roll variety, respectively. Bread does not usually come sliced, but most shops can do it for you.

Other types of bread, such as *arabský chléb* (pita) and various whole-grains can be found in bakeries, as can a long line of pastries. Czechs use a lot of spiced rum in their cakes, as well as chocolate, nuts and whipped cream. The most common pastries include the following:

koláč	a flat sweet bread with fruit, cream or poppy seed toppings
dort	cake
kobliha	jelly doughnuts
závin or *štrůdl*	apple strudel
bábovka	bundt cake
věneček	puff pastry with egg crème
oplatky	filled wafers

Weights and Measures

- *deset deka*—10 decigrammes = 100 grammes
- *dvacet deka*—20 decigrammes = 200 grammes
- *třicet deka*—30 decigrammes = 300 grammes
- *čtyřicet deka*—40 decigrammes = 400 grammes
- *půl kila*—half-kilogramme = roughly 1 pound

- 1 kilogramme = approximately 2.2 pounds
- 1 pound = almost 0.5 kilogrammes
- 4 litres = roughly 1 gallon
- 1 litre = approximately 2 pints
- 1/2 litre = approximately 1 pint

Toiletries and Pharmaceuticals (Léky)

Potraviny and supermarkets often carry a supply of soap, dish detergent, toothpaste, shaving cream and toilet paper, though you might have to go to yet another shop for these. *Drogerie* are, despite the name, shops that carry personal items.

As with food, Czech toiletries are of good-enough quality, though you don't always have the variety or top quality available at home. You can find recognisable brands in most places you look.

Pharmaceuticals, including both prescription and over-the-counter drugs, are sold exclusively at a *lékárna*. Even aspirin and cold medicine can only be bought at a *lékárna*, though these are located all over town. Look for the green sign with the familiar snake-shield logo. Note that many of the over-the-counter drugs you may be accustomed to buying at home are considered prescription medications here (*see section on Health*). For headaches, I've found the best local pain reliever is Paralen.

toaletní papír	toilet paper (This is often cardboard-like and uncomfortable).
papírové kapesníky	facial tissues (Mini-packets of tissues are available, though most Czechs use cloth handkerchiefs).
krém na holení	shaving cream
žiletky	razor blades
mýdlo	soap
šampón	shampoo
vlasový kondicionér	hair conditioner
krém	body lotion
zubní pasta	toothpaste
kartáček na zubi	toothbrush
vložky or *tampón*	tampon
prezervativ or *kondom*	condom

Clothes (Oblečení)

Unfortunately Czech clothing is nothing to shout about. It's not particularly bad, but then it's not particularly good either. Prices can be lower than the glamour international names, and if you're not too fastidious, the quality is good enough. One friend who has lived here for many years says that finding good quality, reasonably priced clothes is one of her greatest frustrations. She, like many, prefers to supply her wardrobe from home.

Nevertheless, you can easily find shirts, trousers, sweaters, jackets, dresses, undergarments, socks and shoes. Large *obchodní domy* (department stores) in many cities stock general clothing needs, and offer both domestic and foreign brands. Small specialised boutiques (*obchody*) flood Prague's centre, selling well known brands such as Levi's, Hugo Boss, Stefanel, Benetton, Reporter and many more. These are the best places to buy casual dress clothes and business attire, although prices are equal to or even higher than in most countries.

Street vendors, many of whom are Vietnamese, also sell clothes, though the quality is often dubious. Finally, second-hand shops (*second hand* or *levné zboží*) are common and well used, and offer a surprisingly good collection of decent clothes.

košile	button-down shirt
mikina	pullover sweat-shirt
tričko	T-shirt
svetr	jumper
sako	dress jacket, blazer
kalhoty	trousers, casual slacks
jeans or *džíny*	jeans
šaty	dress
sukně	skirt
spodní prádlo	underwear
ponožky	socks
bunda	outerwear jacket
bačkory	slippers (An essential item in any Czech household, as shoes are never worn indoors.)

Shoes (Boty)

These are an important item in a country that has a lot of cobble-stone streets and suffers long, cold, wet winters. You are probably best off bringing what shoes you need from home, as you can be assured of quality and expectations. That said, there are many places to buy and repair shoes. The local sales leader is Baťa, originally based in the central Moravian town of Zlín, but whose founder moved to Canada and brought his company with him when he ran into trouble for opposing the rising Communists in the late 1940s. Baťa markets its product all over the world; Czechs consider it a local brand, and it does make a decent, good-value shoe.

boty	shoes
prodejna bot / obuv	shoe shop
opravna bot	shoe repair
krém na boty	shoe polish
tkaničky	shoe laces

HOUSEHOLD FURNISHINGS

This is something you need to decide before you come: do you want a furnished or an unfurnished home? If you want your own furniture, you'll have to arrange shipping, and then will not be too concerned with the information in this section. Department stores and furniture shops are reasonably well supplied, though you may have to make your selection and then order from the shop, which can take a few weeks. Prague has two IKEA outlets which are life-savers to many foreigners.

A special mention should be made of bed linens. Czechs use *peřiny* (duvets), filled with down and wrapped in a linen covering. The idea is to ensure that the whole exterior remains clean, unlike a blanket or cover that is not usually washed and therefore collects dust and dirt.

nábytek	furniture, furniture shop
obchodní dům	department store
kancelářský nábytek	office furniture
postel	bed
peřina	duvet
povlečení, lůžkoviny	bed linen (duvet cover)
deka	blanket
polštář	pillow
stůl	desk/table
lampa	lamp
židle	chair
křeslo	armchair
šatna	closet

skříň	wardrobe
knihovna	bookshelf

Electrical Appliances (Elektriké spotřebiče)

Most flats come with basic kitchen appliances, so you won't need to bring these with you. All brand-name electrical appliances, from radios to fax machines to dishwashers, are readily available at shops throughout the country. *(See the note on electricity in the Housing section for information on different voltages in the Czech Republic.)*

telefon	telephone
televize	television
satelit	satellite
rádio	radio
hi-fi	stereo system
computer, počítač	computer
lednička or *lednice*	refrigerator
mražák	freezer
pračka	washing machine
sušička	dryer
myčka	dishwasher
sporák	stove
elektrický vařič	hotplate
mikrovlnka	microwave
žehlička	iron

GIFTS

A major source of income from tourists, typical Czech household decorations also make the living experience here a bit more authentic. The most noted gifts and trinkets, which are not just touristy but a part of every Czech's daily life, include Bohemian crystal, lace, wooden toys and puppets, and the ever-popular beer and Becherovka herb liquor. Touristy areas throughout the country are a surprisingly

Czech lace is found in all homes and is a popular gift for tourists.

good place to buy these things: they have the best selection and prices are not too bad. These types of things make good gifts for yourself and your friends at home, but it might be the proverbial carrying coals to Newcastle to offer them to a Czech friend.

RECYCLING

There are facilities throughout the country for recycling of glass and paper products. Keep an eye out for large coloured bins on street corners, with signs indicating their intended contents. Recycling of aluminium cans is not in practice here, mainly because most drinks are sold in glass bottles.

Drinks that are sold in glass bottles, such as beer, wine, and some soft drinks, have a 3–5 Kč per bottle deposit tacked on. Bottles can then be returned to the place of purchase, or to any shop that sells similar shaped bottles, in exchange for cash.

TRANSPORTATION
Prague Mass Transit

Prague has an excellent, efficient public transport system, which most of the city relies on daily. The metro system was inaugurated in 1974, and many of the older stations are hilarious testaments to Communist ideology, with plaques and statues dedicated to 'the working people of Prague' and 'the memory of the liberation of Prague by the Red Army in 1945.' Trams and buses fill in where the underground doesn't go, and there is a comprehensive system of night transport between the hours of midnight and 4.30 am.

Tickets (*jízdenky*) for individual journeys remain cheap. There are two separate tickets you can buy: one good for one trip of up to 90 minutes, including transfers (i.e. using any combination of transport), and a separate, slightly cheaper ticket good for a journey of up to four stops on the underground or of 15 minutes above ground. Tickets can be purchased from the orange machines in every underground station, or from most newsagents around town. Tickets must then be validated at the entrance gates to underground stations, or similarly in the little orange boxes you see hanging on poles in buses and trams. The same ticket works in the underground, buses and trams. Note that tickets cannot be purchased on board a bus or tram, so it's a good idea to stock up.

The reason you won't see too many other people validating tickets is that most Praguers possess a system pass, which

Trams and buses complement the well used underground system. Prague has an excellent public transport network.

allows unlimited use of the metro, buses, and trams for a low price. Passes can be purchased for a period of one, three, six, or twelve months, starting on the first day of that respective period—meaning passes are valid from the first to the last day of every calendar month, quarter, half-year or year. Buy your base pass (*legitimace*) at an underground station ticket window (not all stations have such windows), and insert a passport photo. For each respective calendar term, you buy a small stamp called a *kupon* which you insert into the little plastic window. These are available as *měsíční* (monthly), *čvtrtletní* (quarterly), *půlroční* (half-yearly) or *roční* (annual).

Transport officials carry out random spot-checks, so while it may seem that you don't need to pay your way, you can hit an angry ticket-controller and face a fine for 'riding black.' Ticket checkers may be plain-clothed or may be in uniform; you will know them for sure when they flash a small badge at you. Their frequency is low, so some people don't mind testing their luck, but the fines are fairly substantial compared to the ticket price.

Underground trains run every 3-6 minutes during the day. Buses and trams are almost as frequent. Each bus and tram stop is marked by a signpost with the name of the stop and a schedule of times.

It is important to give up your seat to an elderly or disabled person on any public transport vehicle. You'll notice people offering their seats to the *babičky* (old ladies) who potter around the trams, and this is actually part of the system's regulations.

Taxis

Prague's taxis long carried a deservedly bad reputation, although the city appears to have cracked down on some common abuses, and taxis are generally safer now than during most of the 1990s, a time of notorious rip-off artists as well as daring and obnoxious drivers. Taxis must have the rate posted on the door of the cab and should have a meter inside to measure this. Just to be sure, however, to check this rate before you get in, and try to determine with the driver how much approximately the trip will cost. Reputable taxi companies are listed in the Resources Guide at the back of this book.

Domestic Transportation

The country has a remarkably efficient and still-inexpensive bus (*autobus*) and train (*vlak*) network. Although the standard is nothing to shout about, both systems are extensive and usually operate right on schedule. The bus system is the most comprehensive, and many people use it in favour of the railways because it's often faster and more direct. Prices are generally similar between bus and train. For destinations on the main train lines (see below), where service is regular and fast, you'll probably opt to travel by train; for many other destinations you'll probably find yourself travelling by bus.

Czech Airlines (ČSA) flies between Prague and Ostrava; although the airline claims to serve Brno and Karlovy Vary as well, this is actually a bus connection designed for passengers connecting on flights through Prague; in any case the country is small enough that most Czechs would have a hard time believing you would actually fly domestically.

By Bus

There are direct buses between Prague and virtually all sizeable towns throughout the country, and towns and villages of practically all sizes are linked with regional service. Weekday service is quite thorough, as many Czechs rely on regional and inter-city buses to travel to and from work, and Friday and Sunday evenings are especially busy with weekend travellers; on Saturdays there is often a lull in service. The former state-run bus company, ČSAD, still maintains an extensive route network throughout the country, but this is now complemented by a plethora of private bus companies. Quality of service can vary, with many older buses on the road, often with rather small seats lacking a proper headrest. Happily, there is an increasing number of newer, more comfortable buses entering service as well. (Buses on long-distance international routes are generally of a high standard).

Bus tickets are usually purchased on board from the driver (in cash only), though on Friday and Sunday evenings it's a good idea to try to get a seat reservation in advance, as the system is jammed with people going home or to the country for the weekend. To do this, you have to go to the station at which the bus originates. In Prague, tickets for all buses can be purchased from the main bus station at Florenc, but not all buses actually leave from Florenc. Seat reservations come with a specific seat marked on the ticket, and buses often board passengers with reservations first. Remember if you do not have a reservation that you could get booted by a passenger coming along with a reservation for the seat you are sitting in. Bus drivers often will allow passengers to stand if it gets crowded, but there is still the possibility that the bus could fill up, so it's a good idea to arrive at least 20 minutes early. Keep in mind that if you're bringing luggage with you, you may have to place it in the undercarriage and pay a separate (though small) fee. Keep your ticket with you during the trip, as technically inspectors may come on board to check, although in practice this is extremely rare.

One distinct problem with the bus system is that the printed schedule is virtually impossible to decipher, and workers at the information windows are invariably rude and unhelpful. Having a Czech speaker on hand is immensely helpful.

Reading the Bus Timetable

A few common bus schedule symbols are:

X (or two crossed hammers)—Weekdays only

V—Friday only

S—Saturday only

N—Sunday only

† (cross)—Sundays and holidays.

Be sure to follow the printed route schedule from your starting point through to your destination—printed timetables often have many different bus schedules for the route, and some routes go express and may skip your stop, or some routes may be truncated and stop short of your destination.

Greatly alleviating the difficulty of reading bus timetables is the availability of schedules on the Internet, in English, at http://www.idos.cz. You can enter in departure and arrival stations and times and the computer will return the relevant buses.

By Rail

Most cities are served by trains as well, though there are only a limited number of trunk lines radiating out from Prague, which can slow down the proceedings considerably if you are not travelling between major cities connected by a main line.

Main Rail Lines from Prague

- West: to Nürnberg (Germany) via Plzeň and Cheb
- North: to Berlin (Germany) via Děčín and Dresden (Germany)
- East: to Ostrava, via Pardubice and Olomouc
- Southeast: to Bratislava (Slovakia) or Vienna (Austria) via Brno
- South: to České Budějovice

Train tickets can be bought at the station, and it is not necessary to do so in advance. Train tickets remain generally cheap, with the exception of routes on major international lines (such as Prague-Brno on the Prague-Vienna or Prague-Bratislava lines) which may have a Euro-City (EC) or Inter-City (IC) supplement—which should at least guarantee a good-quality train. České Dráhy (ČD) is the national rail company, which has long operated at a loss, and hence has often discussed curtailing service to try to reign in costs. Many of the trains are throwbacks to prior eras, and can be dirty and smoky, although there is a good mix of newer, more comfortable trains as well. Schedules are quite easy to figure out; just look for the yellow sign boards indicating departure (*odjezd*), versus the white boards which are for arrivals (*příjezd*). Schedules can also be found in English at http://www.idos.cz.

Be sure when travelling that you choose the right type of train: in addition to the EC and IC trains, *rychlík* (fast) and express trains make only major stops, while *osobní* trains stop at every last spot on the way.

Cars

Czechs for the most part are horrible drivers, plain and simple. It's not that they don't know how to drive, it's that they take the rules of the road much more liberally than they should. Speed limits are often ignored, lane changes can be sudden and tailgating is common practice; hence, the accident rates are about double what they are in the US and western Europe. The problem is in enforcement of traffic rules: local and municipal governments have simply allowed a lot of the abuses to go unchecked. However, after some particularly bloody recent years, and pressure from the EU, the authorities say they are finally making an effort to crack down with more traffic police monitoring motorways and intersections. We'll see if the situation improves.

Czechs always seem to be in a mad rush on the road – even Prague's narrow one-way streets can be made to feel like a racecourse, and if you're going slower than the guy behind you wants to, you'll be shot past and glared at as if you'd committed some rude act. Driving in Prague is particularly nerve-wracking; it simply isn't made for cars. Many of its streets are one-way, many are torn up sporadically as pipe lines are replaced, and many are cobblestoned. When these are wet, drive especially carefully, as they can slip out from under you like ice. Many main streets have tram lines as well, some of which run down the middle or off to the side, though many share a single lane with cars. The opening of some major outer motorways and cross-city connector roads in Prague is at least beginning to help ease some of the congestion.

Beware of the usual rush hours—approximately 6:00 am–9:00 am and 3:00 pm–6:00 pm. Traffic patterns in Prague are a confounding mystery—some days it all moves smoothly enough, and some days it can be so bad you may as well just leave your vehicle where it is and take a tram.

The speed limit in towns and cities, including Prague, is 50 kmph unless otherwise noted. On two-lane country roads it's 90 kmph, and on four-lane motorways and roads marked in yellow on your road atlas it's 110 kmph, though most drivers tend to ignore all of these.

When a policeman does pull you over for a moving violation you're expected to pay a fine in cash on the spot. Appeals for leniency could work, and you may be able to talk him down a little, but in any case you are expected to pay in cash. Ask him to write up a proper ticket to insure

Roadsigns & Rules of the Road

Czech roadsigns are the same as those in Europe; if you've never driven in Europe be aware of a few differences:

- A sign with a yellow diamond on a white background indicates that you are on the main road, with right-of-way over all incoming traffic. Many intersections don't have stop signs, as they use this right-of-way system instead. As you approach an intersection, watch for a sign with the yellow diamond; it will often be accompanied by a scheme of the upcoming intersection, with a thick line indicating the main road, and thinner lines coming into it. In similar fashion, if you approach an intersection and the scheme indicates you are not on the main road (the yellow diamond has a slash through it), you'll have to yield to incoming traffic. The reason for these signs is that it is not always clear who should have right-of-way.
- A white circle with a red border means do not enter.
- A circular blue sign with a red X means no parking any time; with a red slash means no standing any time, and hence, no parking.
- Trams always have priority—if you're blocking a tram track, and the streetcar driver in either direction wants to go ahead, he can smash you and it will be your fault. Be aware of trams when making a turn.

that it doesn't go into his pocket—the temptation to do so must be irresistible.

Drinking and driving is a serious offence here, and police often do random spot-checks at night. Any hint of alcohol showing up in a breathalyzer is enough to do you in—not even one drink is tolerated, and penalties can range from a 10,000 Kč fine to confiscation of your license to imprisonment. Don't do it.

Car Ownership and Documentation

A regular driver's license issued from any European or North American country is valid here. An International Driver's License comes in handy if you hail from elsewhere.

If you are moving to the Czech Republic with your car, you will have to register it locally. This process is smoother for cars registered in other European countries than for those shipped from overseas. I strongly recommend not doing the latter: it is costly and immensely frustrating and time-consuming. Speak with your dealer at home for information, and consider that to register you car, you must first have a valid long-stay permit ('green card'). With this in hand, pick up a registration form from the local traffic police which you must bring to an inspection station (STK), before to the traffic police will issue your papers and license plates.

To use any of the country's four-lane motorways, you must have a motorway sticker called a *dálniční známka* visible in your windshield—these start at 200 Kč (depending on length of time—they are valid for up to one calendar year), and can be purchased from any border crossing, post office, or petrol station.

Emergency Service

For emergency road service, call Žlutý Anděl at 1230 or ABA at 1240 for English-speaking assistance.

Insurance is not required here, though judging from the number of wild drivers out there, you'd be irresponsible not to have it. Contact one of the insurance companies mentioned in the Resources Guide at the back of this book. In case of an accident, you must not move the vehicle from the spot at which it stopped moving. A police car will come around and monitor the situation.

Parking in Prague

Not only was this city not made for driving, it was certainly not made for parking either. City planners were woefully blind to future trends in this regard, and the ever increasing number of cars on the road has made parking a real problem. All sorts of illegal parking jobs are performed daily, whether it's simply ignoring the 'No Parking' signs, parking in someone else's reserved spot, double parking, parking in front of a garage entrance, or driving up onto the sidewalk. I've done all of the above at one time or another.

The traffic police do monitor the situation, and are now quicker to place boots (clamps) on errantly-parked vehicles. If this happens to you, they will leave a sticker on the driver's side window, with a number to call; tell them the street name and nearest building address and they should come within 20 minutes to relieve you, after you pay the fine in cash. The chaotic compactness of the centre should be enough to convince you to leave your vehicle at home and take the underground. For those who must drive, though, there are zoning regulations for the city centre. Certain streets are reserved for short-term parking (up to 2 hours), others for mid-term (up to 6 hours), and others for those who have Prague 1 parking permits. Check the street signs carefully. There are a few parking garages in the central area, and some streets have designated short-term parking areas monitored either by an attendant or by a meter. If uncertain, seek a parking garage or monitored street parking area. Hourly rates are not unreasonable.

Parking permits for Prague 1 (city centre) are issued to residents of that district and to companies who pay for the privilege. It is possible to reserve a spot on the street anywhere in the city, which will be marked by a sign with either your company name or your car's license number.

Třeboň in south Bohemia—a typical town square with Gothic and Baroque features.

This is a pretty good way to insure yourself a parking spot, though it would still take a while to call a tow-truck if someone decides to ignore the sign.

Reserved street parking does not protect you against car theft or break-in, which is a serious problem in Prague and throughout the country. Protect your car with an alarm, a steering-wheel clamp, and whatever other measures you possibly can.

Street Names and Building Addresses

Streets almost never have the word 'street' or 'avenue' written; instead it's just the name and the number. Building numbers always follow the street name.

You may be confused to see two addresses written on an envelope or letterhead, and two signs with different numbers on the building itself; for example, you may see the address Dlouhá 53/4, and when you go to the building you'll see a blue sign with the 4 and a red sign with the 53. The number on the red sign, usually the longer number, is the building plot number, which used to be used as the address until someone figured out that these numbers don't necessarily go in order. So a new logical numbering system was developed, and blue signs were placed on buildings in the order they stand on the street. These are generally the ones used now—why they keep the old numbers is a mystery.

MEDIA
The Printed Press

Competition in the newspaper and magazine field in Prague is ferocious. This city of 1.2 million people supports numerous daily papers of all editorial slants. Some are of excellent quality and some are trash, and the locals eat them up, often buying two or three to get them through the day. This isn't hard to do—all newspapers are compact, concise

A newsstand in Prague is loaded with local and international papers.

publications, with condensed news stories and not much advertising, making it a quick task to read. Of course, it will take quite a while to develop your Czech language skills to a level of comprehension. Attempting to read the daily paper is a great way to build vocabulary though.

The best, straightforward, unbiased paper is probably *Mladá Fronta Dnes*, followed by the more right-leaning *Lidové noviny*, while leftist publications include the still popular former Communist party rag *Právo*. Specialised papers include *Hospodářské noviny*, a business daily, *Práce*, the Czech Trade Union daily, and *Sport*. Sliding rapidly down the quality scale are the sensationalist papers *Blesk*, *Express* and *Večerník Praha*.

English Language News

The established source of English-language news in Prague is *The Prague Post* (http://www.praguepost.cz). It appears every Wednesday and is available from many newsagents throughout Prague and larger cities in the country. The emphasis is on local news, with sections on business and finance, sports, culture, travel and an extensive rundown of the week's entertainment. It's invaluable if you want to know what's going on.

Other, more business oriented papers include the *Central European Business Weekly* and the *Czech Business Weekly* (http://www.cbw.cz). *The Prague Tribune* (http://www.prague-tribune.cz) is an interesting monthly news/business/culture magazine published simultaneously in English and Czech.

The Fleet Sheet is a valuable daily English-language newsletter delivered by fax and email (http://www.fleet.cz). Another useful news source is Radio Prague's website, http://www.radio.cz, which has great cultural information as well.

Major international papers can be bought from newsagents in central Prague, though are hard to come by elsewhere. These include the current day's issues of the *International Herald Tribune*, *USA Today International*, *The Guardian*, *Frankfurter Allgemeine*, *Le Monde* and other major western publications. Magazines such as *Time,*

Newsweek, Figaro, L'Express, Stern, even *National Geographic, Rolling Stone,* and *Elle* (in Czech!) are often available as well.

TV and Radio Broadcasting

There are four regular network TV channels in the Czech Republic: ČT 1, ČT 2, TV Nova and Prima. Česká Televize, the state-run TV service, operates ČT 1 and 2, similar in content to the BBC networks in Britain. ČT 1 offers mainstream entertainment, while ČT 2 provides good public television with classic films, nature programmes and news commentary. The state's ownership of Česká Televize is quite a controversial issue, as it has often been criticised for being too closely linked with the political fancies of the irascible Václav Klaus and his conservative ODS political party.

Česká Televize has not been nearly as successful as TV Nova, which has swept the market since its inception in 1994, offering up a steady stream of American and British soap operas, game shows and talk shows (dubbed into Czech), and sports. As popular as such shows are, many decry the negative foreign influence that they bring: new obsessions with image and money, and people glued to their TV sets every night after dinner. Nova has also had its own share of sensationalism, as its former Czech CEO, Vladimír Železný was accused by the station's American investors of essentially running off with the profits. The Americans took the case all the way to the international court at the Hague, which ruled that the Czech government had not adequately protected the investment.

A fourth TV station, Prima, is another private channel, though its viewership is well below ČT 1 and 2 and TV Nova.

Cable and satellite TV is also prevalent throughout the country; many apartment buildings and homes have cable or satellite connections, with access to a broad range of European and American programming.

Specific programme information can be found in most newspapers as well as the *Pro-Gram* magazine guide, available at most newsstands.

Radio broadcasting is excellent. For English-language programming, the BBC comes in on 101.1 FM (http://www.bbc.co.uk/czech), with regular news broadcasts in English. For music, rock and pop stations abound, and this is a good opportunity to hear Czech bands. Classical, jazz, and even country radio stations also thrive.

There are nominal monthly service charges for TV and radio; the bill comes in the post and is payable at any post office.

POSTAL SERVICES

Post offices in the Czech Republic serve not only the purpose of sending mail, but also of paying many bills. There are different windows for buying stamps, paying your utility bills, and if you live in a state flat, paying rent. Post offices are open Monday to Friday 8:00 am–6:00 pm. The Main Post Office in Prague, at Jindřišská 14 just off Wenceslas Square, is open 24 hours.

Postal service costs are quite cheap, yet speed of delivery is at least as good as anywhere else. A regular letter sent to or received from North America takes about seven days. Within Europe it takes about five days, and within the country it should be a two day job, though as anywhere, you shouldn't necessarily count on these times. All post is priced according to weight, so unless you are only sending one page letters or post cards, you'll probably want to visit the post office directly to have your post properly stamped. Post sent within Europe is automatically sent air mail, though if you are sending mail overseas, be sure to write *par avion* or *letecky*, or ask for an air mail sticker from the post office.

Paying Bills

Utility bills can be paid at the post office as well—though you may have an arrangement with your landlord that he pays the bills for you. If you pay bills yourself, take them to the window marked *výplata/příjem peněz*, hand the bills and the cash (no other method of payment is accepted) to the bank staff and take your receipt. Not a word of spoken Czech is required other than a simple 'thank you'.

If speed is of the essence, you can send letters *expres*, and if you need security you can send them *doporučeně* (registered), both of which cost about double the normal rate. To send a registered letter, look for the small slips of paper marked *podací lístek*, which usually sit in a pile on the counter. Fill in the recipient's address on the top line, and your address on the line below it.

Parcels over two kilogrammes must pass customs clearance, which is quite a confusing process if you don't speak Czech. The main post office of most cities has a customs department, which will provide you with forms to fill in. They may inspect the contents of your package as well. In Prague, there is a special customs post office, which you must visit if you are sending or receiving heavy packages. It is located at Plzeňská 129, Prague 5. Bring a Czech speaker along with you to avoid immense frustration.

All post offices have a *poste restante* (general delivery) service. In Prague, this is commonly done at the Main Post Office; if you want letters sent to one closer to you, find out the address of that post office. Be sure to have *poste restante* written under your name.

Courier Services

All the big international courier services, such as FedEx, DHL, UPS and so on, have offices in Prague. Note that the cost of sending letters or packages through them is significantly more expensive than in many other countries.

TELECOMMUNICATIONS

Like many things in this country, the telephone service has improved by leaps and bounds with the introduction of market forces.

Land Lines (Pevná Linka)

A well worn joke here from earlier days (i.e. up until the late 1990s) was that half the country is waiting for a telephone, and the other half is waiting for the dial tone. It wasn't long ago that applying for a telephone line at home often took several years of waiting, simply because the national telephone utility was underfunded and underincentivised to install lines.

ZOOM

TRIGG.

Now, after substantial foreign investment, that wait has been cut to a few days or weeks at most. However, if your new flat or house does not have a phone installed, your landlord may hesitate to put one in as his name will have to go on the bill, and he may fear you running out on the bill at the end of your lease. One common feature of lease contracts is a fairly hefty deposit for the phone bill. Your phone bill comes monthly, and is paid at the post office or through bank transfers. As with electricity and gas bills, however, you may make an arrangement with your landlord to pay the bills through him.

Mobile Phones (Mobil)

Meanwhile, virtually all Czechs use mobile phones for personal and business use. In fact one of your first purchases in the Czech Republic may well be your mobile phone, and with the prevalence of mobile phone usage here as in many countries, people often skip the land-lines in favour of more convenient mobile phones.

The Czech mobile phone industry is controlled by three operators, Eurotel, T-Mobil and Oskar, and a variety of plans are available. Services are generally paid for either through a monthly subscription service, or through a pay-as-you-go approach, deducting minutes from the SIM card in your phone via a pre-paid phone card called *karta na mobil* that you buy at a newsagent (*tabák* or *trafika*) or post office. When your available minutes get low, you buy a new phone card to recharge your SIM card. Czechs are also avid users of SMS (short messaging service), given how cheap and easy it is to use.

Dialing

Note that all telephone numbers in the country now have nine digits, and you must dial all nine, even when dialling within the same city. (When dialing to the Czech Republic from abroad, add the international prefix, then 420, then dial the nine-digit number). Note that when dialling a mobile phone from a land-line phone, you will be charged a much higher rate than dialling from land-line to land-line or from mobile to mobile. Also, note that rates go down after 7:00 pm.

It is important to have a telephone card if you ever need to use public pay phones, as there are very few coin phones around. Phonecards can be purchased at newsagents and at post offices, and work on a principle of subtracting units from the amount on it. This figure will appear on a little window on the telephone, and you'll watch it declining in value as the minutes tick by.

Internet

Czechs are very internet-savvy, and internet access is not too terribly difficult to arrange. Through your land-line telephone, internet dial-up and DSL access is fairly straightforward to arrange through services provided by operators such as Český Telecom, Česká Radiokomunikace, Contactel, Tiscali and others. Some of these provide free dial-up service, after which you only pay per-minute phone charges. Others have monthly subscription fees for which you get more premium services such as web domains and larger email storage, or a package of these with unlimited connection time. You can also buy computer cards through mobile operators such as Eurotel or T-Mobile where you get unlimited, albeit relatively slow mobile connections. Your other options are to get internet service through your cable operator (although this is currently much more expensive), or microwave service. Microwave antennas became common in the late 1990s as a means of skipping the long waits for land-line service at the time, and these can be adapted to internet use. Internet cafés are also abundant throughout the country.

PUBLIC TOILETS

Toilets in public areas such as train stations and cheap pubs can be pretty foul. Not only are they dirty and smelly, you often have to pay for them! There's usually a poor old pensioner sitting inside who collects your 3-5 Kč and hands you a puny piece of non-absorbent toilet paper if you need it. There are very few public toilets on the street. Prague's underground system has toilets in each station, and some cities have public facilities in parks, though many men have no qualms about finding the nearest tree.

LAUNDRY SERVICES

There aren't too many of these around. Most Czechs have their own washing machine at home, so there isn't much need for public launderettes.

Prague has a few western-style launderettes where you can do the wash yourself, though it's not cheap. A few are listed in the Resources Guide in the back. Old-fashioned laundry maid services are available from a few *prádelna* shops that you find around town. These are mostly used by hotels and restaurants, though it is possible to give them your load of laundry and have them do it for you.

EATING AND DRINKING

CHAPTER 6

'*Kde se pivo pije, tam se dobře žije*'
(Where beer is drunk, the living is good)
—Czech folk song

ONE FACT OF EAST EUROPEAN COOKING in general is that it relies heavily on a meaty and starchy basis. One often thinks of Polish sausages, Hungarian goulash and potatoes all around; throw in some cabbage sauerkraut and you've got the makings of a hearty peasant meal. Such traditional dishes have been handed down, and are still served today with a particular pride in the folk-country root and the image that this inspires.

Czech food fits the description well. Typical dishes include generous portions of meat and either potatoes or special Czech dumplings, often laden with a thick sauce and washed down with a half-litre of beer or a glass of Moravian wine. In the most traditional pubs and restaurants, the setting is a smoky wood-panelled beer cellar, with red-checkered table cloths and possibly a grizzled old man playing accordion in a corner; a waiter in a dusty old tuxedo walks around the room with armfuls of beer mugs and steaming plates.

Though the sentimental value is one of its strong points, Czech food is the subject of much debate amongst foreign palates. Czechs for their part take enormous pride in visitors to the country who indulge themselves. Many first-timers indeed gush at the simple heartiness of it, soaking in the atmosphere with self-satisfied abandon. Connoisseurs of fine dining, meanwhile, cannot come to a consensus. Perhaps it's not surprising that Czech food hardly holds international status, compared with, say, French, Lebanese or

Japanese cuisine: maybe meat and potatoes isn't so refined after all. Although there is little overall variety in content or presentation, Czechs have developed many nuances in the standard offering.

The Carnivorous Czechs

If you're a meat lover you'll have a carnival indulging in the standard beef and pork fare, and at first you may feel like a child, suddenly free of the reins of your mother's insistence on a balanced diet. Czech cooking almost seems a conscious attempt to ignore nutritional advice and simply indulge in our predator-prey instinct. Imagine ordering a beefsteak topped with a slice of ham, a slice of cheese and a fried egg; or try a deep-fat-fried pork chop with mashed potatoes swimming in a pool of butter. Some quip that the real purpose of Czech food is to line and fill the stomach, for the sake of the beer that accompanies and follows the meal.

Czechs are indeed unabashed carnivores. Not only is meat the centrepiece to virtually any meal, it is additionally served as an ingredient in soups and salads, and you may easily eat more than one animal in more than one form at one single setting. The dietary habits are almost shocking. Not only are animal products the basis of most meals, the very preparation of the meals relies on excessive use of oil and lard for frying and in gravies. Vegetables are served almost as an afterthought.

One thing that makes Czech meat dishes exceptional and intriguing is the variety of sauces used, most of which contain very simple, basic ingredients, yet lend a distinct flavour and edibility to them. There are many varieties of sauces and gravies poured over the meat: paprika, tomato, garlic, butter and dill sauces are common, and each gives an enticing twist to what would otherwise be a monotonous offering. Plenty of potatoes and dumplings fill the plate, serving to soak up the gravy and balance the weight of the meat.

Czech food also happens to be a bit less on the sweet side than many other cuisines. Salty meat, sauerkraut and lots of strong onion- and garlic- flavouring renders Czech cuisine strong and hardy.

Beer, meat and music are the ingredients for a good time.

Healthy Fare

Those who appreciate more healthy fare may find it overwhelming at first, but dig around a bit and you'll learn how to cope. Traditional Czech dishes seem to have a strange aversion to fresh fruits and vegetables: though they are sometimes present on restaurant plates, their appearance is disguised in such a way that it seems they don't want to admit they're eating them. Most vegetables served in restaurants are either pickled or fried, even if they say it's fresh. The mushroom- and cauliflower- entrées (comprising the 'vegetarian' selection on the menu) are breaded and deep-fried. The cucumber salad you order is invariably going to be shredded and soaked in sugar-and-vinegar water, while the expected vegetable accompaniment to the entrée is rarely more than a pickle, a dollop of cabbage or a couple of wedges of tomato with a piece of parsley. It can be frustrating. Chicken and fish are popularly consumed as something a bit 'lighter.'

Much of the food scene just described is what you typically encounter in pubs and cheaper restaurants, which, unless you have immediate inroads to a Czech home, will be your most likely point of entry. But keep in mind the local ties to nature. Czech country cottages invariably have gardens, which are carefully tended. And as most Czechs have a connection with the countryside, including city folk that escape at weekends, Czechs consume much more fresh fruit and vegetables at home than you might realise if you dine in pubs all the time. One reason for the traditional abundance of pickled and canned fruits and vegetables is that the winter is long, and Czechs don't have too much tolerance for artificially-enhanced produce, such as that shipped in from truck farms in the middle of February (although contemporary society benefits from better trading policies since 1989, with better quality fruits and vegetables imported from warmer Mediterranean climes). With a quite discerning palate, Czechs are quick to recognise freshness. So when the season is right, home pantries as well as fruit and vegetable stalls and greengrocer shops in towns overflow with fresh produce.

Given this, you'll never really be in need. With the profusion of supermarkets and hypermarkets in recent years, in addition to some speciality shops in the bigger cities, you won't have too much trouble obtaining most of the ingredients you want for your own cooking. It's up to you to be creative.

In restaurants too, there are options. Soups are sturdy and wholesome; cabbage cream soup, for example, is delicious; the Czech version of potato soup is absolutely wonderful, with lots of onions and garlic; and tasty pea and bean soups are also quite common. And of course, you are not limited to the standard offering in all restaurants: many places do in fact have decent healthy dishes. In Prague and other larger cities too, ethnic and vegetarian restaurants are becoming something of a fad, and newer, slightly more upscale Czech restaurants are even offering more healthy variations on the traditional theme. In addition, practically every town in the country has a plethora of pizzerias by now, many of which also offer decent salads.

A Question of Taste

All in all, Czech food is hearty and delicious, though it may take some time to get used to. Many foreigners who are not used to a meat-and-potatoes diet usually comment that this is in fact the toughest thing to adjust to, though they immediately admit that it's not so bad—it's just easy to complain about. Some, this author for example, think quite highly of it.

THE DAILY MEALS

You may come to think that Czechs somehow have different stomachs than others, but in fact their palate is quite discerning when it comes to freshness and quality, and they are keenly aware of body rhythms; there are certain rules to when one should and should not take a meal. Breakfast (*snídaně*) is a quiet, reserved affair, perhaps because it's still dark for a good half the year as most people rise, but also because a meal of eggs or doughnuts is considered too heavy in the morning—the body can't focus on the day's tasks when it is digesting. So breakfast tends to be little more than a cup of coffee, bread and cheese or jam and/or a piece of fruit or yoghurt.

Lunch (*oběd*) is often the main meal of the day, usually a bit more substantial than dinner unless one is specifically going out to eat in the evening. During the week, lunch is usually taken with colleagues and friends, and it is not a particularly drawn-out affair. Business-people and workers often go to a pub or office cafeteria for lunch, and children eat a full hot meal in the school canteen. The increasingly hectic work week now means that people are skipping or shortening their lunch breaks, and many are doing away with the formalities as they grab a sandwich when they find time.

Meal Times

Lunchtime is generally between 11.30 am and 2.00 pm. At the weekends, the family usually gathers for a meal prepared at home and served as the main meal of the day, at around noon. This is normally a more relaxed affair than the Monday-Friday crunch, with everyone lounging around, drinking, talking and watching television.

The size and formality of the dinner (*večeře*) depends on whether it is enjoyed at home or in a restaurant, and on the whims of those who prepare it. Home meals are often simple, sometimes just a sausage, a bowl of soup or even fruit filled dumplings, though sometimes dinner is a proper hot meal. When one goes out to dinner, the meal is more relaxed than it is at lunchtime. Dinner is usually consumed no later than 8:00 pm; in fact many restaurants stop serving by nine or ten o'clock.

THE ORDER OF THE MEAL

The best and mostly likely place for you to mingle with the locals and eat traditional Czech food is in a pub. The food typically served in these establishments is the same idea as that which is served at home, though due to Czechs' intensely private nature you aren't likely to be invited to friends' homes for dinner very often. Because of this, I've arranged the following section according to the menus you're likely to see when eating out. Common menu items are written in the text in Czech and English. *(For food items in list form, please refer to the Shopping section in the previous chapter, Settling In).*

Czechs don't give a lot of pretence to the meal itself. Lunch or dinner is rarely more than a soup or salad and an entree, and when the food itself arrives it is often downed quickly. Conversation during the meal follows a similarly light-hearted trend. Deep discussion or playful argumentation on political or moralistic issues seem extraneous to the act of eating, a distraction to what should be a time of mental and physical relaxation. One therefore tends to speak about recent travels, plans for the weekend, a current film or perhaps an issue in a relationship.

Be Prepared

Note that restaurants occasionally 'run out' of selections, so think of a couple of options while making your choice.

Appetisers (Předkrmy)

Appetisers such as those discussed below are in fact rarely ordered in restaurants nor are they served at home, as they are often quite heavy themselves. These are rather taken as snacks if you're stopping in for a drink, or as the meal itself if you're not very hungry.

Cheese platters (*sýrová mísa*) are common, and are composed of slices of *eidam, hermelín* (camembert) or *niva* (blue) cheese with a chunk of butter, a dash of paprika, and perhaps a pickle and a basket of rolls. A rather new item on many menus is *nakládaný hermelín*, a chunk of camembert-style cheese dripped in oil and usually accompanied by spices, fruit or nuts.

Eggs

Eggs, usually scrambled, called *míchaná vejce* occasionally pop up on menus too. You might also be able to ask for *hemenex* (ham and eggs)—fried eggs and ham.

Meat platters are similar, though with slices of ham (*šunka*) or various salamis (*salám)* in addition to, or in place of, the cheese. Some places serve *tlačenka* (head cheese), basically animal parts in their own gel.

A bit more substantial are the working-man's sausages available, such as *párek* (bunless hot dogs) and *klobása* (*kielbasa*, or thick Polish sausage). *Utopenec* is a thick pink pickled sausage brewing in big jars on the countertop, and looks especially foul, but I happen to like it.

Pickled or smoked fish include *zavináč* (roll-mops, or very vinegary herring), *sardinky* (dried sardines), and *makrela* (smoked mackerel).

Soups (Polévky)

Although only a preview to the upcoming entree, Czech soups are wonderful and in some cases are more the highlight. There are two basic types of soup: thick and hearty, and light and brothy.

The sturdy soups are almost a meal in themselves, with thick bases of flour and cream, and a few pungent spices to liven them up. Czech potato soup, called *bramborová polévka* though often referred to more intimately as *bramboračka*, is a marvellous concoction of potatoes, mushrooms and onions, with lots of garlic and marjoram. Once you've tried it you'll want to take the recipe home. Equally good is the cabbage cream soup (*zelná polévka)*, with a base of sauerkraut and milk or cream, pieces of sausage to bulk it up, and often flavoured with caraway seeds. Mushroom soup (*houbová polévka*) is another popular soup, made from large dried forest mushrooms and spices such as marjoram and garlic. Pea soup (*hrachová polévka*) is a little less common; it is a good split pea-and-ham type. White bean soup (*fazolová polévka*) is similar. Another Czech speciality is tripe (cow's stomach) soup, known as *dršťková*.

Soups of a brothy nature are also common and very good. Chicken and beef broths (*slepičí* and *hovězí vývar*) often have small pieces of meat, liver and noodles in them. Even better though are onion soup (*cibulová polévka* or *cibulačka* for short) and garlic soup (*česneková polévka* or *česnečka*), both often bulked up with pieces of potato and shredded cheese, and topped with croutons.

Salads (Saláty)

Most pub menus offer what they call fresh salads; in fact, very few of them are. Your best bet for a genuine fresh salad is *šopský salát*, a healthy mix of diced peppers, tomatoes, cucumbers, and onions in a vinegar-water dressing, with salty Balkan cheese (similar to Greek feta cheese) sprinkled on top. You can usually be sure of fresh ingredients. Restaurants usually offer a tossed *míchaný salát,* a fresh mixture of lettuce with tomato and cucumber.

Other so-called salads are usually made of fresh vegetables, though they are often mercilessly shredded and soaked in sweet vinegar water. These may appear as *rajčatový* (tomato), *okurkový* (cucumber), *mrkvový* (carrot) or *zelný* (cabbage) salads. Cabbage salad, basically shredded fresh or pickled cabbage in mayonnaise, makes regular appearances throughout the menu.

Grocery shops and cheap eateries often have buckets of what they call salad in display cases. These are invariably cold, thick salads such as potato salad, egg salad, fish salad, and so on, all coagulated in mayonnaise. Some of the better places offer decent salads comprising of tofu, pasta, rice and vegetables.

Entrées/Main Courses (Hlavní jídlo)

The heart and soul of Czech cooking lies in the hefty main course platter. Home-cooked meals are a real treat, especially if you've grown accustomed to restaurant food, but in either case your eyes are bound to pop when they see that pile of meat and potatoes or dumplings.

Menus are often divided into types of meat, so you can better choose which type of *hovězí* (beef), *vepřové* (pork), *kuře* (chicken) or *ryba* (fish) you'd like. Pubs usually have a list of ready-made dishes (called *hotová jídla*), such as goulash and *vepřový řízek* (Wiener schnitzel), which come as a fixed plate with a side order, such as potatoes, included. Better pubs and restaurants also prepare food to order (*jídla na objednávka*).

One of the quintessential Czech dishes is roast pork with either flour or potato dumplings and sauerkraut, whose proper name (*vepřová pečeně, houskový/bramborový knedlík, zelí*) is affectionately shortened to *vepřo-knedlo-zelo*. It must be downed with a beer.

Another excellent typical dish is *svíčková*—beef sirloin, again with flour dumplings and a rich gravy made of celery root, carrots, onions, ginger and thyme, all topped with a piece of lemon and a spoonful of cranberry sauce.

Classic Czech Dishes

MAIN DISHES

Svíčková–Beef sirloin in a rich creamy gravy of celery root, carrots, onions and spices, with flour dumplings, often garnished with lemon, cranberries and a dollop of whipped cream.

Vepřo-knedlo-zelo–Roast pork in sauce with flour or potato dumplings and sauerkraut.

Vepřový řízek (Weiner schnitzel)–Fried pork wrapped in bread crumbs, usually served with cold potato salad. *Kuřecí rizek* is the same, with chicken instead of pork.

Guláš (goulash)–Beef or pork stew in a dark paprika sauce, with flour or potato dumplings

Kapr (carp)–Roast or fried carp with cold potato salad. Served primarily for Christmas dinner, but occasionally during the year.

SNACKS

Chlebíčky–Small, open-faced sandwiches, usually with a layer of potato salad topped artistically with any combination of ham, salami, cheese, egg, pickles or other ingredients. Often served as a snack for guests or during Sundays or holidays.

Koláče–Open-faced pastries carved out at the top and filled with fruit, jam, poppy seeds or curd.

DESSERTS

Ovocné knedlíky–Large fruit-filled dumplings topped with butter, curd, and sugar.

Goulash (*guláš*) is a stew served on a plate, with lots of paprika sauce, pieces of raw onion or pickled red pepper on top, and flour dumplings to soak it all up. The meat is usually chunks of beef (or occasionally pork), sometimes with bits of fat still attached.

There are many other cuts and preparations of meat, generally either *pečené* (roasted) or *smažený* (fried), and different establishments often have different names for and varieties of them. Look for the kinds of meat on offer, then decipher the menu to figure out how it is prepared and what sides and sauces accompany them. Common preparations include *steak* or *biftek* (beef or pork steak), *roštěná* (roasts), *grilovaný* (grilled meats) and *řízek* (pounded schnitzel).

Chicken is a popular product as well. *Kuřecí pečeně* (roast chicken) is often served with either potatoes or potato dumplings and topped with a succulent garlic sauce. You will likely find some form of fried chicken steak or *smažený kuřecí řízek*, or *kuřecí prsa* (grilled chicken breast), sometimes with almonds and canned peaches or pineapple, as well. Some establishments serve *kachna* (roast duck), *husa* (goose), and *králík* (rabbit); these are delicacies here as anywhere.

Fish is quite popular amongst Czechs, due to the large number of freshwater streams and lakes and the country's passion for fishing. Trout (*pstruh*) and carp (*kapr*) are the most common, either roasted or fried, and usually served with, again, potatoes or potato dumplings. Trout is the most common freshwater fish in the land, and it appears on many a dinner table. Czech carp is a little different from the bottom-dwelling fish in other parts of the world; it is raised in cleaner fish ponds and is eaten when still young. It has a meaty texture and lots of tiny bones. Try it with garlic sauce—called *kapr na česneku*—it's excellent. In recent years, the improving state of the environment has seen salmon return to Czech rivers, and the global salmon farming industry has penetrated the Czech market as well. *Losos* is therefore a more common menu item these days. Other fish appearing on menus include *treska* (cod), *hejk* (hake) and *úhoř* (eel).

Vegetarian Entrees
(Bezmasá or Vegeterianská jídla)

Yes, there are meatless dishes to be ordered too. One of the most popular is *smažený sýr* or fried cheese, a thick slice of eidam or *hermelín* cheese, breaded and deep-fat-fried. It's sinfully rich and unhealthy, especially when taken with *hranolky* (chips, pommes-frites, french fries), and it's usually served with tartar sauce. Wonderful. Be sure to eat it quickly, while the cheese is still runny.

Smažené žampióny (fried mushrooms) and *smažený květák* (fried cauliflower) are the other options here, again breaded and deep-fried. *Čočka* (lentils) are often available, usually served in huge proportions with a fried egg resting on top, but sometimes accompanied by a sausage.

Sides (Přílohy)

Knedlíky (Czech dumplings) are a matter of national pride. They're quite unlike the dumplings one normally comes across, and in fact you may not even recognise them as such when you first see them. There are two types, flour dumplings (*houskový knedlík*) and potato dumplings (*bramborový knedlík)*; both are boiled as round loaves and sliced into thick chunks. You'll be served three or four of them to soak up the sauce on your plate. There are a few varieties of dumplings, for example *špekový knedlík* have bits of bacon mixed into the batter, and there are apparently subtle distinctions in quality which any blue-blooded Czech will quickly determine. The home-made ones are always the best, and most people scoff at the shop bought mixes available—such things require special attention. Perhaps because Czechs are so proud of their *knedlíky*, foreigners are quick to ridicule what appears to be little more than boiled bread, though most agree they have their merits. When eating these thick dumplings, one picks up a piece with the fork in the left hand and slops sauce on top of the bready substance with the knife in the right and carefully raises it to the mouth.

Potatoes come in the usual styles: *vařené* (boiled), *kaše* (mashed), *opékané* or *opečené* (roasted) and as *hranolky* (chips or fries), though they are in fact of pretty uniform quality, with little of the assortment of potatoes eaten in some other countries. One fairly recent addition to the pototo roster is *americké brambory* (roasted wedge-shaped potatoes). *Rýže* (rice) and *těstoviny* (pasta) are less common in traditional Czech cooking, but are consumed with some dishes, and in main course menu items such as *rizoto* (risotto) and *špagety* (spaghetti).

Side orders are sometimes included as part of the dish; if not, they will be listed at the end of the menu and are not included in the price.

Desserts (Moučníky or Dezerty)

Desserts are always included in restaurant menus, and are occasionally served at home, though Czechs rarely indulge in more than coffee after the main course. In fact, your waiter will probably not ask if you want a dessert, so you'll have to request the menu again if you do. Keep in mind that desserts are often just as heavy as the food that came before it, so save some room. There are a few particular ones which you must try.

The Ultimate Sweet

The king of sweets in this land is the fabulous fruit-filled dumpling called *ovocný knedlík*. Large round flour dumplings are filled with strawberries, blueberries, cherries, plums or apricots, dripped with butter, and sprinkled with curd and sugar. Coming after an already heavy meal, this is the height of gluttony, though you really must try it.

One popular dessert is light crepes, known as *palačinky*, rolled up and filled with jam or fruit and occasionally topped with whipped cream.

Štrůdl or *závin* (apple strudel) is well-liked here as in Germany and Austria; it's especially good straight from the oven, topped with whipped cream.

Zmrzlina (ice cream) is more commonly bought on the street from a vendor, though a type of ice cream sundae called *zmrzlinový pohár* is usually available in restaurants. It is often topped with *kompot* (canned fruit), though sometimes chocolate is poured on top of that, with little regard for clashing tastes.

Oh well.

Drinks (Nápoje)

Beer and wine accompany the meal, though if you abstain you can always order a *mineralka* or *sodovka* (mineral or soda water), *kola* (cola), *čaj* (tea) or *káva* (coffee). Beware of *džus*, pronounced and intended to be 'juice'. Unless it specifically states that it is 100 per cent juice, it will be a powder-mix neon-orange sugar water. *(For more on drinks, see the Drinking section below).*

SNACKS

Czechs consume lots of meaty snacks at all times of the day, often stopping at a street stand to pick up a sausage or a roll. You'll never be far from a counter from which you can buy a hotdog wrapped in a bun (*párek v rohlíku*). Street stands in many towns serve thick hearty sausages called *klobása*, accompanied by a hunk of bread and a dollop of mustard on a paper tray. You're meant to eat it with your fingers. Cheap pubs serve it too—this is the mainstay of many. Greasy potato pancakes (*bramborák)* are made of shredded potatoes and lots of garlic fried in lard—a nightmare for the arteries and breath, but a tasty treat nonetheless.

Lunch spots and grocery shops often have an extensive selection of small, open-faced sandwiches called *chlebíčky*. Three or four of these could make a poor-man's lunch. These usually have a layer of potato salad topped with ham, salami, egg, cheese or fish, and a garnish of pickle, onion or parsley. There may be an additional dollop of mayonnaise as well. It makes for a tall mouthful: eat carefully, or you may get it all down your shirt. *Chlebíčky* in fact are considered a delicacy; though the ingredients are rather basic they are arranged artistically—you'll likely see them offered at balls and during intermission at the symphony. If you spend time in a Czech home, you may be offered *chlebíčky* as a snack or before or after the main meal as well.

Sweet snacks are eaten regularly. Ice cream is immensely popular in warm weather, and street stands across the country have lines of people forming to indulge in small cones with minuscule scoops of average ice cream. The quintessential Czech pastry is the *koláč*, a round sweetbread carved out at the top and filled with curd, poppy seeds or fruity paste; it looks almost like a mini-pizza. Cafés and bakeries usually also serve several varieties of cakes cakes (*dort*) as well.

SEASONAL SPECIALITIES

There are a few seasonal specialities to spice up the usual offerings. These for the most part are consumed at home, though good restaurants may play their part and serve the following as well.

Within a week or two at the end of April or beginning of May, everyone opens their windows, and a funny thing happens: people start eating fresh fruits and vegetables again! The seasons dictate the diet to some extent, and while it's normal to eat pickles and sauerkraut for six months, all of a sudden it's part of the celebration of spring and summer to eat fresh strawberries, tomatoes, cauliflower and peppers again. So refreshing!

Autumn is the traditional harvest time, and there are a few culinary pleasures to be discovered. As mushrooms pop up in the forests, people head out with wicker baskets to pick them—and these aren't just regular mushrooms. Czechs have a sharp eye for fungi, and they quickly fill up on monstrous beautiful creations recalling images of *Alice in Wonderland*. These are then taken home where they are dried and fried or put into thick soups.

Christmas, of course, has a traditional meal, but the surprise here is that the dish is not meat based. Throughout November and December, the carp ponds of south Bohemia are harvested and the chunky foot-long fish are wheeled into town in large barrels, where they are sold live. The faithful take them home and let them swim in the bathtub until the 24th, when the fish are fried up and served next to a bed of cold potato salad. I had always thought

A Winter Ritual

In the dead of winter many villagers perform an almost ritual pig slaughter, called *zabíjačka*. The poor beast is strung up by its haunches and gutted, and all body parts are used to make chops, sausages and goulash. Although this is something of a slowly dying custom, it is still an occasion in the countryside, where neighbours and friends gather for a full day's killing, eating and drinking.

this was summer food, but the custom on Christmas day is delightful.

DRINKING
Beer

Pivo (beer) is the pride, joy and ritual passion of the Czech people. Czechs were in fact one of the very first nations to brew and drink beer. The word 'pilsner' itself comes down to us from the Czech beer-producing town of Plzeň, which is recorded as selling a famous malty ale in 1307. So devoted were the city's inhabitants that they rioted when the recipe was subsequently altered. Plzeň is still home to one of the country's (and hence the world's) finest brands, Pilsner Urquell. Pilsner Urquell, called Plzeňský Prazdroj in Czech, is a lager that became so popular after its founding in 1842 that it spawned a series of German imitations (the Czech lands were heavily populated by Germans at this time), marketed under the type name 'pilsner.' The company then had to add the qualifier *urquell* in German, and *prazdroj* in Czech ('source'), to identify it as the original. Great German beers thus owe a tip of the hat to the Czechs for setting them on the right track in this regard.

Another beer word you're probably familiar with is Budweiser, whose name is taken from Budweis, the German name for the south Bohemian city of České Budějovice. Not only the Germans, but also the Americans have exploited this name for their own weak imitations. The American company Anheuser-Busch is currently embroiled in a long-running dispute with the Budějovický Budvar brewery over the international trademark, to such an extent that the Americans would like to buy a majority share in the Czech label to protect their turf from the vastly better Czech brand. Fortunately for connoisseurs, it doesn't look like it will happen, and the Czech government, which still owns the brewery, is doing all it can to keep the Americans at bay. It is indeed a matter of national importance.

In recent years, corporate acquisition activity has greatly concentrated the Czech beer market. In fact, it can be difficult to find the more local brews outside their own domains.

A number of Czech breweries are now owned by foreign multinationals, who while thankfully are not yet interfering with the recipes, are trying to introduce more global tastes into local brews. Hence, in addition to the major Czech labels on the following pages, a number of new brews have hit the market, such as Velvet (a smooth red-brown porter) and Kelt (a decent imitation of Guinness). These are predictably not nearly as popular as the standbys, not least because they are more expensive, although the younger cosmopolitan crowd at least has an ongoing curiosity for them.

Foreign ownership of Czech breweries also means that a number of Czech brands are now aggressively distributed and marketed abroad. SABMiller, the South African/US conglomerate that owns Pilsner Urquell, Gambrinus, Radegast and Velkopopovický Kozel, has in fact declared Pilsner Urquell to be its global flagship brand, and plans to increase production as much as five-fold in the next several years. Interbrew, the Belgian global brewer, owns Staropramen, and has likewise begun to export it more aggressively worldwide. Budvar is also widely available outside the Czech Republic now—it is marketed as Czechvar in the US to get around the trademark disputes.

Czech advertisers have come up with some clever eye-

grabbers in recent years expounding the local adulation. One effective ad for Staropramen beer, for example, showed a classic smoky old beer hall with bearded robed men worshipping at the table, chanting "*Bud' pochválen*" ("Be praised") while the waiters pour the loving nectar in slow motion. Pilsner Urquell plays on its own name, selling itself as '*Prazdroj naše hrdost*'—'The source of our pride.' Little wonder then that Czechs consume far greater quantities of beer per capital than anyone else in the world.

The drink itself is indeed honourable: full-bodied, foamy, and fit for a king. Hop growing is an art form, and a jaunt into parts of north and west Bohemia will lead you through massive wooden hop frames filling the fields. It is not really known why, but Bohemian hops simply produce the best beer, and in fact are exported to many foreign manufacturers, including, ironically, Anheuser Busch. Domestic brewers say it is simply the method used and the care given to the brewing that produces such a fine drink.

Czech beer is not produced in such varieties as elsewhere. There are two kinds, light and dark, and there are different grade strengths within each. Variations such as bitter, white, amber, porter or fruity beers, as available in countries such as Britain, Germany, Belgium or the US microbrewery phenomenon, are not considered 'real' beer by Czech connoisseurs.

Proper Czech beer is a golden lager or pilsner brew, commonly referred to as *světlé* ('light'), though not at all to be mistaken for the low-calorie stuff. It is invariably well toned, just a little hoppy and bitter, not sweet, and comes in two strengths—10°, called *desítka,* and 12°, or *dvánactka.* These do not indicate percentages of alcohol but grades of sugar content. The heavier the degree of sugar, the stronger the beer. Ten-degree beer is lighter in colour, often a little sweeter and contains about 3-4 per cent alcohol. Regular pub-goers often prefer it because the stomach can process more of it during a lengthy drinking session. Twelve-degree beer is stronger and heavier—it normally contains about 4-5 per cent alcohol—with a thick golden-brown colour and frothy foam that doesn't want to go down. It is said that the best way to judge a good beer is if a wooden matchstick, placed vertically in the head, stays afloat for more than ten seconds. If you intend to really go out drinking, moderate your intake of 12° beer; even life-long veterans can wake up with a vicious headache if they down more than four or five.

Dark, or 'black' beer, known as *tmavé* or *černé,* is indeed almost black and often very sweet—many drinkers find it too sugary. For this reason it is less commonly drunk than regular beers, though it is often mixed with light beer and referred to as *řezané*, literally 'cut' beer.

The best place to consume is in the pub, where beer is drawn fresh from the tap. Most pubs offer both the 10° and 12° varieties. Bottled beer is available everywhere, and most shops offer a decent selection. You may soon develop your favourite brands, though for the most part each is similar enough and good enough that beginners won't easily distinguish among them.

> **Not for the Faint Hearted**
>
> Beer is traditionally served in sturdy half-litre glass mugs, or sometimes in large tall glasses. Czechs sometimes order a *malé* (small) beer at lunch and when they only want a taste. As much as they enjoy their national claim to fame, though, they tend to swallow it in gulps rather than sip it gracefully.

The Major Labels

While there are several major labels marketing their products across the land and abroad, consolidation in the beer industry has meant a more predictable selection, with the majority of pubs and restaurants in Prague and around the country offering one of the following national brands:

- Pilsner Urquell (referred to by regular drinkers as simply Plzeň) is the export leader, with the green, gold and white label familiar to most educated beer drinkers around the world. This is one of the country's, and the world's, premier brands. Most pubs that serve it serve the 12° brew, which is particularly strong, a bit bitter and excellent.

- Gambrinus, also brewed in Plzeň, is similarly top-of-the-line—the 12° variety is arguably the very best in the land, although most pubs and restaurants commonly pair the Pilsner Urquell 12° with Gambrinus 10°.

- Budvar, the original Czech 'Budweiser', is at least as good as Pilsner Urquell and Gambrinus; sturdy and just a tad less bitter than Pilsner Urquell. Again, the 12° is preferred over the 10°.

- Staropramen is Prague's main producer, with a large brewery on the banks of the Vltava in Smíchov. This is working-man's beer; both the 12° and 10° beers are very drinkable.

- Krušovice is a smaller brewery in western Bohemia, producing a slightly more pale pilsner with a faintly metallic-bitter aftertaste. The 12° is especially good; Krušovice also produces a 10° pilsner and a sweet black beer.

- Radegast, from Ostrava in Moravia, makes fine 10° and 12° beers.

There are dozens of local brands as well, and a trip to any town out of Prague should include a sampling of the local product. Some of these include the following:

- Bráník and Měst'an are smaller Prague breweries, both producing decent lagers. Měst'an makes one of the best dark beers in the country.

- Velkopopovický Kozel, produced just south of Prague, also has good 12° beers, though some have been turned off by their sexy ad campaigns, which make a pun of their name: *kozel* means goat, and the creature is indeed used on the brand's label, though the word is also dangerously similar to that for breast.

- Regent, from Třeboň in south Bohemia, has a slightly sweet, light beer.

- Bernard, from Humpolec in south Bohemia, produces an unpasteurised 12° beer that garners praise from dedicated adherents.

- Samson lives in the shadow of its more powerful peer Budvar in České Budějovice, but the 10° is both light and tasty.

- Krakonoš is an excellent golden lager from Trutnov, near the Krkonoše Mountains in east Bohemia.

- Nová Paka, a town in east Bohemia, produces a rare 18° beer, which does not taste quite as powerful as it is, so beware!
- Starobrno is the main local beer from the Czech Republic's second city, Brno.

Wine

It's often commented that Bohemians are enthusiastic beer-guzzlers, while Moravians are slightly more refined aficionados of their wine. South Moravia indeed is an endless stretch of vineyards, and its red and white wines are enjoyed throughout the country. Although it doesn't quite match up to the finest French or Spanish or Italian vintages, Moravian wine is still very drinkable and goes well with certain foods. It is often a bit more acidic, even somewhat sour in its most extreme instances, appealing to Czech tastes. In addition to the Czech wines listed below, many other European varieties are much more readily available now, so for home consumption or at the finer restaurants at least you won't go lacking for Merlot, Cabernet Sauvignon, Chardonnay or Pinot Grigio.

The wine drinking establishment is a common gathering place, admittedly more reserved and genteel than the pub, and usually offering a slightly more sophisticated ambience for a quiet dinner. Wine is often sold right out of the barrel at wine bars called *vinárna*; if you bring your own bottle you can walk off with a good, fresh, yet inexpensive brand. Speciality wine shops are also becoming more commonplace, at least in the bigger cities.

The chief Czech wine-producing regions are around the towns of Znojmo and Mikulov in south Moravia, though there are also respectable wines bottled in north Bohemia around Mělník. Seasonal festivals celebrate the harvest and fermentation of local wines. In October, wine-producing regions erupt in jolly *burčák*, or 'young wine' festivals. The honoured drink is an extremely fruity liquid, very cloudy in appearance and almost indiscernible from plain old grape juice in taste. This, of course, is part of the popularity of it: the alcohol is so masked by the fresh flavour that you don't even realise how much you've drunk before it's too late! Be forewarned.

In the wintertime hot mulled wine or *svařené víno* is a popular balm. Red wine is warmed with stick cinnamon and cloves, and sweetened with sugar and lemon. The cosiest sensations of winter involve strolling the Christmas stalls with a cup of hot wine, or relaxing in a snowbound cottage with friends and plenty of mugs.

Šampaňské or *sekt* (champagne) is drunk at special occasions, and there are a few reasonable local brands, such as Bohemia Sekt, although Czech champagne tends to be a little bit rough. Russian champagne is also available, while French champagne is still beyond the budget of many and not too well known.

Red Wines

- Frankovka is a dry, acidic, full-flavoured wine akin to German and Austrian varieties, produced by many domestic vineyards.
- Vavřinecké is generally a bit sweeter and smoother, but can also be sturdy enough to accompany red meat.
- Rulandské (known elsewhere as Pinot Noir) is somewhat fruitier, and also full-bodied.

White Wines

- Ryzlink (Riesling) is a semi-dry, often neutral wine, a good accompaniment to fish dishes. Some vintages are quite powerfully fruity and acidic (i.e. sour), which has great appeal to some.
- Veltlínské (Veltliner) is also semi-dry and somewhat acidic or citrusy.
- Müller-Thürgau is a bit sweeter, and is the most commonly produced white wine in the country.

Other Alcoholic Drinks

Besides beer and wine, Czechs enjoy a good shot or three every now and again, and there are several interesting national specialities that you may not encounter outside the country.

Czechs are proud possessors of a special herb liquor called Becherovka. This drink is difficult to describe, quite unlike anything else of its ilk. The ingredients in fact are a well protected secret—the recipe is literally locked safely away, and only one person is entitled to blend the concoction. Its most immediately recognisable components are chamomile and cloves; if you have a highly distinguished palate you may be able to identify more. It is rather sweet and Christmasy, but drunk year-round.

Becherovka is made in the spa town of Karlovy Vary (Karlsbad), where it was created as an additional salve for patients who spent their days imbibing mineral water, soaking in steam baths and walking in the fresh air. Because of this, it is reputed to have medicinal properties. A little drink after work is said to calm the nerves in a more wholesome way than say, scotch; it is sometimes drunk as an aperitif; and when taken as an after-dinner liqueur it is said to aid in digestion. Some even use it liberally to cure colds.

Slivovice (slivovitz or plum brandy) is another local speciality, produced and drunk more in Moravia and Slovakia, from whence it comes. This is powerful stuff—clear, distilled from plums and served in tiny shot glasses. It is also purported to have medicinal qualities, though to be swallowed in moderation. The leading producer of *slivovice* is Jelínek, which makes a smooth, fruity variety that best approximates the *domácí* (home-made) *slivovice* that purists herald as the best. Similar schnapps-type drinks are distilled from apricots (*meruňkovice)*, pears (*hruškovice)* and cherries (*třešňovice)*. Quality can vary dramatically—a cheap brand or a poor home-distilled drink can be pretty awful, while the good ones can be glorious.

Czech rum is popular in wintertime, especially when poured into a cup of hot water and garnished with a lemon, called *grog*. Czech rum is distilled from sugarbeets, not sugarcane, and therefore has a dark brown colour and powerful, sickly-sweet flavour. To adhere to EU regulations, Czech rum producers have been forced to adopt the moniker *tuzemský*, meaning 'domestic,' to distinguish their product from rums of local origin produced from sugarcane; this means that rather than naming it 'rum,' they label it '*tuzemský rum*' or *tuzemák* for short. I personally can't drink it.

Equally bad in my opinion is Fernet, an even darker brown, thick, bitter drink whose ingredients are a secret, and therefore are said to include fermented bugs. It can be mixed with tonic water to create a drink that looks like beer, and hence is jokingly nicknamed *bavorské pivo*—Bavarian beer.

Vodka and gin are also produced locally, though their quality pales in comparison to their international counterparts. You also occasionally see folks in pubs throwing back shots of fluorescent green peppermint liqueur (referred to simply as *zelená*—'green'); not very appetising.

Perhaps surprisingly, the Czech Republic maintains an active market for absinthe, the dangerous drink distilled from wormwood that was a hit among Paris Left Bank artists and poets in the 1920s. To properly enjoy it you are supposed to light a teaspoon of sugar aflame, then stir in the melted sugar before drinking.

Other western alcohols, such as whisky and tequila, are popular as novelty items, as they were largely unavailable until the 1990s. They remain highly-priced, however, and so are not as commonly drunk.

Coffee and Tea

Czechs truly enjoy a quiet cup of *káva* or *kafe* (coffee). The brown bean is said to have made its way to Bohemia via Turkish traders in the 16th century, and since then has been an important component of the daily diet. Perhaps falling back on such tradition, Czech coffee is often served as *turecká* ('Turkish-style'), with boiling water poured directly over finely ground beans. This lends it a decidedly rich, silty effect. Stir it well, and let the grounds settle to the bottom—and when you get to the bottom of the cup, be sure not to swallow the last mouthful or you'll get a throat full of mud.

Coffee-machine coffee called *presso* or *překapávaná* is more commonly served now, as the country further integrates itself into western Europe, and in fact in many places now you will have to specify if you want it Turkish-style. Finer preparations such as espresso and cappuccino are offered in many cafés and restaurants as well, as brands such as Lavazza have won a broader following. Decaffeinated coffee, however, is still very rare.

The coffee custom seems frozen in time, and sitting in one of Prague's glorious coffee houses such as Café Slavia gives the sensation of being transported back to the 1920s. Czechs claim that they have always had the best coffee—even under Communism, they had it shipped specially from Cuba. Most people add sugar, though milk is usually left out.

Special preparations of coffee add excitement to the pleasure of drinking it, especially in cold weather. *Videňská* (Viennese) coffee is a robust blend topped with whipped cream, served in an appropriately elegant handled glass. Even more heartwarming is *alžírská* (Algerian), with a drop of egg liqueur atop the whipped cream.

Tea has unfortunately never been an important drink in these parts. Czech tea is pretty bland stuff, though foreign made brands are now widely available. It is usually served black, with lemon and sugar. Fruit teas and herb teas are widely available as well. Perhaps as an adverse reaction to all those smoky pubs, many towns around the country now have speciality tea shops with a relaxed atmosphere and wonderful selection of blends from China, India and elsewhere.

Water

In a land famous for its spas, mineral water is excellent and widely drunk. In addition to the beer and Becherovka produced here, a particular brand of mineral water called Mattoni completes the trinity of special, top quality drinks. This is a wonderfully fine, slightly fizzy water with a light, refreshing taste, served in many restaurants and sold in most shops. *Sodovka* or *perlivá voda,* (soda water) and non-carbonated (still) water, called *neperlíva voda,* are also prevalent. Dobrá Voda is the market leader here; other good brands include Aquila and Bon Aqua. Bottled waters are very popular as tap water is never served in restaurants nor drunk at home. Tap water is in fact drinkable—there are no especially harmful elements therein—but it can taste pretty foul.

EATING AND DRINKING OUT: PUBS AND RESTAURANTS

The basic drinking establishment in the Czech Republic is the pub, and there are subtle differences between the types of pubs and the drinks and food they offer. The very word of course implies beer, and many pubs exist for the sole purpose of pouring half-litres of the foamy stuff. A *hospoda* is your basic pub, serving beer on tap, bottled wine and an assortment of liquors. A *hospoda* normally serves a variety of prepared meals. A *hostinec* or *pivnice* is usually a simpler and more intimate version of a *hospoda*, with a more limited food offering; some in fact have only bags of potato crisps and maybe a sausage. Pubs traditionally until recently served only one brand of beer, and many pubs were named or referred to simply for the beer on tap. With the beer industry consolidating, however, this has changed to some degree, and you will often have a choice of at least two or three brands. The price of beer remains very cheap compared with international standards—most Czechs in fact seem to consider affordable beer a birthright, so the breweries make their living off the high volumes rather than prices. Czech wines in pubs and restaurants are also quite cheap.

Another interpretation to the idealised vision of a traditional pub mentioned in previous sections is the general dirtiness of many: crowded, noisy and incredibly smoky rooms with dirty tablecloths, and waiters mumbling and shuffling about. This is still the norm in the cheaper joints. Glasses aren't always properly washed: every bar has a sink full of water into which glasses are dunked, swished around and stacked to dry. Drunken patrons who spend every evening of their lives at the same table unfurl occasional shouts. It's all quite funny, and all it takes is a little lightening up and hunkering down to fit in.

Restaurace are categorised as proper restaurants, though the difference between a good *hospoda* and a cheap *restaurace* is nominal. The original sense of the word 'restaurant' implies food, while 'pub' implies beer, and because of this, *restaurace* generally have a better variety and quality of food.

Lower end pubs and restaurants serve cheap, albeit greasy meals. Keep in mind when choosing a place to eat that Czechs are avid smokers; nonsmoking sections are practically unheard of, ventilation is poor, and in most pubs you'll be overwhelmed by a blast of hazy blue-grey smoke when you enter.

Moving up the scale, better restaurants pay closer attention to food preparation. The difference between a goulash thrown together at a cheap joint, and one prepared with a careful blend of seasonings at a respectable restaurant, can be substantial. So where you might be driven away by the idea of Czech food from a cheap pub, you'll gain a real appreciation for the specialised art of Czech cuisine at a decent restaurant. For this you'll pay something closer to western standards, though still fairly cheap in comparison.

Ethnic foods are becoming increasingly popular. Prague especially is full of pizzerias, and Mexican, Irish, Chinese, Lebanese, Italian, Thai, Indian and American restaurants dot the city's streets, many of them run by expatriates, and many by now at standards comparable to the best in their home countries. Most small towns around the country have at least a pizzeria and a Chinese restaurant as well. You'll undoubtedly seek occasional refuge in the variety and the vegetables they serve. Pizzerias keep prices low to remain affordable, while most ethnic restaurants charge prices similar to what you would expect to pay in North America or western Europe, perhaps a little less. Please note: if you want quality ethnic food, don't look for it at a Czech pub. Though lots of places now serve 'Chinese meat' or 'Milanese spaghetti,' it will most likely be a poor imitation.

Pub Culture

Because of the inherent difference in standards between a cheap pub and a good restaurant, there are different (unwritten) rules for behaviour in them. Where service in a good restaurant is similar to what you would expect anywhere, pubs are a bit rougher and it helps to understand the mentality so as not to upset anyone. Here are a few do's and don'ts of drinking out.

- Waiters and waitresses in pubs are generally inattentive, though customer service is slowly becoming a part of the Czech vocabulary. The main reason for this is that they are underpaid in the first place, they receive only nominal tips, and therefore they have no incentive. At the same time, the waiter is on a power trip; this is his domain and you'd best respect it. Be patient. Don't attempt to draw attention to yourself by signaling the waiter; he'll come to you in his own time.

- In most restaurants and pubs you are expected to seat yourself. Pubs rarely have tables for two—patrons tend to sprawl out along the bench-like tables, and it's perfectly normal to share a table with someone you don't know. In fact, this is often your only option. If you see free space at the end of a table, ask with appropriate hand motions if the spot is free, and seat yourself. Do not, however, move chairs around without first consulting the server. Remember, you are in his house!

- Many establishments have coat racks, though it is fine to drape your jacket over the back of your seat. Better restaurants have cloakrooms, where you often pay a few crowns to hang your bags and coats. Many older citizens often dress up a bit when they go out. As pubs are still the central focus of Czech social life, a tradition remains of respecting the institution. Casual dress and jeans are perfectly acceptable, of course, and only very rarely will a restaurant look down their nose at you for being under-dressed.

- In the real pubs, you rarely need to order beer, as it is simply plopped down in front of you—after all, isn't this why you came? Your waiter will place a tab on the table, with lines to indicate the number of beers consumed. A glance at your neighbour's tab may well reveal a whole slur of lines; if you really want to integrate you can try to play catch-up. Don't by any means write on or rip your tab—it can potentially cause confusion when adding it all up in the end.

- Always toast your friends before taking your first swallow of the evening, and always look into your companion's eyes when doing so. This is part of the ritual of drinking. Never pour beer from one glass to another: the half-litre is sacred, and you may draw a few harsh stares if you don't

A typical Czech pub–focus of much of the social activity in the country.

so honour it. After clinking glasses, many then tap their glass on the table before taking the first sip, as if to seal the moment.

- One curiosity of eating in a pub is that it can take a while to place your order and get someone to come and add up the bill, though for some reason your plate seems to be whisked away the moment you lay down your fork.

- Paying the bill often seems to take a long time. Often the person who collects your money is different from the one who has served you. When you're ready to go, say to your waiter or the person with the money purse, "*Zaplatíme*" ("We will pay"). He will then invariably ask, "*Dohromady?*" ("Altogether?"), hoping to save himself extra work, though it is fine to pay *zvlášt'* (separately). When your dining or drinking companion is on even keel with you, this is common enough, though if someone does the inviting or otherwise feels obliged, he often takes the tab himself. You as a visitor will probably have difficulty trying to pay, as your friends and colleagues will perpetually want to welcome you. Credit cards are rarely accepted in the lower end and non-touristed establishments, so have cash on hand.

- In the cheaper pubs, the tab is usually calculated by hand right there at the table. Rip-offs do still occur though this is much rarer now than in the early 1990s, when foreigners were hapless prey to greedy waiters; it is unlikely that you'll be cheated now, but be sure to verify the prices and the final addition. As the calculations are done at the table, there is potential for honest mistakes to be made, though it is considered pretty bad form to check the bill's final count unless you're sure that something is amiss.

- Tipping is limited to rounding up the tab to the nearest reasonable figure. The person who takes your money may not be your waiter, anyway, so he doesn't deserve any particular tip. If you have a beer tab for 92 Kč, round it up to 100 Kč and the guy will thank you. If your meal comes to 335 Kč, round up to 350 Kč. Better restaurants, especially foreign owned ones, expect higher tips, but it is still nowhere near the 15 per cent or more expected in some parts of the world. Such roundups are always done on the spot: when the waiter tells you the amount, tell him how much you would like to pay. Never leave money on the table; it will be snatched up by the next guy who sits there.

- Remember that many pubs and restaurants close by around 11:00 pm.

Here are some helpful phrases you can use when dining out or visiting a pub:

je tu volno?	is this space free?
máte? …	do you have? …
já si dám … / dám si… / já bych si dal (m.)/*dala* (f.)	I would like …
na zdraví!	cheers!
dobrou chut'	*bon appetít*
zaplatíme	we would like to pay
dohromady	all together
zvlášt'	separately

ENTERTAINMENT AND CULTURE

CHAPTER 7

'The Bohemians... display a reserved, melancholy,
but not infrequently crafty turn of mind. They are
superior... not only in profundity and inner depth
of feeling but also in tenaciousness of will.
The distinct stamp of these character traits
shines forth in their national music as well.'
—Hermann Krigar, a German musicologist who wrote
in the journal *Musikalisches Wochenblatt* in 1879

THE CZECH NATION HAS A REMARKABLY RICH cultural and artistic history, and many visitors today are struck by the vibrancy of cultural life. The architectural legacy is of course immediately noticeable throughout the country, and many people are familiar with such Czech luminaries as the painter Alfons Mucha, the composer Antonín Dvořák or the writer Milan Kundera. There is a very rich vein of creativity throughout the ages, which continues to find new expression in writers, musicians and filmmakers today.

Culture, entertainment and leisure time are important elements of Czech life. Czech cities maintain an active calendar of concerts and other cultural events, including seasonal activities. In addition, Czechs are active outdoorspeople and sportspeople: hiking, cycling and skiing are popular activities. And of course, part of the experience and adventure of living here is travelling around the country to visit castles, chateaux, towns and spas, as well as forests and mountains.

THE ARTS IN THE CZECH LANDS
Throughout its history, much of the architectural development of the Czech nation was in fact the result of the work of foreign masters commissioned by kings and nobility. These served to bring the general European movements to Czech artists, who then produced their own work within the style. Czech painters, sculptors, composers and writers similarly did not begin many trends of their own, rather they were

influenced by Continental movements, to which they added personal and national elements. A few Czechs reached international stature through the years, but it wasn't until the 19th century and the National Revival that Czech artists really came into their own.

Much of the Gothic glory of Prague, from St Vitus' Cathedral to Charles Bridge, is the work of Peter Parler (Parléř to Czechs), an Austrian who from age 22 spent most of his professional life in Prague, and also designed important edifices such as the Cathedral of St Barbara in Kutná Hora and Karlštejn castle outside Prague. Much of the country's Renaissance architecture is influenced by Germans such as Benedikt Reith and Italians such as Octavio Broggio, the latter particularly active in the north Bohemian town of Litoměřice.

During the Hapsburg era, a host of German, Austrian and Italian artists came to the Czech lands to bring the age of the Baroque to flower. Some of the greatest names of this era spent substantial portions of their careers in Prague, and much of their work is still standing. Bavarian architect Christoph Dientzenhofer and his son Kilián Ignaz (born in Prague) designed dozens of churches in the capital city and around the country. Prominent sculptors include Matthias Braun, an imported Austrian, and the native-born Ferdinand Maxmilian Brokoff. One particular feature of the Baroque that emerged in the Czech lands is the peculiar semi-onion-dome steeple which sits atop literally hundreds of churches across the country. This is in fact a common feature of the Baroque in central Europe, most prominently on display in this country.

It is curious to note the ties that the arts have had with politics in the Czech lands, particularly in the past two centuries. In the 19th century, Czech art began to take on a personality of its own, and the growth of nationalism through the arts had enormous consequence on political developments into the following century. Much of the 20th century was marked by painful political oppression, which created in the artistic underworld a sentiment of both despair and hope, so eloquently brought out especially by novelists of the 1960s and 1970s.

The National Revival

During the late 19th century, Czech artists and thinkers began a movement which came to be known as the National Revival or (*národní obrození*). Three hundred-odd years of Austrian rule weighed heavily on the intellectual spirit, and a sense of national awakening, or reawakening, had begun to snowball into a political movement by the end of the century.

There are several explanations for the rise of this movement. This was the Romantic era in the arts, a time when an appreciation for natural beauty, along with a new awareness of folk elements, produced an enthusiastic output of literary and musical material. In addition, the Industrial Revolution during this century brought great numbers of Czechs from the countryside into cities to work in factories, thereby condensing Czech populations in these cities which up to this point had substantial populations of Germans and Austrians.

The revival was 'launched' by intellectuals, whose spiritual leader was the politician and writer František Palacký. A staunch supporter of the emerging pan-Slavic movement, Palacký wrote his *History of the Czech Nation in Bohemia and Moravia* in 1836, a landmark work that was instrumental in creating a sense of national awareness and pride, and its contents helped give rise to a plethora of artistic developments in the succeeding decades.

The poets Karel Hynek Mácha and Božena Němcová are true Romantics, writing of country themes, love and death. Alois Jirásek is famed for his collection of Czech folk tales, while Jan Neruda

> Very few of the writers and artists of the time are well known internationally, but this fact only serves to increase their endearment to the Czechs.

is similarly held in high regard for his touching stories of life in Prague's Malá Strana district. Painters such as Mikoláš Aleš likewise are held dear at home, while are little known abroad.

Similarly, much of the music that comes from this time follows the Romantic inclination. Bedřich Smetana is the darling of Czech composition, particularly for his epic work

Má Vlast (*My Country*), incorporating the mythology and sonorities of the Bohemian countryside into a large scale symphonic poem. Antonin Dvořák is perhaps better known throughout the music world; his intricate and powerful works in nearly all genres incorporate a strong folk element into what has been described as an irrepressible positiveness.

Architecture soon followed suit, and in Prague, the construction of the National Theatre, National Museum and the Rudolfinum concert hall were landmark achievements. Funding for these enormous projects came literally from the pockets of the locals, and their establishment as centres of Czech theatrical, musical and cultural expression and concentration rendered them important showpieces. Of equal symbolic importance was the progress taken to finally complete the Cathedral of St Vitus, begun in 929 by the nation's patron saint, Václav.

By the end of the 19th century, these influences had begun to forge a political movement. With the onset of World War I and the political rise of Tomáš G. Masaryk, Czech intellectuals pushed for an independence which was finally gained in 1918.

The 20th Century

Czech culture in the 20th century takes in all the fits and starts of this schizophrenic time, expounding them with the suppressed energy of a proud nation. Emerging from the 400 year hold of the Austro-Hungarian Empire into a mere 20 years of freedom, only to be knocked down by crushing back-to-back Nazi and Communist rule, the country's artistic output demonstrates the anguish and stagnation of repressed pride. This century produced an oddly steady series of twisted, at times subversive, artists which somehow retain a playful, typically Czech skeptical attitude toward existence.

Cubism caught on here like nowhere else; the Czech lands are one of the only places in the world where cubist architecture went beyond the design stage

Architecture

In the field of architecture, the Art-Nouveau and Secessionist periods brought flowery and angular commercial and residential palaces into streetscape scenes.

and into real buildings. The basic principle of cubism is to rebel against such fundamental architectural features as surface uniformity—the country's cubist buildings utilise new spatial dimensions in a truly revolutionary creation: triangular window edgings, jutting corners and oval staircases predominate. Examples include Prague's Dům U černé Matky Boží and the Fárový dům in the south Bohemian town of Pelhřimov.

Sculpture became acutely expressive at this time—Czech artist such as František Bílek and Jan Štursa created particularly moving images out of wood and bronze, and their work is quite well regarded within their respective circles. The best known Czech painter of this era is undoubtedly Alfons Mucha, who made a living in Paris for much of his life off his Art-Nouveau graphic art posters, though he returned home toward the end of his life to produce a series of epic paintings on Slavic history and mythology.

Perhaps the most tangible expression of the tumultuous 20th century in this country is to be found in the wealth of superb literature, which would not have come into existence were it not for such destructive external forces. One of the first great works of this century's fiction is *The Good Soldier Schweik*, written (largely under a drunken stupor) by Jaroslav Hašek in the midst of the collapse of the Hapsburg Empire during World War I.

20th Century Czech Composers

Twentieth century Czech composers are numerous and their output voluminous. Composers such as Leoš Janáček (who in fact belonged to both the 19th century Romantic era and the 20th century Impressionist and Expressionist movements), Bohuslav Martinů and Vitěslav Novák are fiery, emotional and at times incoherent. Where form begins to dissipate in many of their works, raw energy instead bursts forth.

Although Franz Kafka spent his entire life in Prague, he was a member of the German community and a Jew, and so had no real home in Czech society—a cruelly fitting predicament for this dark, schizophrenic novelist. His works are often set in a city which could be Prague, with characters that could be typical government officials of the time, and it's the very acuteness of his absurdly vague settings that make him so

Czech puppets at Havelská market.

popular. To consider Kafka a Czech is a fallacy—though the tourist industry often chooses to overlook this.

Writers in the Communist era faced severe censorship and risked imprisonment for speaking the truth. This of course only encouraged them more, and a generation of excellent playwrights and novelists emerged in the 1960s that produced some truly outstanding works of subtle social commentary. Their means of expression in fact were very carefully conveyed, and a handful of the most challenging writers were kept on authorities' blacklists for years. Some in fact were able to leave the country in 1968: Milan Kundera left for Paris, Josef Škvorecký immigrated to Canada and film-maker Miloš Forman moved to the US. Meanwhile Ivan Klíma, Bohumil Hrabal and Václav Havel, among others, endured through the 1980s; their perseverance is a source of admiration and inspiration.

The central theme in most works by these writers is that of human relations, particularly in the scope of living under oppression. Škvorecký's *The Engineer of Human Souls* is a particularly insightful and poignant collage of stories about life under Nazism and Communism, presenting many dark images, yet related in a typically ironic, casual air of seeming indifference. Kundera is internationally recognised as one of the finest living novelists. His works incorporate images of the Czech countryside and people into his often insightful, often funny, and often sexually deviant stories. Hrabal likewise writes bawdy stories of playful characters seeking satisfaction despite an undertone of impossibility. Klíma, on the other hand, sheds a more realistic and depressing light on the reality of living under an oppressive regime, while Havel's writing is divided between absurdist theatre and direct commentary in essay form on the immense frustrations and injustices of the Communist state. *(Refer to the reading list at the back of this book for a more complete rundown of individual works of these writers.)*

The 1990s and Now—Film and Music

Cultural expression since the end of Communism has perhaps not surprisingly continued to probe rather cerebral themes such as trying to come to grips with the changes in society. Happily, much of this is accomplished while still being highly entertaining—indeed, popular culture here retains a creative, edifying stature. This is perhaps most evident in film, where young producers such as Jan Svěrák, Jan Hřebejk and David Ondříček have produced touching commentaries on life under Communism and on changing democratic and capitalist society, all with the typical Czech sense for black humour: playfully seditious characters doing their best to deal with all the difficulties of life.

One of the best known Czech films is *Kolya* (*Kolja* in Czech) (1997), which won an Academy Award as best foreign film, produced by Jan Svěrák and whose main actor is his father, the popular actor Zdeněk Svěrák. *Kolya* is a story about an ageing bachelor musician whose career is halted for his failing to join the Communist Party, and who unwittingly becomes surrogate father to a small Russian boy. As charming as the tale is of the relationship between a hapless Czech man and an exuberant Russian boy, the point of the film is just as much the observations of life in the oppressive 1980s, and the newfound glory of freedom upon the 1989 revolution.

There are several other films of this ilk, all equally excellent, including Petr Nikolaev's *Báječná léta pod psa* (*The Wonderful Years of Lousy Living*) (1997), Hřebejk's *Pelíšky* (*Cosy Dens*) (1999) and *Pupendo* (2003). Viewing any of these films is an important way to gain a sense of the Czech experience and spirit, although Czechs themselves aren't always keen to relive what can indeed be bad memories.

Other popular films by producers such as Ondříček have included the wacky *Samotáři* (*Loners*) (2000) and *Jedna ruka netleská* (*One Hand Can't Clap*) (2003), both of which weave tales of goofy, if somewhat troubled, youth amid the absurd settings that contemporary life has bestowed upon us. Another hit was the 2002 film *Rok d'ábla* (*Year of the Devil*) by Petr Zelenka, a marvelous rockumentary/comedy featuring two of the country's biggest musicians, the Moravian folk-rock band Čechomor and singer Jaromír Nohavica.

Meanwhile, Czech popular music has likewise maintained an organic, animated quality. As previously discussed, the folk element remains deeply embedded in much of Czech society, and musicians—many of whom are from Moravia —have flowered in a creative age. Their popularity has not unfortunately managed to extend much beyond the national borders—due in part no doubt to the language barrier. If you can build your Czech language capability to a point where you can understand some of the lyrics, much of this of course becomes much more accessible, but even absent this understanding, the tunes and the instrumentation can be otherworldly.

Among the most popular folk/rock musicians, Jaromír Nohavica is intriguing for his blend of the dark, the comic, the earthy and the grotesque. Combining the acoustic poeticism of Bob Dylan with the occasional bizarre sounds of Tom Waits, and with a deep baritone voice and songs rooted in Moravian folk, he strums and sings poignant melodies of life, death and whatever comes to mind. Albums such as *Divné století* (*Strange Century*) and *Moje smutné srdce* (*My Sad Heart*) give an indication of the sentiment.

Vlasta Redl is another popular Moravian who alternates between simple folk and some harder-edged (and occasionally weird) stuff; one of his best albums is *Staré pecky* (*Old Favourites*). Žalman, the nickname taken by Pavel Lohonka meaning 'psalmist,' is somewhat more reserved, with beautiful albums such as *Láska a smrt* (*Love and Death*) evoking a simpler life. Bluegrass is quite popular throughout the country, and bands such as Druhá trava (meaning 'second grass') and Cop (pronounced 'tsop,' and meaning 'braid') light it up throughout summer festivals. If you've any inclination toward this uniquely American form of music, you'll be amazed at the genuine versatility of these two bands in particular; if not, the driving banjo and mandolin sounds may seem silly at first, but that's all part of the fun.

Folk/Rock

The Moravian folk/rock band Čechomor (Českomoravská hudební společnost) became widely popular in the late 1990s and early 2000s for their exuberant presentation of ancient Slavic folk songs. Albums such as *Master serie (Master Series)* bring forth exhilarating accordian, trumpet and fiddle sonorities amid an electric background, while *Proměny (Transformations)* sets some of these same songs to the accompaniment of the Czech Philharmonic Orchestra.

A bit more in the traditional vein is Hradišťan, yet another Moravian group that has evolved over several decades, and performs mostly traditional Czech and Moravian folk songs in a highly refined and sometimes ethereal style, using a variety of instruments that can include violins, flutes, oboes, double bass, hammer dulcimer and hurdy gurdy. Much of the musical structure draws from the Renaissance, but the group brings a freshness and vitality to its deeply traditional settings; you may even detect ancient Celtic sounds deep within. Some of Hradišťan's most beautiful and accessible albums include *Ozvěny duše* (*Echoes of the Soul*) and *O slunovratu* (*Solstice*). Other popular folk bands include Spirituál kvintet and Neřež, both of whom bring in more international influences.

Well-ingrained rock bands on the scene include Buty and Chinaski, both of whose funky dance rhythms are a big draw in clubs and stadiums throughout the country. Among the heavier, hard rock bands, some of the most popular are Lucie and Alice. One of the most popular singers over the past decade or so has been Lucie Bílá, a striking woman with an equally striking voice, whose style ranges from funky to heavy.

Karel Gott

Standing on his own is the legendary crooner Karel Gott. One of the few Czech performers to strike it big outside of his homeland, Gott is a massive commercial success in Germany and has done the Las Vegas circuit as well. With a voice and style like Frank Sinatra or Neil Diamond, Gott has been a fixture in Czech pop culture since the 1960s, and while his arrogance and corniness are often scoffed at, his voice and track record ensures longevity. Virtually all Czechs over the age of about 40 have Karel Gott records at home, and he continues to win singer of the year awards now even though he is well into his 60s.

CONCERT LIFE

Prague has a never ending run of top quality concerts, operas, ballet, theatre and club shows, and most other cities maintain cultural programmes as well. Tickets for most are still quite cheap, though not at the expense of quality—the Czech Philharmonic is internationally regarded as an excellent symphony orchestra, and Prague's numerous theatres and concert halls draw top names from around the world. Many of the performance halls in the city are architectural showpieces in their own right—the National Theatre, Estates Theatre and Rudolfinum Concert Hall in particular are spectacular venues in which to absorb the arts.

Information on shows in Prague can be obtained from the listings in the weekly newspaper *The Prague Post* (http://www.praguepost.cz), the monthly booklet *Kultura v Praze* (this also includes extensive listings on events throughout the country in a section titled *Česká kultura* (http://www.ceskakultura.cz), or from the signs posted around town. If you're a dedicated follower of classical music, theatre or dance, stop by the box offices of the major halls and pick up a monthly programme. It is usually possible to purchase tickets at the door, though stopping by the ticket office at least a day or two before the show is always safer. It is also possible to purchase season tickets, or series of tickets: both the Prague Symphony Orchestra (FOK) and the Czech Philharmonic run

Rudolfinum Concert Hall–home of the Czech Philharmonic and an example of architecture during the National Revival.

concert cycles, which may feature the music of Beethoven, for example, or the piano repertoire or contemporary music. There is usually one concert a month within each cycle, and the savings are substantial.

Check the Listings

Smaller venues, including theatres, clubs and community cultural centres, regularly put on plays and shows as well. Again, check *The Prague Post* or *Kultura v Praze/Česká kultura* for listings.

(Concert halls, theatres and clubs in Prague are listed in the Resource Guide at the back of this book.)

Jazz, Rock, and Dance Clubs

Jazz and rock clubs are also very popular—if you don't have tickets for bigger-draw shows in advance, it will be difficult to get in. For walk-in-off-the-street clubs, you will probably want to get there early to be sure you get a seat.

Jazz has a small but dedicated following. In addition, there are some great Czech bands playing everything from pop to bluegrass, to reggae to thrash metal. Major rock shows have

Rock and dance clubs are scattered throughout Prague, and all cities have discos and nightclubs to keep a mainly younger crowd pumped. hit Prague, as the city becomes a regular for concert tours. Several big name rock bands who have played Prague since 1989 include the Rolling Stones, Pink Floyd, Guns n' Roses, Neil Young, Michael Jackson and REM.

OTHER CULTURAL SPOTS
Cafés and Teashops
In addition to the endless selection of pubs, Prague and many other Czech cities have several good cafés (*kavárny* or *café*) and tea shops (*čajovny*) many now offering the setting and ambiance of café culture as it is practiced in many other European cities. Although tea is not a culturally rooted phenomenon here as it is elsewhere, Prague and many other cities now have a number of delightful teashops.

Bookshops
For English-speakers, there are a few bookshops in Prague which stock a good selection. Some of these offer events such as poetry readings and low-key performances. *(We list some of these in the back of this book.)*

Foreign Cultural Centres

Many countries have cultural centres linked with their embassies, with the purpose of spreading their nation's culture and customs to the local population. They also serve as magnets for homesick foreign nationals with their libraries and programmes. *(Check the Resources Guide at the back of this book for a partial listing, or contact your embassy.)*

FILMS
The Czech film industry is remarkably active, considering how small the country is and how many American films flood the cinemas these days. In fact, many Czech films outdraw the blockbuster Hollywood films. Unfortunately for most, Czech films only very rarely have English subtitles. Hollywood films

are indeed very popular as well, arriving soon after their premieres in the States. Nearly all foreign films are shown in their original language with subtitles in Czech, though movies are occasionally dubbed—check this before you buy tickets. Film signs and ticket kiosks will usually indicate *dabing* (dubbing).

The film studio AB Barrandov releases new films regularly, many of which are of exceptional quality, and many of which tend toward the cerebral *(see the section on film and music above)*. Czechs seem to like films that invoke a response and pose a question or two. Incidentally, the Barrandov studios have become an in-demand locale for Hollywood producers seeking lower-cost yet highly skilled personnel.

SPORTS AND LEISURE

Despite what often appears to be a sluggard population of boozers and heavy eaters, fitness is in fact an important part of many peoples' lives, and Czechs are very active in sports and the outdoors. Spectator sports are also a common leisure activity.

Hockey and football are the two national sports, and both national teams are among the best in Europe. Czech *hokej* (hockey) in particular has produced an astounding number of topnotch players—dozens play professionally in the NHL in North America. The Czech Republic won the 1998 Olympic gold medal and the 2000 and 2005 World Championships, with teams mostly made up of NHL stars. *Fotbal* (football) is also immensely popular, and as with hockey the Czechs have produced a huge number of players that have been snatched up by the top club teams in Europe. The Czech national team finished runner-up in the 1996 European Championships, and made the semi-finals in 2004 in this event heralding a new era of talent and interest in the sport. Getting tickets to hockey and football matches is rarely a problem, except for the big international events or top rivalries.

Czechoslovakia produced two of the top tennis players of the 1980s—Martina Navrátilová and Ivan Lendl—though both moved to the US during their careers. The tradition continues

Skating and hockey are popular pastimes—even in the grey high-rise suburbs, local residents take advantage of the outdoors.

today with numerous players in the top-20 ranked ATP and WTP. However, despite such huge success, tennis is oddly not a popular spectator sport at all.

Fitness centres are becoming more and more popular, and the prevalence of weight training centres, aerobics classes, indoor swimming pools and other facilities is spreading throughout the country. Many major hotels have fitness centres open to the public. *(Refer to the Resources Guide herein for some listings.)*

Everyone enjoys the outdoors in all seasons, whether it's lounging around the cottage, gardening or engaging in more strenuous activities. The countryside is well-patterned with hiking trails, which often become cross-country ski trails in winter. Trails are very well worked, with excellent maps. Downhill skiing is also popular, with the slopes in the Krkonoše mountains offering the best runs. There are adequate facilities for equipment rental both in Prague and in the mountains. Ice skating on frozen ponds is a common activity too, and cycling on country roads is practically a year-round sport.

In summer, everyone heads off to one of the country's rivers for canoe float trips. *"Jedu na vodu"*—"I'm going to the water"—is a common reason to take a few days off, and it's great fun to just float down a river and pitch a tent. It's also possible to rent rowboats on the Vltava in Prague, or to hop aboard a river cruise. Fishing and hunting are common pursuits as well.

Billiards and table tennis are popular indoor activities, and other sports such as bowling are catching on as well.

CULTURAL AND TRADITIONAL CALENDAR EVENTS

Czechs take a very festive approach toward everyday life, whether it's leaving work early, celebrating someone's name day, going to the pub for the evening or participating in one of the numerous festivals that mark the calendar at regular intervals. Traditional cultural events make up an important part of the social calendar, and organised festivals are also an integral part of Czech social life. Here's a sampling of the fun to be had, by season—some official, some just generally observed. (The ones marked with an * indicates a public holiday.)

- **1 January**
  New Year's Day*
- **January–February**
  Zabíjačka (pig slaughter), family and friends gather for a pig slaughter, then spend the entire day cooking and eating pork chops, sausages and lardspread.
- **February**
  Masopust, somewhat akin to Mardi Gras, this is a celebration of meat (as if the Czechs need another one), to mark the last chance to eat meat before Lent (as if the Czechs care). Parades, costumes and pig roasts predominate.
- **April**
  Easter Monday*, both a celebration of Christ's rebirth and, more importantly to most, of the rite of spring.
- **30 April**
  Čarodějnice (Burning of the Witches), a pagan leftover, celebrating the burning away of winter's evil spirits with a witch effigy in front of a campfire.

- **1 May**
  May Day*, the traditional beginning of spring, celebrated as a day of love.
- **8 May**
  Liberation Day*, the day the country was liberated from Germany at the end of World War II.
- 12 May 12–2 June
  Prague Spring International Music Festival, one of the finest classical music festivals in the world.
- Middle of May
  Olomouc Flower Festival, the main square of this small city becomes a giant flower garden.
- **5 July**
  St Cyril and Methodius Day*, celebrates the introduction of Christianity in the 9th century.
- **6 July**
  Jan Hus Day*, honours the death of Protestant leader Jan Hus.
- **Late June**
  International folklore festival in Strážnice that is located in southern Moravia.
- **Early July**
  Zahrada, outdoor festival of folk and country music in Náměšť na Hané in Moravia.
- **Early July**
  Chrudim Puppet Festival.
- **End of June**
  International Film Festival in Karlovy Vary, lots of famous movie stars come for this celebration of film.
- **Middle of August**
  Chod folk festival, celebration of the Chod people of Domažlice in south Bohemia, with traditional folk dress, bagpipe music and dance.
- **September to October**
  Burčák (young wine) festivals, fall harvest festivals in parts of north Bohemia and much of Moravia celebrate the production of the year's wine, accompanied by food, song and dancing.

- **Early October**
  Beer festival in Plzeň
- **28 October**
  Independence Day*, commemorating the creation of Czechoslovakia in 1918.
- **17 November**
  Freedom and Democracy Day, commemorating the anti-Nazi student demonstrations of 1939 and anti-Communist student demonstrations of 1989.
- **6 December**
  St Nicholas' Day, when neighbours dress up like St Nicholas, accompanied by a devil and an angel, visit homes to bring presents to good children and coal to bad ones.
- **24 December**
  Christmas Day*, better known as Štědrý den or Generous Day, when families gather for the traditional meal and gift-giving in the evening.
- **25 December**
  First Christmas Holiday*
- **26 December**
  Second Christmas Holiday (St Stephen's Day)*

Spring

Easter Monday: Don't forget this is not a religious nation, so Easter Sunday is merely the middle day in a three-day weekend. Easter Monday is the first official day off since 1 January, so it comes as a welcome respite.

The Burning of the Witches, or *čarodějnice*, on 30 April, is a pagan tradition of sorts in which people build an effigy of a witch out of straw and old clothes, then burn it on a bonfire in their backyard. The timing is symbolic: the witch represents winter, and the act of burning her gets rid of the last vestiges of a stubborn winter, ushering in the spring. City folk tend to guffaw at the tradition, though in the country it's a great excuse to roast sausages outdoors.

In The Name Of Tradition

Czechs still take part in an amusing tradition, which some find shocking: my first year in Prague was a surprise introduction to it. I was an English teacher at a Czech primary school, and on the Friday before the Easter weekend as I walked down the corridor to class, a group of my giggling 10-year-old girls ran up to me with sticks in their hands, then dutifully formed a line in front of me—and bent over as if to be spanked! I looked over, disconcerted, at a colleague, who motioned that I should indeed administer a whipping. In the US I would likely lose my job over this, so I really hesitated, but a crowd had formed by now, urging me on. So I cautiously lifted the stick and let it fall gently on the upturned behind of the first in line, at which point everyone shouted, "Harder! Harder!" I was mystified. It turns out this is part of an age-old belief that when young girls are whipped with weeping willow sticks on Easter Monday, they will be guaranteed fertility from the sapling branches. Receiving it from a baffled American seemed to be extra promising.

The Prague Spring International Music Festival is a highly-acclaimed festival of classical music, running for three weeks from 12 May to 2 June. The festival starts on the day of composer Bedřich Smetana's death, and naturally opens with a performance of his nationalist work *Má Vlast* (*My Homeland*), attended by the president; the final show is always a rousing performance of Beethoven's incomparable 9th Symphony. Throughout the three weeks there are several concerts daily, and you can choose from among series of orchestral performances, soloists, chamber groups, ancient music and contemporary music. There is also a prestigious competition held for a different instrument every year. The festival naturally attracts world-famous performers.

Prague Spring Concert Tickets

Tickets for Prague Spring are sometimes obtainable at the door, though you're more likely to succeed in getting tickets by going to Ticketpro (http://www.ticketpro.cz) in December when they go on sale; you can find out the program and further ticket information at http://www.festival.cz.

Summer

Summertime sees lots of folk festivals throughout the land. One of the most popular, which draws visitors and performers from as far away as Lithuania and Scotland, is the international folk festival held at Strážnice in south Moravia in the last weekend of June. Traditional music, dance and crafts are on offer. Further information is available at the city's website:

http://www.straznice-mesto.cz.

The outdoor folk museum at Rožnov pod Radhošťem in north Moravia is open all summer long; the country is dotted with other such *skanzen*, but Rožnov is the biggest and the best.

Karlovy Vary has an international film festival starting the last weekend in June and running for eight days, drawing top name international actors, actresses and producers to the screenings.

Český Krumlov hosts an international classical music festival in mid-August, not nearly as grand as the Prague Spring festival, but the location is charming nonetheless.

Autumn

There is yet another festival of classical music in Prague in September, appropriately named the Prague Autumn. This is a month-long series of classical music concerts of all genres, though again, it is not nearly as impressive as the spring version.

Folk traditions come alive again in the autumn, as this is harvest time. One of the most important crops is grapes, and Czechs have a special way of producing a sweet 'young' wine called *burčák*, which is drunk with abandon at weekend celebrations throughout wine country. Moravian towns such as Hodonín and Mikulov fest the fruity drink with barrels in the town square throughout late September and early October, while towns in north Bohemia, such as Litoměřice, host medieval and renaissance festivals concurrently. On a more mundane level, everyone heads into the forest to gather mushrooms in the autumn.

Winter

Christmas: The entire Christmas season is festive and joyous, as stalls open up around city centres from early December to sell wreaths, wooden charms and hot mulled wine, while nativity scenes and blacksmith shops add a touch of the olden days to the atmosphere. The sixth of December is Mikuláš—St Nicholas' Day, when St Nick comes around to leave little gifts for children—this is Santa Claus, three weeks early. Unbeknownst to the youngest, neighbours and friends in groups of three dress up as St Nicholas, as an angel and as a devil, and St Nicholas frightens the children by demanding if they have been good or bad: if good, the angel gives them sweets or fruit or little toys; if bad, the devil threatens to carry them away. Christmas is actually celebrated on the 24th, not the 25th as elsewhere, and the entire proceeding is a bit different from what most are used to. Again, this is not really a religious day. On the evening of the 24th, families decorate the Christmas tree, often with homemade ornaments, and gather together for a traditional meal of fried carp and potato salad—the carp is usually bought live from large barrels rolled into the city and some bring them home

Cross-country skiing is a popular winter sport and many people spend their holidays on the snow.

alive to swim in the bathtub until the 24th. On the night of 24 December (*Štědrý den* or 'Generous Day'), Jesus himself comes and leaves a second round of gifts for children under the tree—parents have to be crafty and sneak them there sometime during the meal, adding to the magic of discovery. The 25th and 26th of December are also holidays.

To lighten the heavy burden of a five-month winter, balls are held regularly throughout February and March. These can be anything from black-tie proms to 1930s big band shows to country/bluegrass hoedowns. It provides a pleasant (if usually drunken) pause in what is a dreary time of year.

Winter is also prime time to celebrate meat, in its various forms. January and February is the time for pig slaughters, called *zabíjačka*. Family and friends gather for a full day of killing, eating and drinking. The animal is strung up and gutted, and all body parts are used to make chops, sausages, and lard. *Jitrnice* is a particularly gruesome, though delicious blood sausage. Just before Lent is *masopust*, a meat-eating binge often accompanied by parades and concerts, to fatten up the body in preparation of the long fast to come.

Name Days

Every day on the calendar has a first name associated with it—these were originally days assigned to honour saints, though now every Czech name has its own day (*svátek*). In fact, Kafkaesque as it sounds, there exists a government office on names, which is supposed to be consulted if you choose to give your baby a name other than one of those on the calendar! Czechs rarely stray though, and therefore name days such as Jan, Josef, Jana and Eva are exceedingly busy.

It is very important to be aware of your colleagues' and friends' name days—they are in fact almost a second birthday to Czechs. Offices often let loose at lunchtime or after work for a celebratory bottle. Flower shops run a brisk trade, and many post the day's name of honour on a billboard outside. You can also find name days mentioned on many calendars, and most newspapers print the day's name of honour.

PRAGUE LORE: FOLK TALES
AND SEMI-TRUTHS

The legends swirling about Prague are older than the city itself. Many of course are purely fairy tales, though they have a special power that the natives respect. Some have elements of truth in them, or emerge from true scenarios and events, and some are historically documented facts, odd and intriguing enough to merit mention.

The origin of the city is a legend in itself. Around the 7th century or so, Libuše was princess of the Slavs who settled on the hill at Vyšehrad, and whose social structure was largely governed by women. She is said to have foreseen a great city rising from the opposite banks, whose glory would 'touch the stars.' A couple of centuries later, Hradčany became the seat of the first Přemyslid dynasty in the Bohemian lands.

Vyšehrad was also an important Přemyslid stronghold, which included at one time a prison. A Bohemian prince, Horymír, was sentenced to death here, though was mistakenly granted a last request: to ride his horse one last time around the castle grounds. The horse knew what to do and leapt the wall, sliding down the cliff to the Vltava, where his rider swam away to freedom.

Protector Of The Nation

Sometime around the Přemyslid era, a great Bohemian warrior and traveller named Bruncvík wandered the earth with his lion and magic sword, now supposedly buried in Charles Bridge. Upon moments of great national danger, prince Václav, the patron saint, will grab his sword and shout "Heads off!" and all the nation's enemies will disappear.

Prague's streets are littered with monsters and ghosts, the most famous of which is the Golem. A creation of Rabbi Löwe, who in fact was the chief rabbi of the Jewish Quarter in the 16th century, this brute was brought to life by a piece of donkey skin which Rabbi Löwe placed under his tongue (modern interpretation has the Golem's soft spot in his forehead). As all man-made beings, though, the Golem started to become dangerous and uncontrollable, wreaking

The Golem–fairy tale monster of Prague's Jewish Quarter.

havoc throughout the quarter until his master was forced to destroy the donkey skin pergamen and bury the Golem in the attic of the Old New Synagogue.

Several lesser critters of the Old Town include the stone knight of Platnéřská Street, who killed the local blacksmith's daughter after she refused his love. He then turned to iron and returns once every 100 years to find her—though nobody knows when the last visit was. The Karolinum is haunted by the ghost of an exceedingly tall man who sold his corpse to Charles University for the benefit of science—he now begs money from tourists to buy back his skeleton. Several of Prague's pubs are haunted by the Vodník, a little man in an overcoat who lives under Charles Bridge, wooing little girls into his lair. He can be detected by the pool of water under his pub seat. The ghost of a merchant Turk and his former lover lurk around the Hotel Ungelt, where he killed her in a romantic fury—the headless body of the girl supposedly lies in the basement.

Unfortunately true is the character of Mydlář the Axeman, who is responsible for the beheadings of 24 Bohemian noblemen on 21 June 1621 as a Hapsburg punishment to the instigators of the uprising that ended in defeat at Bílá Hora. Perhaps the rebels were asking for it though; three years earlier they had thrown two of the ruling governors out the window of the Ludvík Wing at Prague Castle in the second defenestration of Prague. The first defenestration was a similarly rebellious bloody effort by the Hussites, who did the same from the New Town Hall on Karlovo náměstí in 1420.

Medieval Old Town Prague suffered numerous floods over its first few centuries, finally prompting the residents to raise the street level several metres. This contributed to the rich Gothic make-up of the city, though much of the Old Town's ancient foundations are now buried underground.

During the reign of Rudolf II, the city was a European cultural centre, with one of Europe's richest collections of fine art (which was subsequently pilfered by the Swedes during the Thirty Years' War). Rudolf also surrounded himself with astronomers, astrologers and alchemists—he was more intent on exploring the heavens and turning lead into gold than in ruling the Austrian empire. Results were mixed; while Edward Kelly never managed to turn lead into anything but molten lead, astronomers Tycho de Brahe and Johannes Kepler made significant advances in our knowledge of the heavens.

A Stroke Of Luck

Chimney sweepers or *komínící* are to this day considered a lucky charm. Though the practice is dying, it is still a sign of luck if a coal-dusted chimney sweep brushes against you; even more rewarding is to rub the button on his lapel.

BRIEF TRAVEL GUIDE TO THE CZECH REPUBLIC

While this is not intended to be a proper travel guide, I do feel it is important and useful to highlight a few choice travel destinations within the country. This is only a sampling of some of the most interesting destinations, any of which could easily make a weekend getaway. Your appreciation for the Czech Republic will only grow by visiting different parts of the country, and especially if you live in Prague, you will find it enriching to travel outside the city, for the Czech Republic really is so much more than just its capital. *(For listings of museums, galleries, restaurants and the like in Prague, refer to the Prague Listings-Entertainment and Leisure section in the Resource Guide on page 271.)*

West Bohemia

The spa region is the second-most visited part of the country after Prague, and the towns of Karlovy Vary (Karlsbad) and Mariánské Lázně (Marienbad) offer beautiful spa architecture, curative waters and fine walks in the parks around. Many people come just for the ambiance, with oom-pa-pa bands and fountains, and to sample the high mineral-content waters, but these are in fact active spas, with pools available to cure ailments or just to relax. Karlovy Vary is the granddaddy, with wedding cake architecture and graceful promenades, but Mariánské Lázně is in many ways more pleasing, as it is greener and quieter. Not far from Karlovy Vary is a stunning hilltop castle in the village of Loket.

The largest city in the region, Plzeň, is of course known for its beers, but other than the interesting tour of the Pilsner Urquell brewery, there isn't too much to hold your fancy.

Top Destinations in the Czech Republic

With such a wondrous variety of cities, quaint towns, castles, chateaux and beautiful countryside to explore, it is difficult to isolate the best of the best; here at least is an attempt.

Cities and Towns
- Prague
- Český Krumlov
- Karlovy Vary
- Olomouc
- Telč

Castles and Chateaux
- Loket (west Bohemia)
- Jindřichův Hradec (South Bohemia)
- Rožmberk nad Vltavou (South Bohemia)
- Kuks (East Bohemia)
- Pernštejn (South Moravia)

Outdoors
- Šumava Mountains (South Bohemia)—hiking, cycling, camping, canoeing, cross-country skiing
- Hřensko/České Švýcarsko (North Bohemia)—hiking, cross-country skiing
- Český Ráj (East Bohemia)—hiking, cycling, camping, sightseeing (castles and sandstone rock formations)
- Krkonoše Mountains (East Bohemia)—hiking and downhill skiing
- Beskydy Mountains (North Moravia)—hiking and sightseeing (outdoor folk museum at Rožnov pod Radhošťem)

South Bohemia

This is the treasure trove of Bohemia, with multiple enchanting small towns and castles dotted amidst a rolling countryside, and buffered by the thickly forested Šumava mountains along the Austrian border.

Tábor is a small, pretty city, home of the Taborites in the 15th century, and whose twisty cobblestone streets and maze of underground tunnels are fun to poke around. Písek is another pretty town with a medieval footbridge that actually pre-dates Prague's Charles Bridge. Further south, the Třeboňsko region is the swampy home of numerous carp ponds centered around the pint-sized medieval town of Třeboň. Nearby, the larger town of Jindřichův Hradec sports a fascinating array of architectural styles, and a wonderful Renaissance chateau.

České Budějovice is the biggest city in the region. In addition to its Budějovický Budvar brewery, it has an enormous cobbled square and a fine tower from which to admire the scenery. A short distance south is the fairy tale town of Český Krumlov, whose medieval backstreets scatter through an S-shaped bend in the Vltava river, all lorded over by a fantastic castle. Given its location near the Austrian border, it has become a favourite border-hopping day trip as well as something of a backpacker's hangout, but nothing can take away from its beauty, especially at night when the crowds disappear.

South of Český Krumlov, past the charming village of Rožmberk nad Vltavou, the low Šumava Mountains begin. Aside from simply disappearing into the thick pine forests, whether on foot or by bicycle or canoe (rentals are available), the Šumava is home to enticing small towns such as Prachatice, Kašperské hory and Klatovy.

North Bohemia

Slim pickings here, but what attractions there are certainly are worth the trip. Less than an hour from Prague, the town of Mělník has a fine castle set above the confluence of the Vltava and Labe rivers. Further north, the town of Litoměřice hosts some excellent Renaissance buildings. Just a few kilometres away is the former concentration camp at Terezín (Theresienstadt).

Through the impressive hills of the České středohoří, the Labe river passes through some tough industrial towns such as Ústí nad Labem before slipping through the pretty, forested sandstone region of Hřensko—great for hiking.

East Bohemia

East Bohemia's topography shifts from dead flatness east of Prague to the rolling hills of Český ráj to the highest mountains in the country, the Krkonoše. Appealing towns include the medieval mining town of Kutná Hora, with a fabulous cathedral and a gruesome ossuary—a church decorated with thousands of human bones—in nearby Sedlec; Hradec Králové, with a nice square and an excellent modern art museum; and Litomyšl, with a pretty arcaded square and an extensive chateau.

The countryside is the real draw, however: Český ráj is a luxuriant landscape of forests and sandstone 'cities'—weird rock formations that are great fun to scramble through; Adršpach further east has more of the same. The Krkonoše Mountains offer the country's best skiing in winter (particularly at Špindlerův Mlýn and Pec pod Sněžkou) and great hiking in summer.

North Moravia

North Moravia suffers the same perception problems as north Bohemia, again due to its heavy industrial base. That said though, Olomouc is a glorious city with a sprawling cobblestoned square and absorbing gothic cathedral. North Moravia has some wonderful scenery and intriguing folk centres as well: the Jeseníky Mountains near the Polish border are deep and fairly remote, while the Beskydy region along the Slovak border holds a rich heritage of folk traditions. The large *skanzen* (open-air folk museum) at Rožnov pod Radhošťem is a fascinating exploration of historical Moravian village life; nearby Štramberk is a hillside town with original wooden cottages; and the village of Hukvaldy contains a museum in the former home of composer Leoš Janáček. The Beskydy Mountains themselves offer excellent hiking.

South Moravia

Centered around the country's second city, Brno, this region encompasses an array of attractions, from the lovely rolling Českomoravská vrchovina (Czech-Moravian Highlands) in the west to broad vineyards and chateaux in the south to important religious sites in the east.

While Brno cannot approach Prague in terms of breadth of historical sites, it is certainly worth a visit, with a collection of handsome squares, the grand Cathedral of Saints Peter and Paul, the imposing Špilberk fortress that saw use from the Swedish invasions of the 1600s to the Nazi occupation, and a fascinating collection of mummified remains of prominent citizens in the Capuchin church. Just outside of Brno is the famed battlefield site of Austerlitz (Slavkov to Czechs), where Napolean defeated the united Austrian and Russian troops.

Telč, in the highlands region that forms a loose border with Bohemia, sports a stunning square and a kaleidescope of Renaissance and Baroque architecture. To the south, the border region with Austria is the country's wine-producing heartland, with summer and autumn festivals breaking out in interesting towns such as Znojmo and Mikulov and lovely chateaux such as Lednice and Valtice. Further east, the landscape and culture blends into Slovakia. Impressive ecclesiastical sites such as Velehrad host important pilgrimages, while the town of Kroměříž is home to an admirable archbishop's palace and gardens.

COMMUNICATING

'Strč prst skrz krk'
(Stick a finger through your neck)
—Czech tongue twister

LANGUAGE

One of the most difficult aspects to living in a foreign country, of course, is the language. In the Czech Republic especially, you'll find it extremely frustrating to live day by day if you don't acquire at least a basic vocabulary. Relying on friends and colleagues to interpret for you is a poor means of getting by, and you'll soon find yourself floundering if you don't make an attempt.

Native English speakers are fortunate that this has rapidly become the 'international language,' and in the Czech Republic, as in most of Europe, many people are able to communicate in English. Most educated people speak some English, and many do so with near-fluency. The universality of the English language is probably due to the expanse of the former British Empire, whose former colonies, including the United States, have become important international powers. British and American pop culture have undoubtedly influenced many; in fact many Czechs confess to having started learning English through the Beatles!

It is arrogant and wrong, however, to assume that everyone you meet will understand English, and that you will be able to get by with it. True, you'll make yourself understood somehow, but to spend time in a foreign country without trying to assimilate into something so basic as communicating is not only an injustice to yourself, but also a mark of disrespect to your host people.

That said, you are up against a monstrous task, for Czech is an extraordinarily complex language that takes incredible patience and stamina to learn, and even Czechs themselves readily acknowledge this. Many foreigners living in Prague become so intimidated by it that they quickly give up. This is undoubtedly compounded by the fact that many are too busy with their daily jobs, family and social calendars to really apply themselves to the task, and also because so many of the Czechs they meet are eager to improve their command of English. As understandable as this is, keep in mind that your standing is raised a thousandfold if you are able to communicate with Czechs in their own tongue.

Because Czech is so difficult, and because it is (unfortunately) so insignificant outside of the country itself, Czechs are extraordinarily receptive and appreciative of anyone who make the remotest attempt to acquire even a basic vocabulary. The utterance of even a few random words is invariably met with, "Oh! You speak good Czech!" which is wonderful for the ego but can easily lure you into a false sense of security.

LEARNING CZECH
The formal language that Jan Hus systematised in the early 1400s has been noted by linguists as the perfect legal language, as the subtleties of expression leave no room for

Basic Rules Of Courtesy

- Always ask first if the other person speaks English.
- Speak slowly and clearly, but not overly so: many who claim to speak only a little English in fact speak very well, and too much slow motion acting comes across as condescending.
- Those with North American accents should be aware that many Czechs learned textbook British English and therefore have a hard time deciphering the typical American twang.

doubt as to their meaning. This of course means that it is especially difficult to master. Even Czech children need to be formally taught the nuts and bolts, as well as pronunciation, before they are able to use it properly.

It takes a lot of textbook work to make headway; Czech is not a language that you can simply 'pick up' without systematic study. Progress is invariably slow, and you'll likely only notice it long after you've been in the country and 'suddenly' find yourself understanding bits and pieces. It's always easier to follow a conversation on a topic with which you're familiar; listening to the radio or picking up on a random conversation is always the hardest thing to do.

Many students choose to enrol in a language course to learn the fundamentals of grammar and pronunciation, and this is a good idea, at least in the beginning. Real learning, though, is achieved only through independent study and sheer willpower.

The obvious starting points are pronunciation, basic greetings, numbers and food and drink items to use in restaurants. Learn how to say hello, please, thank you, and learn a few critical nouns and verbs and you'll have a foot in the door. Then you can try to tackle the complexities of verb conjugation; declension of nouns, pronouns and adjectives; formal and informal speech; and the subtleties of expression. Below I have provided some simplified rules for conjugation of verbs and declension of nouns. This is a far cry from a comprehensive grammar lesson; rather it is a set of simplified models and tips that I believe can help break through some of the initially overwhelming barrage of information that humbles most first-time Czech language learners.

THE CZECH LANGUAGE

The Czech language is a member of the Slavic family of languages, and is therefore similar in many ways to Russian, Ukrainian, Polish, Slovak, Slovenian, Croatian, Serbian and Bulgarian. In fact, if you have a grasp of any of these languages, you will find Czech much easier to learn. (There is no relation to German other than a few words and names that have jumped the border). Czech uses the same alphabet as English (unlike Russian, which uses the Cyrillic alphabet) and is perfectly phonetic once you are familiar with the letter sounds.

Letters and Pronunciation

Where the English alphabet has 26 letters, Czech has 40. Diacritic marks above letters render them completely different letters: *c* and *č* are considered different letters, and there are lots of lines and hooks, to the point where there is scarcely a word without such extra signs. These are easy enough to pronounce once you know the rules, though there is one letter, *ř*, which is so difficult that even children have to be taught properly how to say it. It's a hard *r*, rolled but once, followed immediately by *zh*; it's all one sound, and it comes out like a crash of glass. This letter only appears in the Czech language, a fact that many Czechs are perversely proud of.

Strict phonics means that each letter has a specific sound, and therefore each word has a perfect pronunciation based upon the letters in it. Once you learn the letters, you can pronounce any word. This is not to say that Czech words

are easy to pronounce, however! Whereas English words are formed with the whole mouth, Czech words are for the most part formed with the front of the mouth; the tongue and the lips can quite easily get entangled as you try to get everything out. Czechs consider their language very 'soft'; it contains many *sh* and *zh* sounds, for example, whose soothing sonority is admired. At the same time, though, there are some awful consonant clashes in words such as *skříň* (skrzheenye) and *chci* (khtsee), which take a lot of practice to get right, and still end up spilling out of the front teeth in a confused splutter.

Czech words often contain a lot of consonants, and the letters *k* and *z*, uncommon in English, seem to turn up with frustrating regularity in Czech. Two letters, *l* and *r*, can function as syllables, producing some marvellous words such as *vlk*, *krk*, *mlč* and *smrt*.

The Czech Alphabet

a	*a* as in *cat*
á	*ah* as in *father*
b	*b* as in *boy*
c	*ts* as in *cats*—Havel's first name, Václav, is pronounced *Vahtslav*
č	*ch* as in *church*
d	*d* as in *dog*
d'	*dy* as in *due* or *duty* in British English
e	*e* as in *egg*
é	*eh*, pronounced as a prolonged *e*, not *ay*
ě	*ye*; this letter softens the syllable preceding it; for example the word *děkuji* is pronounced *dyekwee*.
f	*f* as in *father*
g	*g*—always a hard *g* as in *good*
h	*h* as in *happy*

ch	*kh*, with an airy sound. The letters *ch* together are considered a single separate letter, coming after *h* in the alphabet. It is pronounced as a soft airy sound made by pushing the back of your tongue up to the rear upper palate, almost like clearing your throat, though without the gargle, as in the composer Bach or the Scottish *loch*.
i	*i*—short *i*, as in *ship*
í	*ee*—long *i*, as in *sheep*
j	*y* as in *yellow*
k	*k*, but without the airy sound
l	*l* as in *love*
m	*m* as in *mother*
n	*n* as in *no*
ň	*ny*, as in *new* or the Russian *nyet*
o	*o*—short *o*; the vowel sound is cut off at the end; not as round as in American English; pronounced as in *box* in British English
p	*p* as in *pill*, but less airy
r	*r*, rolled softly once by the tip of the tongue on the hard palate, as in Spanish
ř	*rzh*—a sound unique to Czech and very difficult to make. It is a rolled *r* followed immediately by *zh*, all spilling off the tip of the tongue through the front teeth.
s	*s* as in *sad*
š	*sh* as in *shalom*
t	*t* as in *tipsy*, but less airy
t'	*ty* as in *Tuesday*
u, ú, ů	*oo* in varying degrees, as in *blue*
v	*v* as in *very*
w	*v*—the letter *w* does not exist except in foreign words and is pronounced like a *v*
x	*x* as in *fax*

y	*i*—short *y*, as in *ship*
ý	*ee*—long *i*, as in *sheep*
z	*z* as in *zebra*
ž	*zh* as in *pleasure*

A Few Starters

Here are a few phrases to get you started.

dobrý den (formal)	hello
ahoj (informal)	hi
jak se máš/máte? (formal/informal)	how are you?
těší mě	pleased to meet you
mluvíte anglický?	do you speak English?
nemluvím český	I don't speak Czech
nashledanou (formal)	goodbye
čau (informal)	bye
prosím	please
děkuji	thank you
co to je	what is it?
pivo prosím	beer, please
kolik to stojí?	how much does it cost?
dobrý	good
ano	yes
ne	no
kdo	who
co	what
kdy	when
kde	where
proč	why
jak	how

All Czech words are accented on the first syllable. This makes it easy to know how to pronounce a word, though long words seem to dwindle off at the end. The name Navrátilová, for example (as in Martina the tennis player—she's originally Czech) is always mispronounced internationally.

CONJUGATION (ČASOVÁNÍ) OF VERBS

The infinitive of virtually all verbs ends in the letter *t*, usually *-at, -et* or *-it*. Verbs are conjugated according to a system of models, and there are different endings for each based on the personal pronoun (I, you, he/she/it, we, you, they). Personal pronouns are not usually used: as each conjugation is distinct, the personal pronoun is unnecessary. Fortunately, there are only three tenses: simple past, simple present and simple future.

The Present Tense

The present tense of verbs is conjugated according to four general models, as below; look to the ending patterns in these conjugations:

-t: dělat	to do/ to make
*já děl**ám***	I do
*ty děl**áš***	you do
*on/ona/ono děl**á***	he/she/it does
*my děl**áme***	we do
*vy děl**áte***	you do
*oni děl**ají***	they do

-et and -it: bydlet	to live
*já bydl**ím***	I live
*ty bydl**íš***	you live
*on/ona/ono bydl**í***	he/she/it lives
*my bydl**íme***	we live
*vy bydl**íte***	you live
*oni bydl**í***	they live

-ovat: pracovat	to work
*já prac**uju***	I work
*ty prac**uješ***	you work
*on/ona/ono prac**uje***	he/she/it works
*my prac**ujeme***	we work
*vy prac**ujete***	you work
*oni prac**ují***	they work

Irregular forms: jít	to go
*já jd**u***	I go
*ty jd**eš***	you go
*on/ona/ono jd**e***	he/she/it goes
*my jd**eme***	we go
*vy jd**ete***	you go
*oni jd**ou***	they go

In addition, as explained below, it is very useful to get the conjugation of 'to be' correct: it is irregular, but follows recognisable patterns:

být	to be
*já js**em***	I am
*ty js**i**/js**eš***	you are
*on/ona/ono j**e***	he/she/it is
*my js**me***	we are
*vy js**te***	you are
*oni js**ou***	they are

The Past Tense
The past tense of verbs is formed by creating a two-part word, using the relevant form of 'to be', with the past participle of the verb being conjugated. The past participle is usually formed simply by replacing the t at the end of the

infinitive with *l*. The past tense can be expressed in either of two inverse ways, as shown below.

pracovat	
*já js**em** pracoval* or *pracoval js**em***	I worked
*ty js**i** pracoval* or *pracoval js**i***	you worked
on/ono pracoval or *pracoval*	he/it worked
ona pracovala	she worked
*my js**me** pracovali* or *pracovali js**me***	we worked
*vy js**te** pracovali* or *pracovali js**te***	you worked
oni pracovali or *pracovali*	they worked

The Future Tense

The future tense is relatively simple in most cases, formed by conjugating the word 'will' as if it is a verb itself, and tacking on the infinitive form of the verb you wish to conjugate. The complication here, however, is that some words have their own future tense forms; there are of course just enough exceptions such that you can't be sure without learning which verbs are irregular, but at least you won't be misunderstood if you follow the simple format below.

pracovat	
*ja bud**u** pracovat*	I will work
*ty bud**eš** pracovat*	you will work
*on/ona/ono bud**e** pracovat*	he/she/it will work
*my bud**eme** pracovat*	we will work
*vy bud**ete** pracovat*	you will work
*oni bud**ou** pracovat*	they will work

DECLENSION (SKLOŇOVÁNÍ) OF NOUNS, PRONOUNS AND ADJECTIVES

Not only do verb endings change according to use, but nouns, pronouns and adjectives also all change according to context. For anyone who has not studied Latin, German, Russian or another Slavic language, this is probably the single most confounding aspect to Czech, as English does not use declensions. Even your own name changes according to its use in the sentence, and while it's easy to figure out who Tima Nollena is, it's a difficult task to get it right when you're doing the talking. After years of constant use, I still manage to get the endings wrong half the time. The following explanation of declensions is purposefully oversimplified, just to help you get the concept.

There are seven cases, or declensions, of nouns, pronouns and adjectives. I have found it easiest to consider these cases in terms of (a) the grammatical sense of their use, as well as (b) depending on the prepositions they follow.

- Nominative   the root form of the word, or subject of the sentence.
- Genitive   possessive (in English, such as 'his' or 'the boy's' in which the genitive ending takes the place of 's in English). Also used when following the prepositions *do* (to), *od* or *z* (from) and *bez* (without).
- Dative   used with the indirect object (such as 'to him' in the phrase 'give it to him'). Also when following the preposition *k* (toward).
- Accusative   used with the direct object, the object that receives the action of the verb (such as 'theatre' in the phrase 'I see the theatre').
- Vocative   used when calling somebody. For example, when calling Adam, you would say 'Adame', or when calling Jana, you would say 'Jano'.

- Locative   indicates location or place. Used when following the prepositions *v* (in), *o* (about), *u* (at or near) and sometime *na* (on).
- Instrumental   indicates the use of the noun. For example, you travel *autobusem*—by bus. Also used when following the preposition *s* (with).

To decline a noun, you have to be aware of its gender and the declension model it fits within this gender. The letter endings of words are your clue to that word's gender, as well as the declension model that the word fits within the gender. Nouns are classified according to the letter they end in, so the trick is to memorise, or recognise, patterns. Nouns are of masculine, feminine or neuter gender.

Letter endings are generally considered according to whether they are hard consonants (such as *d, g, h, ch, n, k, r* and *t*); soft consonants (such as *c, č, d', j, ň, ř, š, ť* and *ž*); or neutral consonants (*b, f, l, m, p, s, v,* and *z*).

Masculine words often end in hard consonants. Feminine words often end in soft consonants or the vowels *a* and *e*. Neuter words often end in neutral consonants or the vowels *e, i* and *o*. There is a good deal of overlap, however, and because some letters such as *e* and *l* can be used in more than one gender, you will have to keep your dictionary handy to look up unknown words.

Each of these three genders then has four models, which you will simply have to learn, or else wing it like I do. Classification of masculine words depends on whether the word is animate (i.e. living, such as 'man') or inanimate (i.e. not living, such as 'machine'), and on whether the letter ending is hard or soft. Classification of feminine and neuter words is more a matter of knowing whether the letter ending is soft or neutral.

This makes 12 different models, which are represented by the following model words:

- Masculine   *pan, hrad, muž, stroj*
- Feminine   *žena, růže, piseň, kost*
- Neuter   *město, moře, kuře, stavení*

So when you are faced with a noun, you have to figure out, via the letter ending, first what is its gender, and then more specifically which of the four models it falls under within that gender. So if, for example, you come across the word *syn* (son), you have to recognise that this word is masculine, the ending letter *n* is a hard consonant, that the word 'son' is animate, and that the word therefore is declined according to the model word *pan*, as demonstrated below. Then you have to understand which case, or declension, to use depending on the context of the noun. Easier said than done.

Czechs all memorised this strictly formalised grammar in school, and they can all recall the models used to decline nouns. I can never remember all these models, so I have found it easiest to boil things down to common, simple forms: to know the most common letter endings and whether they are masculine, feminine or neuter. I find the most common forms are words ending in the letters *a* and *o*. For other letter endings I try to make educated guesses based on the letter ending, without specifically memorising the model for every word.

Common forms that I use here as examples of declensions include:

Noun (Masculine)	Translation
syn	son
bez syna	without the son
k synu	toward the son
vidím syna	I see the son
syne!	son!
o syne	about the son
se synem	with the son

Noun (Feminine)	Translation
škola	school
do školy	to school
ke škole	toward the school
vidím školu	I see the school
Jano!	Jana!
ve škole	in school
se školou	with the school

Noun (Neuter)	Translation
divadlo	theatre
od divadla	from the theatre
k divadlu	toward the theatre
vidím divadlu	I see the theatre
Ivo!	Ivo!
v divadle	in the theatre
s divadlem	with the theatre

As if this isn't tricky enough, pronouns and adjectives are conjugated as well, always depending on whether the noun that these relate to are masculine, feminine or neuter. I won't go through all the models, but by following the examples above:

Masculine
Nominative: *můj hezký syn* ('my nice son')
Genitive: *bez mého hezkého syna* ('without my nice son') etc.

Feminine
Nominative: *moje hezká škola* ('my nice school')
Genitive: *do mojí/mé hezké školy* ('to my nice school') and so on

Neuter

Nominative: *moje hezké divadlo* ('my nice theatre')

Genitive: *od mojeho/mého hezkého divadla* ('from my nice theatre') etc.

And all this is only for singular nouns, pronouns and adjectives—there is another whole set of rules for plurals! Although, the rules for plurals are simpler, and of course by the time you are at this level you will likely be able to handle it much better.

Note too that Czech does not use the indefinite article ('a' and 'the'), although the demonstrative pronouns 'this' and 'that' are sometimes used.

In short, it's a mess. The last letter of the word is your indication and starting point. But of course there are enough exceptions to throw a wrench in the whole effort. For example, one might expect the words *postel* and *hotel* to be declined the same way, but no! you go *do postele*, and *do hotelu!*. Also, letters can change in the forming of words; for example in the city name *Praha* (Prague), the *h* changes to *z* in the locative case—*v Praze* ('in Prague').

NUMBERS

one	*jeden*
two	*dva*
three	*tři*
four	*čtyři*
five	*pět*
six	*šest*
seven	*sedm*
eight	*osm*
nine	*devět*
ten	*deset*
eleven	*jedenáct*
twelve	*dvanáct*
thirteen	*třináct*

fourteen	*ctrnáct*
fifteen	*patnáct*
sixteen	*šestnáct*
seventeen	*sedmnáct*
eighteen	*osmnáct*
nineteen	*devatenáct*
twenty	*dvacet*
twenty one	*dvacet jedna*
thirty	*třicet*
forty	*čtyřicet*
fifty	*padesát*
sixty	*šedesát*
seventy	*sedmdesát*
eighty	*osmdesát*
ninety	*devadesát*
one hundred	*sto*
two hundred	*dvě stě*
three hundred	*tři sta*
four hundred	*čtyři sta*
five hundred	*pět set*
six hundred	*šest set*
one thousand	*tisíc*
one million	*milion*
one billion	*miliard*

FORMAL AND INFORMAL SPEECH

When your command of the language progresses beyond the 'hello' and 'one beer please' stage, you'll start to notice differences between formal and informal speech.

As in most other European languages (except English) there are different words for 'you' and different conjugations of the verb that follows. When speaking to friends, close acquaintances, family members, and young children, use the informal *ty*. When meeting people for the first few times, and when addressing business contacts and elders, always use the formal *vy*. (This *vy* is also used as 'you' plural, even when addressing a group of friends). Confusing the two can be very embarrassing for both sides. You would never address a client or the bank assistant as *ty*, and you would seem extremely stiff to address a friend as *vy*. Not only must you be aware of which form of 'you' to employ, you must also choose which greeting to use: *dobrý den* and *nashledanou* are the formal 'hello' and 'goodbye,' while *ahoj* and *čau* are spoken to friends and family.

It can be difficult to ascertain when a relationship has developed to such a point that you can switch to the informal. Always address elders and superiors in the formal, even if they use the informal with you, unless they specifically say that you can be less proper. In office relationships and with friends, Czechs usually switch to the informal after the first meeting, to establish a friendly accord. Still, if unsure, you shouldn't use the informal address until the other person initiates it—this can be a funny event in itself, when the Czech person may ask rhetorically, "*Můžeme se tykat?*" ("We can use the 'ty' form with each other?"). This momentous occasion is then often celebrated with a handshake and possibly even a drink. As an example, I always used the formal *vy* with my wife's parents and grandparents before we were married; at the wedding itself, each elder family member made the occasion of announcing that we could henceforth use the informal *ty*, and we marked the event with shots of *slivovice* all around.

Polite Expressions

Whenever you need to approach someone to ask for help or information, don't launch into the discussion without the standard *dobrý den* greeting. This should then be followed with a respectful *prosím Vás*, which is a step above *prosím*, translating roughly as 'I ask of you or 'if you

Small Talk

Czechs do note the superficiality of small talk that many foreign cultures are wont to engage in, and they identify this with lack of real personality. In business settings, try not to broach personal matters beyond the topic at hand. The ho-ho guffaws that Americans in particular are so good at don't go over well here at all.

please'—it serves to acknowledge that you are asking a favour of the other person. Remember that Czechs have a built-in sense of politesse. Even if the people you address may look dour and nasty (especially those in low-paying government or sales clerk jobs) a *prosím Vás* will help to swing them over to your side.

People of many cultures often follow up the 'hello' with a 'how are you?' though Czechs rarely use this artificial space-filler unless they really mean it. Where English-speakers almost always throw out a 'how's it going?' or a 'how's everything?' and the French commonly ask 'ça va?' usually only expecting to hear the standard response, 'I'm fine thanks,' Czech tend to hear the question literally. So if you ask a colleague on a Monday morning, 'How are you?' he may respond with, 'Oh, I'm feeling a bit ill this morning' or 'Yes, thank you, I had a nice weekend.' If you ask a first-time acquaintance or business contact, he will probably express surprise that you're already asking a personal question. Reserve the question for friends for whom you are genuinely interested in the answer.

Titles

The use of titles is strictly adhered to. On business cards and on door signs you usually see the person's name accompanied by his or her professional degree—there is a great respect for education here. Therefore, it is important in both spoken and written communication to address the person with his or her appropriate title. In fact, professionals are often referred to as *pan Doktor* (Mr Doctor) or *paní Profesorka* (Mrs Professor), as a measure of respect, a small form of flattery. One of the most common accompaniments to a name is the classification 'ing.' which stands for *inženýr*, the equivalent of a business or technical degree, which many Czechs possess. (The 'ing.' abbreviation is a vestige from the times of German cohabitation in the country).

First names are not normally used in business situations, except with colleagues and long-established contacts. Americans and British often switch to the first name basis after the initial contact, to establish what they hope to be a friendly, healthy relationship. In Czech business this doesn't necessarily happen right away. Always use the last name and precede it with a *pan* or *paní* (Mr or Mrs/Ms).

Common Courtesies

Don't commence your babbling away in English unless you are sure the other person speaks English. Even if you don't speak Czech, you should at least learn how to say thank you and goodbye. Unfortunately, 'thank you' is one of the most difficult words to pronounce correctly in Czech. A simple thank you is *děkuji* (roughly, 'dyekwee' or alternatively, 'dyekooyoo'). If you want to emphasise this, for example if the person went out of his way to help you, you can say *děkuji Vám*, literally, 'I thank you,' or *děkuji mockrát*, literally 'thank you many times.' Czechs don't get too worked up by formalities, though being able to communicate these simple pleasantries always works in your favour.

> When taking leave of someone, always remember to say goodbye. Czechs often say goodbye, for example, to strangers when getting off the lift, even if they didn't bother to say hello when they got on!

These general tips are especially important in telephone conversations, when personal contact is more limited—so be on your best behaviour!

THE BEAUTY OF IT

Despite, or perhaps because of, all the complexity, Czech is an extremely descriptive and beautiful language, and in this way is very practical as well. Many words have a logical basis; for example the word *vchod* (entrance), literally means 'walk in,' and the word *východ* (exit), means 'walk out;' a farmer is a *zemědělec*— 'earth maker.'

The months are all derived from their relative elements: *leden* (January) means 'ice', *květen* (May) means 'flower' or 'blossom,' and *listopad* (November) means literally 'leaves fall.' The days of the week are similarly descriptive: Wednesday is *středa*—'middle,' while Sunday is the perfectly apt *neděle*—'do nothing.' The poeticism of the language is one of the reasons Czechs are so enamoured by it.

Diminutives

Czech uses a lot of diminutives; in fact, virtually every Czech word can have an ending tacked on to it to make it sound small and quaint. Diminutives are usually formed by changing the end of the word to *-ek, -eČk, -íček, -íčka, -íčko*, etc. Where English has a few such words, like 'booklet' or 'birdy,' any Czech word can be diminutised, some for no apparent reason. Why bother calling a fax machine a 'little fax machine' when it's not? In some ways such diminutives serve a practical function, though; a spoon which is *lžice*, becomes *lžička* when it's a teaspoon.

Czech names are often very descriptive as well, even to the point of silliness. Many Czech names are not just names, they are words with meanings. Some of the more common family names, in fact, are Malý/Malá (Small) and Černý/Černá (Black). Stranger, though, are names you occasionally come across, such as Škvarek/Škvarková (Lardspread), Výborný/Výborná (Excellent), Šourek/ Šourková (Scrotum), Nevečeřel/Nevečeřelová (Didn't-eat-dinner) and Skočdopole/Skočdopolová (Jump-to-the-fields). These are real names!

Women's surnames are always changed to the feminine or possessive ending forms of the male name; the meaning in the traditional sense is that until marriage a girl or woman belongs to her father, but upon marriage, she belongs to her husband. So all women you meet, almost without exception, will have names ending in *-ová* or *-á*. These, incidentally, are the feminine forms of the genitive (possessive) case.

SLANG AND SWEARING

For such a small country, it is remarkable how much dialect, phraseology and vocabulary can vary within the Czech language. I spent most of my time living in Prague, and I have some difficulty understanding friends from southern Bohemia and from Moravia, who both have slightly different accents, and who speak a somewhat different form of the language with occasional differences in vocabulary.

Czechs don't seem to curse as often or as loudly as others—at least in public. The four-letter words that we tend to utter so frequently in English sound especially hard and vulgar in Czech. If you really get upset and start swearing at someone in public, you'll attract a host of shocked onlooking eyes. Czechs are struck by the excessive rudeness of swearing, and usually temper their vocabulary or murmur it under their breath. Needless to say, swearing is reserved for light-hearted communication between close friends and acquaintances, and indeed Czechs can really break loose in these moments.

There is an amusing work in Czech, *vůl*, which is spoken frequently and must be dealt with delicately. A *vůl* is an ox, which seems harmless in itself, but the implications this word has are significant. To call someone an ox is to call them a lowdown, moronic boor, so of course it is extremely insulting; at the same time though, the word is used almost casually amongst close friends as a silly quip to acknowledge camaraderie, almost as Americans use the expression 'man.' It's almost a challenge to say *ty vole* ('you ox') to someone, and it is only used with someone you're very comfortable with, yet within these circles it's spoken with almost careless abandon. Women please note that the expression is extremely masculine. To call a woman a *kráva* (cow) is similarly insulting, though is often apt for some service staff!

Mind-boggling Tongue Twisters

Due to its heavy reliance on crashing consonances, Czech has some of the most difficult tongue-twisters of any language. Even getting through these slowly once is a chore.

The most commonly known, and perhaps most bizarre due to its entire lack of vowels, is the relatively simply '*Strč prst skrz krk*'—'Stick a finger through your neck'. Moving on in silliness of meaning is this warm-up phrase: '*Kmotře Petře, nepřepepřte toho vepře*'—'Godfather Peter, don't over-pepper this pig'. All hell breaks loose, however, and the spittle goes flying while attacking the following: '*Třistatřicettři stříbrných stříkaček stříkalo přes třistatřicettři stříbrnych střech*', whose meaning is secondary to its simple existence, 'Three hundred thirty three silver hoses shoot over three hundred thirty three silver roofs.' A children's favourite is '*Od poklopu ku poklopu Kyklop koulí koulí*'—'From manhole cover to manhole cover Cyclops runs around'. Meanwhile, adults manoeuvre through '*Nenaolejuje-li tě Julie, naolejuji tě já*'—'If Julia doesn't oil you, I'll oil you.'

Those with religious inclinations will be surprised and even shocked to hear the Lord's name taken in vain with reckless alacrity. Remember Czechs are not a religious people overall, so using Christ as a scapegoat is a common form of relieving tension or expressing anger. Once your ears are attuned to Czech speech, you'll start to hear the profane *Ježiši Marie!* ('Jesus Mary') or *Pane Bože!* ('my God'), spoken to mean anything from 'Oh no' to 'C'mon, what now!' to 'What the hell is going on!' Don't take offence.

You may be shocked to hear the expression *fakt jo!* which sounds dangerously like the most offensive sendoff imaginable in English. *Fakt* means 'fact,' and *jo* is the equivalent to 'yeah' so the meaning is something like 'really!' or 'I can't believe it!' Unfortunately Czechs do have the F-word in their vocabulary, so be careful who you may choose to use it on; likewise, don't take offence if someone says it to you.

BODY LANGUAGE

For a people not given to emotional displays, body language is not a particularly noteworthy aspect in communicating. In fact, it's more helpful to be aware of what Czechs don't do that many other people do do in order to avoid offence.

Greetings and their Related Civilities

When greeting someone, anyone, a firm handshake is an appropriate, respectful gesture. In business settings, the handshake is always accompanied with the greeting *dobrý den* (hello); in social meetings, a simple *ahoj* or *čau* (hi) usually suffices instead of the handshake. In a group of people, men always offer their hands to women first, and it is perfectly appropriate for men and women to shake hands, even in social settings.

More physical displays of affection are rare. Men rarely greet male friends with anything more than a handshake; an affectionate hug between men is still seen as a bit queer (*see section on sexual relations*). Women greeting female friends occasionally accompany the greeting with a kiss on the cheek.

The kiss on the cheek between men and women, as practised in many European countries, is reserved for more friendly or romantic relations. When greeting a member of the opposite sex for the first time, do not make the move to kiss him or her on the cheek unless you are comfortable with the person and your standing with him or her, for example a friend of a friend. Similarly, men only kiss women on the hand in a semi-joking cultural affectation. Much lip-puckering has a romantic/sexual connotation and should be avoided unless respectfully intended.

While physical contact is limited, visual contact is very important. When shaking someone's hand, always look them square in the eye. It is said that the eye is the window to the soul, and to Czechs, this is an important means of contact.

When saying goodbye, the handshake is repeated, accompanied by several *nashledanous* or *čaus*. If there are more than two people in the group, it is common for everyone to shake hands with everyone else, though true to their practical nature, Czechs don't make a circus of it. In business meetings, it is common to follow up the goodbye with a comment that you were glad to have met the person, to thank them, and to perhaps mention that you look forward to seeing them again next time.

Other Body Language

Always remember to maintain eye contact. As in many places, this establishes friendship and equality between friends and business associates alike. Remember especially to look the other person in the eye when toasting a drink; it is considered bad form to simply watch the glasses clink, as if the drink is more important than the person. *(More about this in the section on pub culture)*.

International hand signals such as the thumbs-up, the 'OK' thumb-and-index-finger circle, and the raised middle finger, are recognised by all but not actively used.

One body motion you will notice quite often is the exasperated arms-thrown-up-at-the-shoulders. This is usually

a direct 'What the hell are you doing?' or 'What the hell's going on?' seen regularly in traffic intersections in Prague. The exclamation is usually accompanied by a helpless, 'Well, what do you expect?' sort of shrug.

STANDARDS OF APPEARANCE

True to their humble nature, Czechs tend to groom, dress, walk and talk as modestly as possible, obliging themselves of the necessities of good appearance but not going far beyond that. (In his early days as president, Václav Havel himself was occasionally seen in a Rolling Stones T-shirt). Czechs are not obsessed with physical appearance, although fashion trends are becoming more important here, particularly amongst young women and particularly in Prague.

Business attire is similar to most anywhere. Sharp dress is not necessary, so long as it corresponds with the basic coat and tie or skirt and blouse or trousersuit theme. You still see lots of greys and browns, but the wild colour schemes that were prevalent in the early 1990s are much less common now: purple dress jackets and white socks were an amusing sight in the early post-Communist era. Don't try to impress with grand appearances in Armani suits and full-length furs: Czechs are not at all ostentatious in this way (at least outside of film or fashion circles), and they don't look kindly on artificial displays. They are much more interested in what's inside.

Image

Czechs do, however, have a new concept of image. Many have exciting new roles now, and a few choose to play them out in almost comical fashion, picking up the swagger and the accents of the western businessmen, sports and film stars they observe. This often comes off in exaggerated fashion *(as explained in the following chapter titled Doing Business)*: some seem to take themselves too seriously, and the style is as abrasive here as similar behaviour anywhere.

DOING BUSINESS

CHAPTER 9

'Perhaps I don't understand economics, but
economics does not understand me, either.'
Lin Yutang, *The Importance of Living*

Czechs are quickly re-learning the efficiency and prowess which brought them into the top eight world economies before World War II, and they are one of the economic leaders among the EU expansion countries. The 1990s was a period of great learning, and the recession in the latter part of the decade helped tighten some the remaining loose screws. Heavy trade with the west, as well as extensive foreign direct investment, means Czechs have by now had lots of interaction with western business practices. In fact, foreign-owned companies now account for nearly half of Czech GDP, and employ about one-third of Czech workers.

However, Communism did have a strong effect on mentality and the way of going about doing (or not doing) business, from which Czechs are slowly but surely extricating themselves. Though occasional absurdities remain, this school of thought should be blamed not on Czech thinking but on Communist non-thinking. Quality, efficiency and customer services were not practiced in business for forty years through 1989, and the years since have not yet been enough time to unlearn almost two generations of bad management and lack of initiative. Part of the problem in the early years was that the sudden lust for money was often tangled up in unfamiliarity with the process of earning it. Now that the Czech Republic is converging toward EU standards, the differences are less severe, and the level-headed, pragmatic nature of the Czech persona is generally guiding the way.

Certainly, things are much better now than in the early 1990s.

But be aware that the procedure for doing business is not always as clear as what you may be used to: a seemingly straightforward deal may come across unforeseen and with inexplicable problems, while a supposed agreement may not be so sure after all.

You may find the pace of work to be agonisingly slow. In the former system where efficiency of production was irrelevant, getting the job done was a matter of getting around to it. Some workers, especially those who do not deal with western firms, can be painfully slow at accomplishing a task. Offices commonly start to close early Friday afternoon as everyone heads out of town. And when somebody gets sick, even with a common cold or flu, he or she usually takes the entire week off, or even more. Of course this is sensible, allowing the body to recover and not to spread the germs, but it's almost laughable how health clinics are jammed at 7:00 am with people trying to get sick-leave notes signed by the doctor.

At the same time, many Czechs these days are working harder than ever, even to the detriment of family life. Standards are rising rapidly, and EU entry inevitably means a rising economic tide.

The following observations and tips may be a bit on the critical side, and they may not apply to your new colleagues, especially those who have worked or studied in western Europe or North America, and are by now used to the game.

A FEW STARTERS

When it comes to doing business in the Czech Republic, the rules are essentially the same as in North America or Europe, though there are a few important subtleties that you must be aware of. You must have a good sense of how things are done here and in what ways they are different, and this takes a little time to absorb. One company manager I spoke with complains that his single greatest frustration is interpreting between his US corporate policies and the local conditions. This is certainly not a criticism of the Czechs: many westerners (Americans in particular) come in thinking that their way is simply how it should be done, and they make the mistake of choosing not to perceive the reality here. Know your environment before you make judgments or decisions on it.

Time is not quite the critical factor in Czech business as it often is in other countries. Where some are constantly driven by deadlines and incentives, Czechs are a bit more laid-back

Do's And Don'ts

Do's:
- Be flexible.
- Always have business cards handy. You will certainly receive a card from your Czech partners, so be ready to reciprocate.
- Be conscious of maintaining a cordial demeanor in any business situation, enter with a hello and part with a goodbye. This simplicity is practiced by all.
- Dress appropriately.

Don'ts
- Don't enter negotiations with a superiority complex; this is often met with silent refusal. Don't assume the way you are accustomed to doing things is the way things work here. Know your environment before making judgments or decisions. The 'ugly American' can quickly find himself marginalised. Consider your business dealings an opportunity to learn, not to impose.
- Don't, on the other hand, succumb too quickly; understand that your Czech counterpart may have a different sense of timing or priorities, so don't give in too soon.

about getting things accomplished, and this allows them the chance to send out feelers and explore other possibilities. Or perhaps conversely, it is their tendency to check out all the options and let ideas gel in their mind, which takes so much time and can lead to frustrations for those unfamiliar with the practice. You also have to remember that this is a foreign country, with a different language and different laws, and if you don't speak Czech and aren't thoroughly familiar with the local ways, it simply takes longer to get through it all.

Czechs realise that the system they have emerged from was an illogical, inhuman one, which suppressed personality and destroyed entrepreneurial spirit. They know that they need to adapt to western business practice if they want to reintegrate with the international market economy and in many cases they already have. The younger generation especially is extremely flexible, willing, and able. At the same time, however, Czechs do know what they are doing and they are wary of outsiders coming in and monitoring, telling them how it should be done.

The Power Of Acceptance

Flexibility will be your greatest asset—accept the fact that things are not quite the same as what you are used to. One simple rule that I developed early on was to eliminate the concept of 'should' from my mind, and simply to accept things as they came. This is not to say expect the unexpected, or expect the worst; you'll usually achieve what you set out to do, though occasionally in an unanticipated manner.

Establishing a Business Relationship

The most important thing to keep in mind is not to enter with a superiority complex. Many westerners come in assuming that Czechs are still in the dark ages and need to be taught what to do and how to do it. This is an enormous mistake to make, first of all because it's not true, and secondly because Czechs don't take kindly to unsought council. Those who succeed socially and in business are those who respect their Czech colleagues and friends. Those who fail are those who make little or no attempt to mingle and appreciate the culture, who stick to their own communities, and who act haughtily in business deals. Any pretence of superiority will only meet silent refusal.

Because Czechs often base their business relationships on personal sentiment *(see below)*, it is crucial that you establish cordial relations with your potential colleagues, partners and clients. So the question here is, how to get on the other person's side?

Most meetings start off with a short, light prelude—a comment on the weather, or a slight self criticism (for example, "I got off at the wrong metro stop") will set you on the right track. An excellent introductory remark is a simple *"Dobrý den, těší mě"* ("Hello, pleased to meet you") said in Czech. Even with a funny accent, it comes off well, and is endearing to the listener. But don't prolong it. Americans have a tendency to chitchat, acting as if you are close friends from the get-go. This can be conducive to friendly relations if presented in a genuine fashion, but don't linger on it—get down to business, and stick to formal language.

Don't Fake It

It is very important to act genuinely, to present yourself as a real person. Czechs have an intuition and a deep appreciation for sensibility and sensitivity, and any pretence of condescension or inapproachability will immediately work against you.

Be Aware of Emotions

Czechs are very conscious of feelings. In fact, many business transactions succeed or fail based on the opinions formed by one another. I used to work as a real estate broker in Prague, and we often heard from landlords at the initial meeting: "I want a tenant who is *solidní*"—meaning they want someone who is not only financially stable, but also a reasonable person. When it came to negotiating a contract, we often heard comments from the landlord such as, "Well, she seems like a nice person, I think we'll work something out" or conversely, "No, she's too difficult, I can already see there will be too many problems."

This is not necessarily to say that Czechs are emotional in business dealings. The average Czech is not outwardly emotional. Rather, he is inwardly conscious of feelings. This can be difficult to recognise. Non-response from the other party may well be an avoidance of the issue. Remember, Czechs tend to be non-confrontational, and snags or stumbling blocks in the course of a negotiation may become insurmountable walls. It is important to recognise the danger signs: lowered eyes and silence are a signal that there is a problem, which the other party may feel paralysed to overcome. If this happens, take a step back, make a light-hearted remark and proceed from there. *(See below for more on Negotiating.)*

MONEY

One effect of dulled sensitivity to business dealings is that Czechs often think only about their side of the deal. When it comes to money, I've heard it stated simply: *Češi chtějí dostát, ale ne vydělávat*—Czechs want to make money, but not earn it. In this sense, they can be extraordinarily efficient: they want your money, and they can be inordinately tough when trying to get it. They want it all, and they want it now.

There is a sense among some of having been cheated for 40 years, only to be teased by how hard it is now. Now countries such as neighbouring Germany 'have everything' and Czechs 'have nothing.' But some still seem to think that it should just be handed to them. One of the initial reactions to freedom in 1990 was disillusionment: the material things they had wanted for so long were suddenly available, but well out of proportion to the average salary.

THE INDIRECT APPROACH

One thing you will gradually start to perceive is that some Czechs take an indirect approach in business dealings. Your calls may go unanswered, you may find there are hidden other people responsible for various aspects of the transaction, and you may soon get the feeling of being jerked around. There are actually a few reasons for this.

Some Czechs are still a little green when it comes to wheeling and dealing, and they are a bit nervous about taking steps which may be risky. They often take their fine old time, making sure they've thought it all out, and likely conferred with colleagues and friends to validate their concerns, before they proceed.

Take Note

A comically typical negotiation procedure for a house or flat, for example, goes something like this: Day 1, view property and discuss initial terms; Day 2, haggle on kitchen appliances and light fixtures, and discuss a revised rent price for providing this items; Day 3, haggle again on the price; Day 4, whoops! The landlord suddenly is 'ill' or 'out of town' (read: he's taking time to think about it), call again tomorrow; Day 5, at the contract signing, the landlord comes up with a new demand after conferring with his cousin the previous day, that the rent should be adjusted according to inflation after the second year of the lease. Further haggling ensues, and in the end neither side is quite sure if they can trust the other.

Under Communism, responsibility was shattered along with the destruction of the individual. Where the goal was a society of equal people, the individual was a lost entity. Therefore, as Havel writes, the displacement of the self meant the loss of responsibility, and the practical manifestations of this were played out in the lifeless roles assigned to all members of society. In business, this meant the lower level workers simply did what they were told, middle management relayed the dictates of their superiors, and the top brass simply followed the Party line.

So now, taking responsibility for individual actions, and accepting the blame when something goes wrong, is a bit difficult to stomach; it's always somebody else's fault, and if you're not careful, it can quickly be turned back onto you. Instead of admitting failure or defeat, they often try to patch up the problem, covering it up so that it looks alright—remember, most Czechs want to avoid confrontation at all costs.

OTHER EXTREMES

There are, of course, many other styles, some of which are the unfortunate consequences of people who rather suddenly have power or abilities. These individuals can be dangerous, dishonest, and difficult to work with.

One of the most noteworthy is quite the opposite extreme to that just described: this is the type of brash, self-assured manager who clearly has taken white-collar Hollywood films and TV shows a bit too seriously. In some circumstances you may encounter the executive who plays the starring role with precision: juggling two mobile phones, always late to meetings, very curt in his or her conversations, quick-tempered, and therefore almost impossible to carry on a productive meeting with. Decisions are made quickly, even abruptly, and others are forced to wrap themselves around his or her timetable. In such a situation, your degree of success depends on the degree of your leverage—i.e., how badly he or she wants what you have to offer.

Another case is the 'manager,' whose title goes sarcastically into quotes. This is the boss with newfound power over underlings, who therefore has decided that the most comfortable and self-fulfilling course of action is to delegate responsibility to his or her subordinates. The title 'manager' in this case means someone who sits back and supervises while lesser employees do the dirty work. In such situations, you may find it hard to make progress because of the extra layers involved, and because the manager you are dealing with may be hopelessly uninformed or ineffective simply because he or she is not actively engaged in the proceedings—or indeed is often not in the office at all. If you then are dealing with the underlings, your task will also be complicated by the fact that these people may fear the top dog, and hence may have little or no motivation or input themselves.

These, again, are stereotypes and extremes, but they are certainly elements of reality. Think of them as the negative forms that in fact exist just about anywhere in the world. For the most part, you will find your Czech colleagues and business acquaintances to be hard-working and eager to see transactions reach a successful conclusion. Any combination of these traits may play in, so proceed with a clear head and cover your bases as well as possible.

GETTING THE JOB DONE

Performing a task quite often involves finding your own way to get it done. Sometimes this is equally, if not more effective, and sometimes it turns into a comedy of errors.

Learning The Ropes

The indirectness spoken of above is quite simply due to lack of experience; as one Czech colleague of mine says, we in the west have this concept of a market economy built in—we've always lived in a consumer oriented economy, and are naturally cognisant of the marketplace.

The younger generation of Czechs, those with little or no memory of the Communist era, are in fact in many ways free and clear of many of the disruptive influences of that time. In some ways, it is like the old 'don't trust anyone over 30' mantra—in this case, many of those who were over the age of about 30 at the time of the 1989 revolution still have the old ways stuck fast in their heads.

Czechs are fast learners, however, and conditions are infinitely better now than they were in the early 1990s. You may be pleasantly surprised at the dedication of motivated employees, particularly those that are given incentives to succeed. Keep in mind that Czechs are an inherently logical people; in some cases they only need to be taught how to follow the thought process through, and to be given incentives to do well. Employees may only respond to a task with a simple 'OK,' and they proceed to do what they are told, no more, no less. Effective management tactics to bring out the best involve opening the floor to discussion and debate. Brainstorming sessions, where all employees involved are on even keel, are enormously productive; workers are full of ideas, though they may hesitate to challenge an authority. It also helps to explain not only the what but the why when giving instructions—following the thought process through can awaken the logic within.

BEATING THE SYSTEM

Because Czechs never took Communism seriously, they developed ways around the system, and in this manner they are ready and able to overcome a real problem. They are very creative in a utilitarian perspective and they are good at getting what they want. Now that western firms are so active in the Czech Republic, and many Czech firms have restructured to compete and trade with the west, locals are leaping at the opportunities for career advancement and higher salaries. Some even have the sense that westerners are here to exploit: amongst their many virtues, Czechs can be crafty at getting your self-esteem and money.

There is a telling quip from Communist days: *Když neokrádáš stát, o krádáš rodinu—* If you don't steal from the state, you're stealing from your family.

NEGOTIATING

Most sources agree that negotiations are not always carried out fairly—they can be tough, as there is not always an inbuilt desire to please both sides. Again, it's a matter of thinking it all through—the demands that are placed comprise a long list of what your opposing number wants. The key difference is that when a Czech business-person presents an offer, it is not necessarily a basis for bargaining; the offer made is essentially what he expects to get. This is not to say there is no room for flexibility, but don't expect him to give in much.

Where one is generally accustomed to making an offer, having analysed the situation as thoroughly as possible, and leaving room for negotiation within that offer, a Czech may simply lay all his cards on the table, take it or leave it. Beyond that, he is probably waiting to see what more he can get from you. Counter-offers are rarely given: it's not a process of offer-and-counter-offer so much as offer-and-acquiescence—and the cynics out there say he's always trying to pull you more and more towards his end of the deal.

The indirect approach mentioned above comes into play during negotiating sessions. Czechs are exceedingly polite in most business situations, and this can even get in the way of productive haggling. If a sticking point comes up you may notice your counterpart avoiding your eyes, speaking to a third party instead of directly to you, and taking a sort of roundabout approach to the deal. The topic of conversation may change, or a weighty silence may ensue, while he lets the latest thought turn over in his mind. You may find yourself having to lead the whole negotiation, easing the discussion along while trying to cover all relevant points.

Keep The Upper Hand

One company manager I spoke with outlines it thus: the western business-person often infuses a sense of urgency into a deal, while the Czech counterpart often doesn't have the same constraints, so he sits and waits. The westerner then gets nervous and starts to cave in more and more until the final outcome is decidedly in the other guy's favour. This is a big mistake, especially when the westerner does have some leverage. Remember, your Czech partner may want the deal as much as you do. If you approach him on an even keel and proceed with reason, you will get a better result.

Remember to keep your cool, to listen calmly and patiently. It's fine to express disapproval but do so gently; always retain a measure of respect for your interlocutor. Don't ever give an appearance of unfriendliness or condescension—Czechs pick up on this immediately, and respond in one of two ways: either save face at all costs or, conversely, back away and drop everything. In either case, you're up against the wall. If the negotiations start to get tense, you may find the other party becoming defensive, bristling at the notion of having to relent in any way. If he turns non-communicative, he is probably contemplating and may take a while to come back with a reasonable response.

Don't acquiesce too much unless it is really necessary, or he may find you too soft and try to take advantage of it. Retain your position of leverage. A bit of bullying, done gently, can take you far. The best position to be in is when you're very close to finishing the deal, having accepted many of his terms (assuming they are acceptable) from the outset. From here, he'll hold onto his demands even though he sees the end in sight. If you've established a good business accord, you'll find it much easier to wind things up productively.

As a last resort, a threat to just walk away from it all will often scare him and he'll simply give in. He is being as tough as he can, but if he perceives it falling through, he may well drop his hold-out requests. I once was brokering a deal for a client who, in the midst of a final sticking point, looked at his watch and realised he had to make a phone call. He jumped up to get his phone from his jacket, which his adversary perceived as him walking out of the deal, and he immediately dropped his demand.

Stereotypes

Please note that these again are generalisations. Many Czech businesspeople are perfectly comfortable with straightforward negotiations, and you often won't notice any difference in procedure.

FORMAL AND LEGAL MATTERS

Further complicating matters is the unfortunate fact that the Czech legal system leaves something to be desired, primarily in enforcement. Laws that ought to be taken for granted sometimes are not, some laws may be lax, and Czechs know what they can get away with. You as an outsider may not, and this could be used against you.

In its most basic form, this could include something such as lack of protection for tenant rights—are you really going to try to take your landlord to court when the small claims legal system is as weak as it is? At a grander scale, but perfectly indicative of the gravity of the situation, the Czech government was recently forced to pay a huge penalty by the international court in the Hague to Central European Media Enterprises for failing to protect this foreign investment in the Czech Republic's most successful TV station, TV Nova, when the Czech counterpart, Vladimír Železný, basically ran off with the money. At least in this case justice was finally done, but it took a major international proceeding, which would not be seen through to the end in most business dealings. (Železný, by the way, was elected to the Senate from his region of Moravia as a member of the Communist party in 2002, again exemplifying the sometimes twisted state of affairs in this country).

The Czech Republic was in fact ahead of its eastern European neighbours in the 1990s in drawing up new legislation for trade and taxation, and it continues to work on legal frameworks in conjunction with EU norms, but it has continued to fall short in the area of enforcement. Having a good lawyer who is familiar with both Czech law and western practices is therefore essential *(a couple are listed at the back of this book)*. At the end of the day, though, the success of a transaction, whether it is a rental agreement, a supplier arrangement or even an employment contract, may come down to the will of the parties involved to deliver—so your ability to establish trust is paramount.

In most business transactions, the final contract is the most important element and you should never feel at ease until you have this signed. Once the contract is signed, it is generally honoured to the best of one's abilities; most Czechs are respectful of this formality. You may rest easy when the contract is signed, but there is still the issue of getting the money. Cash in hand is the only guarantee: even an invoice does not insure payment, as you may well have to follow up on it to get your reward.

One thing that western companies often overlook in expanding to the Czech Republic is that there are different laws and indeed a different language governing the whole operation. Contracts written in English or other languages are valid, though if there is a Czech version as well, it prevails in case of dispute. All contracts must be carefully checked to insure that they correspond with Czech legal provisions.

Bribes and Other Payoffs

'Hush money' is not the order of business here, and most transactions are happily free of corruption. However, bribes and other forms of corruption do occur, and you should at least be wise to their presence. Fraud and corruption are of course regarded by the general population as exceedingly low-class, a deviation in which Communists, mafiosi and corrupt businessmen (as well as certain politicians) engage. Czechs feel they ought to be above this, and in most cases they are. But there is a paradox here: today's entrepreneurs are also often viewed with suspicion, as if they must have had illicit connections to get where they are. Some, indeed, have: the economic downturn of 1997–1999 brought to light some disturbing cases of tunnelling (stripping the valuable assets from an entity, out of sight of shareholders), and many of today's most successful executives are indeed those who had Party connections before 1989. The deepening entrenchment of western businesses in the Czech Republic is helping weed out some of this ugliness, and dealings made within these spheres are usually straightforward.

Under-the-table payments and little favours are similarly regarded as unethical, though in some cases, it is the easiest way to get things done. The dark comedy of it all is that one really ought not to participate in such deals, though many do. In another example from real estate, I was once part of a deal in which the official rental price was written in the contract as half the real amount, while the remainder was declared as 'payment for services.' This allowed the landlords to escape the higher tax bracket in which the full rental amount would have put them.

The police themselves often work under a quiet system of bribery, and for those willing to veer off the straight-and-narrow, paying off the traffic police can save you hundreds of crowns. On more than one occasion I've been pulled over for a moving violation, which should have met a fine equal to about 1,000 Kč. Just a little bit of protest and plea for sympathy though, and the cop let me off with a 200 Kč 'gimme,' which I assume went straight into his pocket. On a more serious note, a friend of mine was once ripped off at a nightclub in Prague by a bartender who refused to give him his change; this friend of mine went to the police station nearby, only to find when he returned to the club that the cops were in cahoots with the nightclub staff!

You'll notice that many financial transactions are carried out in cash, and there are two reasons for this. First, there is still only a rudimentary system of credit established in the Czech Republic, so personal cheques are extremely limited. Second, and more importantly, payments in cash can slip through the accounting books.

BUSINESS FUNCTIONS

The 'business lunch' is a common social interlude, though it is not commonly used as a medium of meeting and negotiating. More often, colleagues head down to a local pub for a quick bite around noontime. The experience is not necessarily one of exciting food and enlightening conversation, though. You will likely soon tire of the same old meat-and-potatoes, and the locals often down their meals as quickly as possible, seeming to focus merely on the plate and on getting it all in.

There aren't too many activities in the way of company get-togethers, parties and the like. Office parties may spark up on the occasion of somebody's birthday or name-day, and colleagues often head to the pub for a beer or two after hours, where they continue to discuss business or develop a social rapport in a more casual manner. In general, though, Czechs keep their public and private lives separate.

Exhibitions and trade fairs are very important in business. Prague and Brno both have large convention and exhibition centres, which are fully booked months and even years in advance. Business-people take advantage of the opportunity

A Czech business lunch is usually an informal affair and may take place at the local pub.

to make new contacts on a face-to-face basis, and if you want to do the same, you'd be well advised to follow suit.

BUSINESS FORMALITIES

Czechs have strong concept of polite behaviour, and in most situations (shop assistants and waiters sometimes excepted) you will find them humbly, almost painfully polite. Aligning yourself with this simple fact is the key to making a good impression. (*Refer to the sections on polite expressions and body language in the chapter on Communicating*). Remember the importance of a firm handshake.

Vizitky (business cards) are an important instrument. All Czechs have them, and they tend to distribute them generously. Whenever you are presented with a card, be sure you have one of your own to offer; it's a small token, but it makes you look much more professional in their eyes.

Office Hours

Czechs tend to start and finish their day about an hour or two earlier than most. Offices thus open as early as 7:00 am or 8:00 am and most employees go home by 4:00 pm or 5:00 pm, though the influx of western business, and the general Czech drive to success, has affected these hours. Shops open anywhere from 8:00 am to 10:00 am, and generally close by 6:00 pm. Bakeries, grocery shops and news-stands open as early as 6:00 am. More and more shops are staying open later and opening at weekends. Peak hours on the public transport systems are from 5:00 am to 8:00 am and from 3:00 pm to 6:00 pm.

FAST FACTS ABOUT CZECH REPUBLIC

CHAPTER 10

'I believe that there is a kind of
poetry, even a kind of truth, in simple fact.'
—Edward Abbey

Capital
Prague

Currency
Czech koruna (CZK) or Kč

Government
Parliamentary Democracy

Climate
Temperate; cool summers; cold, cloudy winters

Area
total: 78,866 sq km (30,450.3 sq miles)
land: 77,276 sq km (29,836.4 sq miles)
water: 1,590 sq km (613.9 sq miles)

Agricultural Products
Wheat, potatoes, sugar beets, hops, cherries, plums, beef, pork, poultry

Ethnic Groups
Czech: 90.4 per cent
Moravian: 3.7 per cent
Slovak: 1.9 per cent
Other: 4 per cent (2001 census)

Exports
Machinery and transport equipment (52 per cent), raw materials and fuel (9 per cent), chemicals (5 per cent), (2003)

Gross Domestic Product (GDP)
US$172.2 billion (2004 est.)

Highest point
Sněžka (1,602 m / 5,256 ft)

Imports
Machinery and transport equipment (46 per cent), raw materials and fuels (15 per cent), chemicals (10 per cent)

Independence
1 January 1993 (Czechoslovakia split into the Czech Republic and Slovakia)

Industries
Metallurgy, machinery and equipment, motor vehicles, glass and armaments.

Internationally Famous Czechs
Artists/Writers/Musicians
Antonín Dvořák, composer
Bedřich Smetana, composer
Leoš Janáček, composer
Alfons Mucha, painter
Milan Kundera, writer
Miloš Forman, film director
Josef Sudek, photographer

Athletes
Emil Zátopek, Olympic athlete (track and field)
Jan Železný, Olympic athlete (javelin)
Jaromír Jágr, hockey player
Dominik Hašek, hockey player
Pavel Nedvěd, football player

Martina Navrátilová, tennis player
Ivan Lendl, tennis player

Politicians/Religious Figures
Jan Hus, seminal figure in the Protestant movement
Jan Ámos Komenský (Comenius), Protestant leader and educator
Tomáš G Masaryk, founder and first President of Czechoslovakia
Václav Havel, playwright and instrumental figure in 1989 revolution; President of Czechoslovakia and the Czech Republic from 1990–2003
Madeleine Albright, former U.S. Secretary of State, who was born in Czechoslovakia

Born and Lived in the Czech Lands, but Ethnically German, not Czech
Gregor Mendel, scientist (Hynčice, North Moravia)
Franz Kafka, writer (Prague)
Rainer Maria Rilke, writer (Prague)
Gustav Mahler, composer (Kaliště, South Bohemia)
Sigmund Freud, psychologist (Příbor, North Moravia)

Internet Country Code
.cz

Language
Czech

Life Expectancy at Birth
*to*tal population: 76.0 years
male: 72.7 years
female: 79.5 years (2005 est.)

Literacy
99.9 per cent (1999 est.)

Lowest Point
Elbe River at Hřensko, 115 m (377.30 ft)

Population
Total: 10, 241,138 (July 2005 est.)

Religion
Roman Catholic: 39.2 per cent
Protestant: 4.6 per cent
Orthodox: 3.0 per cent
Other: 13.4 per cent
Atheist or *undetermined:* 39.8 per cent

Time Zone
Central European Time (GMT + 1)

CULTURE QUIZ

Now that your introduction to Czech culture is complete, all that remains is for you to experience it for yourself. A willingness to embrace Czech customs and a genuine interest in the people will take you a long way, but be patient in the initial stages as its takes time to adjust to any new social environment. The following questions will help test your new found knowledge and instincts about the country.

SITUATION 1

You've just moved into your new flat and are eager to get to know your neighbours, though nobody seems to pay you any mind whatsoever when they see you in the hall. Do you:

Ⓐ Get offended and ignore them too.

Ⓑ Say hello and move on.

Ⓒ Introduce yourself and try to draw them into conversation

Ⓒ Invite them in to your flat for a house-warming party and a get-to-know-you.

Comments

Although **Ⓐ** is a natural response, remember that most Czechs simply keep to themselves. Saying hello to them may meet with a mumbled reply, though it will still take a while to establish any form of a relationship. After a few such meetings, recognition will set in and the ice may begin to melt. Inquiring into their lives too soon may be seen as probing, so gradual warm-up conversation pieces, such as comments on the weather, are your best way in. Option **Ⓓ**, while it may be a common, friendly gesture in your own country, is far too personal here—it's bit too close for comfort to enter someone's home if you aren't properly familiar with them. For now, **Ⓑ** is the best answer, after which you can progress to **Ⓒ**.

SITUATION 2

You are in a pub after work with your new Czech colleagues. After a beer, the waiter comes around with another handful of mugs and your colleagues start to take in another round. You don't really want to drink, but you don't want to offend your colleagues by not taking part. Do you:

Ⓐ Refuse the drink graciously and leave politely, saying you have another commitment
Ⓑ Order coffee or water instead
Ⓒ Drink on with them, seeing as this is an ice-breaking opportunity

Comments

Meeting after hours with colleagues is a great way to begin the friendly aspect of the relationship which is so important to Czechs. Furthermore, they tend to keep their social schedules flexible, particularly when it comes to meeting someone over a beer. To refuse and leave could be taken as an unwillingness to establish cordiality. To stay, but with a cup of coffee instead, is fine, but seeing how beer is such a part of Czech socialising, it ingratiates you to your hosts if you take part in their activities. Choose **Ⓒ**, and then proceed with moderation.

SITUATION 3

After a few months here you've learned a bit of Czech and feel confident enough to use it when you need it. You are in a shop and need to ask the sales assistant something about the contents of a package, so you lurch into your question in broken Czech—yet she snaps something back at you that you cannot comprehend. Do you:

A Continue as well as you can, ignoring her rudeness and vow to look up the words you don't know when you get home.

B Realise you can't make yourself understood, so start speaking English to her.

C Forget about it and go home.

Comments

Responses **B** and **C** are the ones you will probably prefer but may not be the best course of action. Speaking English to a shop assistant is likely a fruitless endeavour—not only will she probably not understand, she may not appreciate your assumption that she does. Of course, she may feel sympathy and try to help out, in which case, you will have accomplished your task. If you just drop it, you'll get discouraged at your inability to communicate and at the unwillingness of the shop assistant to be helpful—in the 'down' phase of culture shock this is dangerous. Be bold and push through; choose **A**.

SITUATION 4

A male friend of yours makes a comment about women that offends your more progressive views (this could indeed happen whether you yourself are male or female). Do you:

A Tell him that a comment such as that is unacceptable in your country.

B Not respond and let it pass.

C Laugh along with it, not wanting to put a hurdle in the way of your friendship.

D Explain as lightly as possible that you disagree and why.

Comments

Above all, remember that you are a visitor in his country, so any remark which smacks of cultural condescension will put him on the defensive. Meanwhile, not responding, or going along with it, will only encourage such remarks. If you can smile, yet shake your head and make a return comment, you will at least make it clear that you disapprove. The best response is **D**.

SITUATION 5

You are in the midst of a seemingly interminable negotiation in which your company is trying to gain a lucrative deal with a Czech counter-part. You feel your offer is fair, yet the opposing number is waffling and coming up with further demands, which you find unacceptable. Do you:

A Sense that he will not relent and, seeing how important the deal is for you, realise that you will have to make even more concessions.

B Go along with the slower pace, in hopes that he will finally accept your offer.

C Take charge of the situation by pointing out the advantages and disadvantages to both parties, and presenting what you believe is the fairest solution.

D Bully your way through with strong words, trying to out-tough your current rival/potential partner.

Comments

Remember that Czechs put a lot of value into personal understanding, so angry words and emotional displays are automatic deal breakers. Many western businesspeople make the mistake of not recognising that Czechs often take some time to sort things out, all the while coming up with more ways to win. Patience is a virtue in negotiating, though without movement it can turn into a spiral. Therefore, by discussing circumstances in rational terms, maintaining friendly relations, you'll likely work toward a solution. The best response in this situation is **C**.

DO'S AND DON'TS

DO'S
In General

- Be modest. Czechs appreciate modesty and humility in a person. Arrogance, aggression and ostentation are frowned upon. Observe and recognise behavioural patterns, and try to align with them as much as possible.

- Learn as much as you can of the Czech language and about Czech culture. Your standing in the eyes of a Czech person increases infinitely if you show an interest in them.

- Try to recognise Czech sarcasm and dry humour. Czechs are good at making jokes out of virtually any situation, and they even be can be rather harsh about it sometimes. Try not to take yourself too seriously, and don't take commentary too personally.

- Remember birthdays and name-days of your Czech colleagues. Both are considered important. And be cognizant of the semi-formalities that Czechs use. Both events are cause for a token gift or card, or at least a pause for a drink, accompanied by handshakes and expressions of best wishes for future health, luck and happiness.

In Business or Commercial Transactions

- Always have business cards handy. You will certainly receive a card from your Czech partners, so be ready to return the compliment.

- Be conscious of maintaining a cordial demeanor in any business situation, enter with a hello and part with a goodbye. This simplicity is practiced by all.

At Somebody's Home

- Remember to take off your shoes upon entering and accept the slippers you will likely be offered. (This may require you to remember to wear socks without holes!)

- You may bring photos of home or family. This is a common social practice, and since your hosts will want to show you their photos, it's nice to be able to reciprocate.

At the Theatre or Concert Hall

- Dress appropriately. This does not have to mean coat and tie (many do dress as such), but jeans and trainers are definitely looked down upon and may even receive a terse comment.

In a Pub or Restaurant

- Seat yourself unless someone greets you at the door (unlikely except at the better places).
- When paying, remember to tell the waiter what you would like to round the bill up to when he/she tells you the amount or hands you the tab—don't leave a tip on the table.

DON'TS
In General

- In any business or social situation, do not assume your cultural superiority! Many make this unfortunate (often unwitting) mistake. Don't try to impose your cultural values or business principles upon your Czech friends or business associates. Instead, observe and demonstrate humility, but without pandering or flattery.

In Somebody's Home

- Don't talk too much about business and politics. Social situations are to be reserved for social matters, and there is a quite strong divide between work and play in the Czech Republic.
- Don't be messy. Because homes are generally very small, Czechs keep them neat, so try not to spill crumbs. Don't lean on walls, as the paint used in most homes will leave a powder film on your clothes.

In a Pub or Restaurant

- Don't be picky. Special requests are rare, so don't, for example, try order a vegetarian version of a dish.

GLOSSARY

More complete glossaries can be found in relevant sections of the book.

COMMONLY USED WORDS AND PHRASES

dobrý den	hello
ahoj or čau	hi
těší mě	pleased to meet you
ano	yes
ne	no
dobrou chut'	"bon appetit"
nazdráví!	to health! / cheers!
jak se máš?	how are you? (informal)
jak se máte?	how are you? (formal)
mluvíte anglický?	do you speak English?
děkuji	thank you
nashledanou	goodbye (formal)
prosím	please

DINING OUT

restaurace	restaurant
hospoda	pub
já si dám ... / dám si	I would like
káva or kafe	coffee
čaj	tea
pivo	beer
víno	wine
snídaně	breakfast
oběd	lunch
večeře	dinner

zaplatíme	we will pay
zvlášť	separately

SHOPPING

potraviny	grocery shop
supermarket	supermarket
večerka	late-night shop
řeznictví	butcher's shop
drogerie	shop to buy toiletries
léky	pharmaceuticals
elektrické spotřebiče	electrical appliances
obchodní dům	department store
nábytek	furniture
oblečeni	clothes
boty	shoes

TRAVEL AND TRANSPORTATION

autobus	bus
tramuáj	tram
vlak	train
metro	underground train
jízdenka	ticket
auto	car
dálnice	motorway

ACCOMMODATION

pokoj or místnost	room
byt	flat
přízemí	ground floor
pronajmout	to rent

k pronajmu	for rent
zařízený	furnished
nezařízený	unfurnished
elektřina	electricity
plyn	gas
voda	water

RESOURCE GUIDE

GOVERNMENT WEBSITES AND INFORMATION

An official English-language government website, http://www.czech.cz, has comprehensive information for visitors and businesses, with some useful links. Czech centres operate in numerous cities in the United States and Europe, providing business services and organising social events. The website http://www.czechcentres.cz has links to Czech centres in many countries; some specific sites include:

Britain (London) (http://www.czechcentres.cz/london)
France (Paris) (http://www.centretcheque.org)
US (New York) (http://www.czechcenter.com)

Additional Visa Information

You are strongly urged, and often required, to arrange residency and work permits before arriving in the Czech Republic (in some cases this can be done once in the Czech Republic on a tourist or student visa). Arranging long-stay permits in advance can take anywhere from two to six months; be sure to check with the Czech embassy in your country well in advance of departure. If you are relocating with your firm, your firm should handle the details. If you are a student, you will need a student visa, to be obtained before arrival through your school.

The Czech embassies in Canada and the UK seem to provide the most useful general information procedures on their websites; addresses are given below.

Czech Embassy, Canada (http://www.czechembassy.org)
Czech Embassy, UK (http://www.czechembassy.org.uk)
Minister of the Interior (http://www.mvcr.cz).

The Czech Minister of the Interior has much useful information, but in Czech only.

There are also foreign police offices throughout the country. In Prague:

- **Cizinecká policie (Foreign Police)**, Olšanská 3, Prague 3—Žižkov; tel: 974–820–238

EMERGENCY NUMBERS

- **SOS** 112
- **Ambulance** 155
- **Emergency road service** 1230 or 1240
- **Fire** 150
- **Czech state police** 158
- **Prague city police** 156

HEALTH CARE

In addition to English-speaking health care through Prague's main hospital, there are several private health clinics, including some foreign-operated services, in Prague.

- **Nemocnice Na Homolce**, Roentgenova 2, Prague 5–Motol; tel: 257-272-174 or 257-272-146; website: http://www. homolka.cz
  This is Prague's largest hospital, with full services including a special foreigners' division with English-speaking doctors on call 24 hours a day, experienced in all matters of health service including arranging for insurance coverage with your provider at home. This hospital generally has lower prices than the private clinics listed below.
- **The First Medical Clinic of Prague,** Vyšehradská 35, Prague 2–New Town; tel: 601-225-050
  Czech private health clinic with good English-speaking doctors (no foreign insurance policies are accepted).
- **Canadian Medical Centre**, Veleslavínska 1, Prague 6–Veleslavín; tel: 235-360-133 or 724-300-301 after hours. Operated by Canadian doctors and thus charging higher fees, but they do accept international insurance policies.
- **American Medical Centre**, Janovského 48, Prague 7–Holešovice; tel: 220-807-756
  Staffed by American and Czech doctors and nurses, with full medical and dental services; foreign insurance policies accepted but initial payment is steep by local standards.
- **Health Center Prague**, Vodičkova 28, Prague 1–New Town; tel: 224-220-040 or 603-433-833 after-hours; website: http://www.doctor-prague.cz
  Includes service in many languages.

- **American Dental Associates**, V Celnici 4, Prague 1–Old Town; tel: 221-181-121; website: http://www.americandental.cz

INSURANCE

Numerous foreign insurance firms operate in the Czech Republic, in addition to Czech insurers. All offer a broad range of health, life, travel and other forms of insurance.

- **Česká pojišťovna,** offices throughout the country; tel: 267-222-601; website: http://www.cpoj.cz
- **Amcico-AIG Life,** several offices in Prague; tel: 221-033-888; website: http://www.amcico.cz
- **Allianz**; tel: 224-405-111; website: http://www.allianz.cz

Handicapped Information

The Czech Republic is making efforts to accommodate the physically and mentally handicapped, although facilities are still somewhat more limited than they are in much of western Europe.

- **Association of the Physically Handicapped**, Karlínské nam. 12, Prague 8-Libeň; tel: 224-86-976; website: http://www.svaztp.cz
  Comprehensive information on physical and mental handicaps, available in Czech only.
- **Czech Blind United**, Krakovska 21, Prague 1–New Town; tel: 221-462-146; website: http://www.braillnet.cz
- **Czech Association for Mental Health**, Lannova 2, Prague 1–New Town; tel: 224-802-220 or 224-802-328

SETTLING IN
Residential Real Estate Agencies

Dozens of real estate agencies place ads in *The Prague Post*. In addition, I can recommend two agencies, run by former colleagues who have been at it since 1991, and therefore have deep local knowledge and extensive property databases.

- **Prague Realty**, Velehradská 21, Prague 3–Vinohrady; tel: 222-717-249 or 603-422-456; website: http://www.prague-realty.cz

- **Flaks Real Estate Services**; tel: 222-515-898 or 602-283-900; email: flaks.real@login.cz

Moving Companies

- **AGS**; tel: 286-882-160; website: http://www.ags-worldwide-movers.com
- **Allied Pickfords**; tel: 233-090-501; website: http://www.alliedintl.com

Childcare and Maids

There are a number of home help agencies, with English speaking staff.

- **Agentura Domestica**; tel: 257-316-150; website: http://www.domestica.cz
- **Agentura Domov**; tel: 224-216-322; website: http://www.agenturadomov.cz

Laundry

- **Laundryland Praha,** Londýnská 71, Prague 2–Vinohrady; tel: 777-333-466.
  Other locations in the city too.
- **Laundry Kings**, Dejvická 16, Prague 6–Hradčanská; tel: 233-343-743

ONLINE COMMUNITIES

- **http://www.expats.cz**—just what it says, a portal full of information and services for expats living and working in the Czech Republic.
- **http://www.americansinprague.com**—homepage of the American Women's Group in Prague, this is quite an active organisation.
- **http://www.czechinfocenter.com**—web portal for travel and business information.

SOCIAL WORK

- **Czech Catholic Charity**; tel: 296-243-330; website: http://www.charita.cz
- **Salvation Army**; website: http://www.armadaspasy.cz

- **Greenpeace;** tel: 224-320-448; website: http://www.greenpeace.cz
- **Unicef**; tel: 224-915-328; website: http://www.unicef.cz

SCHOOLS

- **International School of Prague**, Nebušická 700, Prague 6–Nebušice; tel: 220-384-111; website: http://www.isp.cz
  Ages 3-18. Housed in a new complex in suburban Prague 6 to accommodate all grade levels, the International School is the most populous school for international children in the country. It operates under the auspices of the US Embassy and follows an American school curriculum.
- **The British International School of Prague**. Located in three separate buildings, one in Prague 4–Kamýk, one in Prague 4–Modřany and one in Prague 6–Bubeneč.
  Tel: 241-431-151; website: http://www.bisp.cz
  Ages 18 months-18 years. British nursery, primary and secondary education.
- **The English College in Prague**, Sokolovská 320, Prague 9–Vysočany; tel: 283-893-113; website: http://www.englishcollege.cz
  Ages 13-19. Located in an eastern suburb (near underground station Vysočanská), the school offers a regular British secondary school curriculum for both Czech and international stuents.
- **Lyçée Français de Prague**, Drtinova 7, Prague 5–Smíchov; tel: 257-317-611; website: http://www.lfp.cz
  The French International School in Prague offers a French curriculum for pupils aged 3-18.
- **Deutsche Schule**, Laudova 29, Prague 6–Řepy; tel: 235-311-725 or 235-312-776; website: http://www.dsp-praha.cz
  German education for all ages situated in a western Prague 6 suburb.
- **Österreichische Schule Prag**, Drtinova 3, Prague 5–Smíchov; tel: 257-322-494; website: http:// www.oesp.cz. Austrian curriculum.

LANGUAGE SCHOOLS

Several language schools in Prague offer Czech lessons.

- **Angličtina Expres**, Kopernikova 2, Prague 2–New Town; tel: 222-513-040; website: http://www.anexpres.cz
- **Berlitz**, Karlovo náměsti 10, Prague 2–New Town; tel: 800-221-221; website: http://www.berlitz.com
- **The Caledonian School**, Národní 11, Prague 1–New Town; tel: 224-237-731; website: http://www.caledonianschool.com
- **The Language House**, Škrétova 8, Prague 2–New Town; tel: 224-231-211; website: http://www.interschool.cz
- **SPUSA (Society of Friends of the USA)**, Na porici 6, Prague 1–New Town; tel: 224-210-813; website: http://www.spusa.cz

BUSINESS SERVICES
Banks and Financial Services

There are many foreign banks and financial services firms in addition to the top Czech banks. We list the biggest Czech banks first, each of which has branches throughout the country, followed by a selection of foreign banks.

- **Česká spořitelná**; tel: 800-207-207; website: http://www.csas.cz
- **ČSOB**; tel: 800-110-808; website: http://www.csob.cz
- **Komerční banka;** tel: 222-432-111; website: http://www.kb.cz
- **Živnostenská banka**; tel: 224-121-111; website: http://www.ziba.cz.
- **American Express**, Václavské námēsti 56, Prague 1—New Town; tel: 222-800-111; website: http://www.americanexpress.cz
- **Bank Austria Creditanstalt**, Revolučni 7, Prague 1–Old Town; tel: 800-100-012; website: http://www.ba-ca.com
- **Citibank** (branches throughout the country); tel: 233-061-111; website: http://www.citibank.cz
- **Deutsche Bank**, Jungmannova 34; tel: 221-292-111; website: http://www.db.com
- **HVB** (branches throughout the country); tel: 221-112-111; website: http://www.hvb.cz
- **Raiffeisenbank** (branches throughout the country); tel: 800-900-900; website: http://www.rb.cz

Taxes

The following all speak English.

- **České daně,** Vinohradská 138, Prague 3–Vinohrady; tel: 272-731-633; website: http://www.ceskedane.cz or http://www.czechtaxes.com
- **Moore Stephens,** Národní 28, Prague 1–New Town; tel: 221-105-282; website: http://www.moorestephens.cz
- **SP Audit,** Korytná 3, Prague 10–Strašnice; tel: 274-815-159; website: http://www.spaudit.cz

Legal

Local firms with English-speaking attorneys:

- **Ürge & Černohlávek,** Jungmannova 31, Prague 1–New Town; tel: 224-494-530; email: office@ur.cer.cz
- **Neštický & Neštická,** Ječná 1, Prague 1–New Town; tel: 224-920-466
- **Wenzel,** Jungmannova 31, Prague 1–New Town; tel: 224-949-494; website: http://www.wenzel.cz

Business Organisations

Many embassies have commercial departments called *obchodní oddělení* listed in the Yellow Pages. In addition, the American Chamber of Commerce and the British Chamber of Commerce maintain active business and social calendars.

- **American Chamber of Commerce,** Dušní 10, Prague 1–New Town; tel: 222-329-430; website: http://www.amcham.cz
- **British Chamber of Commerce,** Pobřežní 3, Prague 8–Libeň; tel: 224-835-161; website: http://www.britishchamber.cz

Translation Agencies

- **Skřivánek Translation Agency;** tel: 241-430-022; website: http://www.skrivanek.cz. Offices throughout the country.

COMMUNICATIONS
Domestic and International Dialing

Czech telephones now all use nine-digit numbers; you simply dial the full nine digits wherever you are in the country. The

Czech country code is 420. When calling a Czech telephone number from North America, dial 011 420, then the nine-digit number. When calling a Czech telephone number from within Europe, dial 00 420, then the nine-digit number. When dialing from the Czech Republic to any other country, dial 00 then the country code, city code and number.
Directory Information, Czech Republic: 1180; International: 1181

Mobile Phone Services

Mobile phone service is quite sophisticated and easy to arrange. The three operators are:

- **Eurotel**; tel: 267-016-701; website: http://www.eurotel.cz
- **T-Mobile**; tel: 603-604-604; website: http://www.t-mobile.cz
- **Oskar**; tel: 800-777-777; website: http://www.oskar.cz

Internet Access Providers

- **Český Telecom;** tel: 840-114-114; website: http://www.telecom.cz
  Provides ISP and DSL services, with information in English on the company's website.
- **Česká Radiokomunikace**; tel: 800-400-200; website: http://www.cra.cz
  Provides ISP and DSL services, the latter branded under the name Bluetone, with information in English on the company's website.
- **Tiscali;** tel: 971-100-811; website: http://www.tiscali.cz
- **Contactel;** tel: 255-755-111; website: http://www.contactel.cz

Cable Providers

- **UPC;** tel: 241-005-100 (Prague)/844-111-112 (outside Prague); website: http://www.upc.cz

Bus and Train Information

Nationwide bus and rail schedule and ticketing information in English is available at:
Tel: 221-111-122; website: http:// www.idos.cz

- **Prague City Transport (MHD)** also provides information in English; tel: 222-623-777; website: http://www.dp-praha.cz

- **Prague Ruzyně Airport** central flight arrival and departure information. Tel: 220-113-321

Prague Taxis

There are at least a couple of reputable agencies in Prague which provide door-to-door service, and speak English:
- **AAA Radiotaxi**—Tel: 14-014
- **ProfiTaxi**—Tel: 261-314-151

ENTERTAINMENT AND LEISURE (PRAGUE)
Budget Hotels

Prague has finally worked through its hotel shortage and in fact now offers a broad range of pensions, B&Bs and hotels. Some have en-suite kitchen facilities, so they are good for arrivals while you're looking for longer term accommodation, or for friends or relatives staying in town. Prices at the places below are in the range of 1,200-2,500 Kč (US$50-100) per double room.
- **Cloister Inn,** Konviktská 14, Prague 1 –Old Town; tel: 224-211-020; website: http://www.cloister-inn.com
  Simple, clean, quiet, and very central.
- **Dům U velké boty,** Vlašská 30, Prague 1 –Malá Strana; tel: 257-533-234 or 257-311-107
  Beautifully situated, well-appointed and well-run B&B.
- **FlatHotel Sibelius,** Jana Masaryka 39, Prague 2 –Vinohrady; tel: 222-521-700; website: http://www.oktours.cz/sibelius
  Comfortable hotel with kitchen facilities in most rooms.
- **FlatHotel Orion,** Americká 9, Prague 2 –Vinohrady; tel: 222-521-706
  Similar to Sibelius (run by the same management), with en-suite kitchens.
- **Pension City,** Belgická 10, Prague 2 –Vinohrady; tel: 222-521-606; website: http://www.hotelcity.cz
  Another pleasant B&B; some rooms also come with small cooking area.

Restaurants

- **Kolkovna** V kolkovně 8, Prague 1 –Old Town; tel: 224-819-701
  Excellent and inexpensive Czech pub, a Pilsner Urquell-themed 1920s throwback.

- **Pivovarský dům**, Lípová 15, Prague 2–New Town; tel 296-216-666
  Fabulous Czech microbrewery with decent food.
- **U sádlů** Klimentská 2, Prague 1–New Town; tel: 224-813-874
  Grilled meats in a purposefully over-the-top gothic cellar.
- **Pálffy palác,** Valdštejnská 14, Prague 1–Malá Strana; tel: 257-530-522
  Elegant setting within the Prague Conservatory; continental cuisine at continental prices.
- **Nebozízek,** Petřínské sady, Prague 1–Malá Strana; tel: 257-515-329
  Located on Petřín hill, at the midpoint stop on the funicular rail—the views are unbeatable, particularly from the outdoor terrace; Czech/continental cuisine.

Cafés and Teashops

- **Café Slavia**, Národní 1, Prague 1–New Town
  Famous Prague coffee house, favourite haunt of Havel and the theatre crowd under Communism, now with the same glorious river views, though it's somewhat overpriced.
- **Obecní dům,** Náměstí Republiky, Prague 1–New Town
  Marvellous atmosphere in this Art Nouveau masterpiece.
- **Institut Français**, Štěpánská 35, Prague 1–New Town
  Long-standing element in the cultural scene here, with French pastries, newspapers and the library and theatre of the French Institute just steps away.
- **Dobrá čajovna,** Václavské náměstí 14, Prague 1–New Town
  Excellent soothing tea room with a fantastic array of gourmet teas. Other branches in cities around the country as well.
- **Velryba**, Opatovická 24, Prague 1–New Town
  Slightly grungy student hangout, with good, cheap food.

Shopping Districts

- **Na příkopě,** which connects Wenceslas Square with náměstí Republiky, is an upscale central shopping street, with several new mini-shopping centres such as Myslbek, Růže and Slovanské Dům and the large Kotva department store on náměstí Republiky itself.

- **Melantrichova**, a small street connecting Wenceslas Square with Old Town Square, is a prime area for finding crystal shops.
- **Havelský trh**, just off Melantrichova, is a year-round street market with a good little collection of arts and crafts stalls, including lace and wooden puppets, in addition to fresh fruit and vegetables.
- **Shopping Park Prague**, at the western end of underground line B at Zličín in Prague 5–Zličín, is a new shopping centre with an IKEA furniture shop.
- **Centrum Černý Most**, at the eastern end of underground line B at Černý Most in Prague 9–Černý Most is a large shopping centre with several western retailers.
- **Anděl**, at the Anděl underground station in Prague 5–Smíchov is a large new shopping centre with an enormous Carrefour department store and supermarket.
- **Vinohradská tržnice**, on Vinohradská street in Prague 2–Vinohrady, is a smaller, boutique shopping complex with good speciality food shops.

Major Concert Halls

- **Rudolfinum**, Alšovo nábřeží 12, Prague 1–Old Town; tel: 224-893-352; website: http://www.rudolfinum.cz
  Houses the grand Dvořákova síň concert hall, home to the Czech Philharmonic, and frequently hosts visiting symphonies and instrumental soloists. Individual tickets plus monthly and yearly schedules are available at the ticket office on the ground floor.
- **Obecní dům (Municipal House),** Náměstí Republiky 5, Prague 1–New Town; tel: 222-002-105; website: http://www.obecni-dum.cz
  A wonderful Art Nouveau building containing Smetanova síň concert hall, home of the Prague Symphony Orchestra. Individual tickets, monthly and yearly schedules are available at the FOK ticket office, housed at the back of the building.

Major Theatres

- **Národní divadlo (National Theatre)**, Národní 2, Prague 1–New Town; tel: 224-913-437; website: http://www. narodni-divadlo.cz

  Built in 1881 only to be immediately burned down and subsequently rebuilt with contributions from private citizens, the National Theatre is an important cultural landmark and a showcase for operas and plays.
- **Stavovské divadlo (Estates Theatre)**, Ovocný trh 1, Prague 1–Old Town; tel: 224-215-001; website: http://www. narodni-divadlo.cz

  Formerly known as Tylovo divadlo, where Mozart conducted the premier of *Don Giovanni*. Lovingly restored in 1991, a gorgeous venue for opera, theatre and ballet.
- **Státní opera (State Opera)**, Wilsonova 4, Prague 1–New Town; tel: 224-227-266; website: http://www.opera.cz

  Prague's third great theatre/opera house, located just between the National Museum and the main train station. It looks a bit out of place with cars whizzing past, but it is a glorious hall inside.

Nightspots

- **Lucerna**, Štepánská 61, Prague 1–New Town; tel: 224-217-108; website: http://www.lucerna.cz

  Large, classy hall for concerts and balls, plus a separate, smaller club for rock and jazz shows.
- **AghaRTA**, Železná 16, Prague 1–Old Town; tel: 222-211-275; website: http://www.agharta.cz. Intimate jazz venue.
- **Reduta**, Národní 20, Prague 1–New Town; tel: 224-912-246; website: http://www.redutajazzclub.cz

  Another popular, slightly larger jazz club.
- **Malostranská Beseda**, Malostranské náměstí 21, Prague 1–Malá Strana; tel: 257-532-092; website: http://www. mb.muzikus.cz

  A variety of shows including folk, jazz and rock.
- **Rock Café**, Národní 20, Prague 1–New Town; tel: 224-914-414.

  Good venue for local rock bands.

- **Palác Akropolis**, Kubelíkova 27, Prague 3–Žižkov; tel: 296-330-911; website: http://www.palacakropolis.cz
  Good-sized club putting on a great mix of bands from hard rock to grunge to world music; the focus is on independent, alternative music.
- **Klub Lávka**, Novotného lávka 1, Prague 1–Old Town; tel: 222-222-156
  Trendy, loud dance club at a great spot on the river.

English-Language Bookshops

- **Big Big Ben Bookshop,** Malá Štupartská 5, Prague 1–Old Town; tel: 224-826-565
  Small but well-stocked.
- **The Globe**, Pštrossova 6, Prague 1–Old Town; tel: 224-934-203; website: http://www.globebookstore.cz
  An expat institution since 1992, with lots of new and used books, a popular café, young crowd and occasional live performances.
- **Kiwi**, Jungmannova 23, Prague 1–New Town; tel: 224-948-455
  Specialises in maps and guidebooks.
- **Knihkupectví U černé Matky Boží**, Celetná 34, Prague 1–Old Town; tel: 224-211-275
  Good collection of books on art, architecture and language.
- **U Knihomola,** Mánesova 79, Prague 2–Vinohrady; tel: 222-729-348
  Upscale, with a good variety of books on art history, architecture, travel, cooking and so on. Also a café with occasional readings and performances.

Foreign Cultural Centres

- **Austrian Cultural Forum;** Jungmannovo náměstí 18, Prague 1–New Town; tel: 224-234-875
- **The British Council**
  Národní 10, Prague 1–New Town; tel: 221-991-111; website: http://www.britishcouncil.cz
  Books, films, current newspapers and magazines as well as lectures.

- **Institut Français,** Štěpánská 35, Prague 1–New Town; tel: 222-401-011
  Excellent cultural centre for anyone with French interests, with a library, gallery, café, theatre, language courses and regular films.
- **Czech-Japanese Association**, Na můstku 8, Prague 1–New Town; tel: 224-216-032
- **Goethe Institute**, Masarykovo nábřeží 32, Prague 1–New Town; tel: 221-962-111
  Centre of German culture, with language courses, a library, films and presentations.
- **Hungarian Cultural Centre**, Rytířská 25, Prague 1–Old Town; tel: 224-222-424
- **Italian Cultural Centre and Library**, Šporkova 14, Prague 1–Malá Strana; tel: 257-533-600
  Regular films and get-togethers.
- **Polish Institute**, Václavské naměstí 49; tel: 224-212-274
  Small, with occasional exhibitions, films and a shop.
- **Scandinavian House**, Zlatnická 10, Prague 1–New Town; tel: 251-019-369; website: http://www.scandinavianhouse.cz
- **US Chamber of Commerce Cultural Center (Americké středisko),** Hybernská 7, Prague 1–New Town; tel: 257-535-194; website: http://www.usembassy.cz
  Very good cultural centre and library under the US Embassy; cultural programmes and occasional exhibitions also on offer.

Libraries
- **Městská knihovna (City Library)**, Mariánské náměstí 1, Prague 1–Old Town; tel: 222-113-111; website: http://www.mlp.cz
  Extensive collection, mostly in Czech.

Physical Fitness Centres
In addition to those listed below, most of the good hotels also have fitness centres which are open to the public
- **YMCA**, Na poříčí 40, Prague 1–New Town; tel: 224-875-811
  Full facilities, including a swimming pool.

- **Plavecký stadión Podolí**, Podolská 74, Prague 4–Podolí
Olympic-size swimming pool, plus outdoor pool open in
the summer.
- **Hotel Axa**, Na poříčí 40, Prague 1–New Town; tel: 224-
812-580.
Swimming pool and weightroom.
- **Hotel Olšanka**, Táboritská 23, Prague 3–Žižkov; tel: 267-
092-233.
Swimming pool, sauna and weights.
- **Esquo Squash Centrum Strahov**, Vaničkova 2b, Prague
6–Strahov; tel: 233-109-301; website: http://www.
squashstrahov.cz
Part of the huge Strahov stadium complex, with lots
of amenities including pool, fitness centre and those
squash courts.

Museums and Galleries

- **Pražský hrad (Prague Castle)**, Prague 1–Hradčany;
website: http://www.hrad.cz
This is the castle itself; admission to the nave of St Vitus
Cathedral is free, but a ticket gets you into the rest of the
cathedral plus other buildings such as the Royal Palace.
- **Jiřský klášter (St George's Monastery)**, Jiřský náměstí,
Prague 1–Hradčany; website: http://www.ngprague.cz
Czech Renaissance and Baroque painting and sculpture,
located within the Prague Castle complex in a mysterious
gothic monastery.
- **Šternberský palác**, Hradčanské náměstí, Prague 1–
Hradčany; website: http://www.ngprague.cz
Just in front of Prague castle, a fine collection of European
art from the 14th to 18th centuries in a grand palace.
- **Židovské muzeum (Jewish Museum)**, Prague 1–Josefov;
website: http://www.jewishmuseum.cz
Most sites in the Jewish Quarter, including the Old-New
Synagogue, Pinkas Synagogue, Spanish Synagogue and
Jewish Cemetery, are run by the Jewish Museum; tickets
cover all sites.

- **Anežský klášter (Convent of St Agnes),** Anenská 1, Prague 1–Old Town; website: http://www.ngprague.cz
  Czech medieval and Renaissance art in a sublime restored medieval convent.
- **Veletržní palác (Trade Fair Palace),** Dukelských hrdinů 47, Prague 7–Holešovice; website: http://www.ngprague.cz
  Excellent gallery of European 19th and 20th century art, including some seminal Czech works.
- **Národní technické muzeum (National Technical Museum),** Kostelní 42, Prague 7–Letná; website: http://www.ntm.cz
  Fun collection of exhibits chronicling Czech technological innovation, from Kepler's astrological gadgets to motorcycles and warplanes from the interwar period.
- **Vyšehrad,** Soběslavova 1, Prague 2–Vyšehrad; website: http://www.praha-vysehrad.cz
  Includes a church and the national cemetery in which virtually all famous Czech cultural figures are buried, plus great views across the river to Hradčany in the distance.

Dance

Ballroom dancing is a popular winter activity. Check listings in *The Prague Post* or *Kultura v Praze*. To polish up on your waltz and polka, or for other classes in ballet, jazz dance and more, try the classes offered at **Dance Perfect**, Národní 25, Prague 1–New Town; tel: 221 085 260.

Alternative Lifestyles

Amigo and *Promluv* are bi-monthly gay/lesbian magazines.

- **A Club**, Miličova 32, Prague 3–Žižkov; tel: 222-781-623.
  Small but popular lesbian bar.
- **Gejzeer**, Vinohradská 40, Prague 2–Vinohrady; tel: 222-516-036; website: http://www.gejzeer.cz
  Prague's largest gay bar and club.

RELIGION

Check *The Prague Post* classifieds section, which has comprehensive listings of religious events and services in English. A selection of religious organisations is below.

- **Church of St Thomas (Roman Catholic)**, Josefská 8, Prague 1–Old Town; tel: 257-532-675
- **Cathedral of SS Cyril and Methodius (Orthodox)**, Resslova 9, Prague 2–New Town; tel: 224-920-686
- **International Baptist Church (Baptist)**, Vinohradská 68, Prague 3–Vinohrady; tel: 604-634-677
- **Šárka Valley Community Church (Baptist)**, Nad Habrovkou 3, Prague 6; tel: 296-392-311; website: http://www.svcc.cz
- **St Clement's Church (Anglican)**, Klimentská 5, Prague 1–Old Town; tel: 284-688-575
- **Old-New Synagogue (Jewish)**, Maiselova, Prague 1–Old Town; website: http://www.bejt-praha.cz
- **Islamic Centre in Prague (Islam)**, Blatská 1491, Prague 9; tel: 281-918-876; website: http://www.islamcz.cz
- **Bahai Center (Bahai)**, Lucemburská 33, Prague 3–Vinohrady; tel: 222-713-496; website: http://www.bahai.org

TOURIST SERVICES

- **Prague Information Services**, Na příkopě 20, Prague 1; tel: 12-444; website: http:// www.pis.cz
  General travel information on Prague and environs.
- **Velvet Voyages**; tel: 233-373-376;
  email: velvetvoyages@chello.cz
  Individual and package bookings and tours in the Czech Republic.
- **OK Tours**, Jana Masaryka 39, Prague 2–Vinohrady; tel: 222-521-700; website: http://www.oktours.cz
  Individual and group tours and programmes in the Czech Republic and throughout central Europe.
- **GTS**, Ve smečkách 33, Prague 1–New Town; tel: 257-187-100. Student trips and cheap air tickets.

FURTHER READING

BOOKS AND PERIODICALS IN ENGLISH
Newspapers and Magazines

The Prague Post—complete newspaper published every Wednesday

The Fleet Sheet (website: http://www.fleet.cz)—concise newsletter rundown of the day's breaking news

The Prague Tribune—business and cultural news magazine

Czech Business Weekly—weekly business news magazine

The Lands of the Czech Crown—a colourful and interesting bi-monthly magazine full of history and culture

Literature
Czech legends and fairy tales make for great light reading.

Prague Tales. Jan Neruda. London: Chatto and Winders, 1993.
- Tales of life in Prague's Malá Strana quarter in the 19th century, funny and intimate.

Old Czech Legends. Alois Jirásek. London: Forest Books (UNESCO), 1992.
- Finally available in English, the very best collection of Czech myths, fairy tales and half-truths, written by one of the giants of Czech 19th century literature.

Czech Fairy Tales. Prague: Vitalis, 2003.
- Contains well-loved fairy tales by Czech romantics Božena Němcová and Petr Erben.

Czech literature, particularly that of the 20th century, is perhaps the most incisive commentary on life here during this tumultuous era.

The Good Soldier Schweik. Jaroslav Hašek. London: Penguin Books, 1973.

- Perhaps the most renowed work in Czech literature, both at home and abroad. Švejk (often written as Schweik in German and English) is the stereotypical non-conformist, beer-guzzling Czech, a reluctant soldier serving the Austro-Hungarian Empire. His rebellious adventures are shamelessly silly, while the underlying theme is a pointed analysis of Czech society.

Toward the Radical Centre. Karel Čapek. Highland Park. NJ: Catbird Press, 1990.

- Čapek is one of the country's most prominent writers of the early 20th century. Written in a semi-absurdist, futuristic style, this is a 'humorous and searching' insight into the root of human mysteries and contradictions. Also, *The War of the Newts*. Highland Park. NJ: Catbird Press, 1990.

The Dimension of the Present and Other Essays. Miroslav Holub. London: Faber and Faber, 1990.

- This renowned biologist/poet uses animal behaviour as his basis for a subtle criticism of government and society, as both a sociobiological theory and an allegory of survival under an oppressive regime. Also: *Poems Before and After*, Newcastle: Bloodaxe Books. 1990—uses myth to enrich his politically charged commentary on life in the 1950s and 1960s ('before' the Prague Spring uprising), and the 1970s and 1980s ('after' the failed revolution).

The Little Town Where Time Stood Still. Bohumil Hrabal. London: Abacus 1993.

- Hrabal is another of the country's great writers, one who, like Václav Havel, stayed put and managed to get his politically conscious stories published. All his stories are subtle criticisms of political and social trends, the central characters of which search for far-reaching meaning in an isolated environment. Yet the mood is always light.

Also: *Closely Observed Trains*. London: Abacus 1990;
I Served the King of England, London: Chatto & Windus,
1989; and *Too Loud a Solitude*. London: Harcourt, 1992.

The Spirit of Prague. Ivan Klíma. London: Granta Books,
1993.

- Collection of essays by this nationally acclaimed writer/
  journalist on events in Prague, dealing with critical events
  in each decade of his professional life: the 1940s and the
  Nazis, the1950s and Stalin, the 1960s and the Prague
  Spring, the 1970s and Charter 77, the 1980s and the Velvet
  Revolution. Other works by Klíma touching similarly on
  life under Communism include *Love and Garbage*. London:
  Penguin, 1991; *My Golden Trades*. London: Penguin, 1992;
  and *Judge on Trial* London: Vintage Books, 1992.

The Unbearable Lightness of Being. Milan Kundera. London:
Faber and Faber, 1984.

- Probably the Czech Republic's most internationally well-
  known novelist who consistently uses sex as a theme in his
  works. This is his best-known work, a probing, intimately
  personal look into human emotions and deed, revealing
  a cry for freedom in a socially oppressive environment
  (the book backflap here says it best: 'Milan Kundera poses
  serious questions with a blasphemous lightness which
  makes us understand that the modern world has taken
  away our right to tragedy'). Also (from the same publisher):
  Life is Elsewhere, 1986; *The Book of Laughter and Forgetting*,
  1982; *Immortality*, 1991; and *The Farewell Party*, 1976.

Darkness Casts No Shadow. Arnošt Lustig. London: Quartet
Books, 1976 and 1989.

- Harrowing account of life in Prague and in the concentration
  camp at Terezín (Theresienstadt) by this Czech Jew who
  survived the ordeal. Luštig made it to the US, where he has
  written and taught for many years; his other celebrated
  works include *Diamonds of the Night* and *Night and Hope*,
  both of which are similar to *Darkness Casts No Shadow* in
  their dark narrative.

The Engineer of Human Souls. Josef Škvorecký. London: Vintage Books, 1994.

- Škvorecký is one of the most important living Czech writers; he immigrated to Canada during the 1968 upheavals. This and several other of his works was banned in Czechoslovakia. As the subtitle explains, 'an entertainment on the old themes of life, women, fate, dreams, the working class, secret agents, love and death'; perhaps the most poignant depiction of life in Czechoslovakia under successive Nazi and Communist governments. The style is somehow so typically Czech: full of darkness and suffering, yet told in a blackly comical manner. Particularly recommended. Also: *The Republic of Whores*. London: Faber and Faber, 1994; *The Miracle Game*. London: Faber and Faber, 1991.

General History

Charles IV, the King from the Golden Cradle. Eduard Petiška. Prague: Martin Press, 1994.

- Full chronicle of King Charles IV and the Bohemian 'Golden Age' of the mid-1300s, written by an eminent Czech historian. Literary and readable. Also: *A Treasury of Tales from the Kingdom of Bohemia*, 1994—great book full of Czech lore, from Libuše to the Přemysls, plus lots of little-knowns.

History of Czechoslovakia in Outline. J.V. Polišenský, Prague: Bohemia International, 1991.

- Reprint of professor Polišenský's excellent 1947 overview of the history of Czechoslovakia. Perhaps the best introduction to the subject, very readable and not too academic, though it leaves off at a critical point, just before the Communist takeover.

The Price of Freedom: A History of Eastern and Central Europe from the Middle Ages to the Present. Piotr A. Wandycz. Toronto: Routledge, 2001.

- The title captures it: a sweeping political history of the region, placing Czech history in a broader context.

Contemporary History

We the People: the Revolutions in 1989 Witnessed in Warsaw, Budapest, Berlin, and Prague. Timothy Garton Ash. London: Granta Books, 1990.

- An eyewitness account of the revolutions in Eastern Europe by an acclaimed British journalist.

So Many Heros. Alan Levy. Sagaponack, NY: Second Chance Press, 1980.

- An update and reprint of the 1972 book *Rowboat to Prague,* a history of the 1968 Prague Spring witnessed by this noted journalist, who was subsequently expelled from the country. Levy returned to Prague in 1990 and served as Editor-in-Chief of The Prague Post newspaper until his passing away in 2004.

Prague, in the Shadow of the Swastika. Callum McDonald and Jan Kaplan. Prague: Melantrich Press, 1995.

- Detailed history of the Nazi occupation of Prague, including the five-day Prague Uprising that marked the end of the Third Reich.

The Walls Came Tumbling Down: The Collapse of Communism in Eastern Europe. Gale Stokes. Oxford: Oxford University Press, 1993.

- Textbook-like chronicle of all the political unrest in Eastern Europe from the 1968 Prague Spring, through the emergence of Charter 77, the 1989 Velvet Revolution, and the 1990-1991 turbulence in Russia.

Social History and Commentary

The Origins of Backwardness in Eastern Europe. Daniel Chirot ed. Berkeley: University of California Press, 1989.

- A poorly-timed release (just before the revolutions throughout the region) which nevertheless probes deeply into the history of political, social and even geographical problems in Russia, the Baltics,

Poland, Czechoslovakia, Hungary and the Balkans. It's quite incisive into why these nations have, for the better part of their histories, suffered foreign domination and internal chaos.

The Gypsies of Eastern Europe. David Crowe and Kolsti Kohn. eds. New York: M.E. Sharpe, Inc. 1991.
- Traces the history of migration of the Romany people, commonly referred to as Gypsies, through eastern Europe, and deals with their culture and the prejudices they encounter virtually everywhere they go.

How We Survived Communism and Even Laughed. Slavenka Drakulič. London: Vintage Books, 1987.
- Touching and revealing description of life under Communism in the former Yugoslavia, the themes of which apply equally to the Czech lands.

Disturbing the Peace. Václav Havel. London: Faber and Faber, 1990.
- President Havel is a renowned philosopher, essayist and playwright, with a keen perception of the evils of political oppression and the position of human morality. This book looks back, with Havel's admirable lack of bitterness, on the events of his life from 1968 to 1989; it is a testament to his method and ideology.

Living in Truth. Václav Havel. London: Faber and Faber, 1986
- A collection of deeply philosophical essays which explicate one of his key concerns: living a conscious and 'truthful' life. Includes his famous open letter to Gustav Husák, for which he was sent to political prison.

Toward a Civil Society. Václav Havel. Prague: Lidové Noviny Publishing House, 1995
- Selection of the president's political speeches.

Open Letters. Václav Havel. London: Faber and Faber, 1991
- Open letters to the Communist government, prose and reflections from 1968-1990. A good complement to *Disturbing the Peace.*

Letters to Olga. Václav Havel. London: Faber and Faber, 1988, 1990, 1991
- Havel's prison conrrespondence with his late wife Olga, revealing not only his repressed political temperament, but also a touch of his personality.

Selected Plays. Václav Havel. London: Faber and Faber, 1992
- Plays, many of which are absurdist, from 1963-1989.

Iron Curtain Rising. Peter Lanfer. San Francisco: Mercury House, 1991.
- An account that goes beyond the politics to examine the social and cultural trends in Eastern Europe. Examining how these differ between the former east and west European nations, the author provides timely insight on the future of this region; his notes on the former Yugoslavia have proven accurate.

The Meaning of Czech History. Tomáš Garrigue Masaryk. Chapel Hill: University of North Carolina Press, 1974.
- Social analysis by the creator and first president of the Czechoslovak republic.

Revolutions in Eastern Europe: The Religious Roots. Niels Nielsen. Maryknoll, NY: Orbis Books, 1991.
- Traces the cultural, especially religious, roots, that spurned the former Soviet East Bloc to revolt.

Questions of Identity: Czech and Slovak Ideas of Nationality and Personality. Robert B. Pynsent. London: Central European University Press, 1994.
- Character study of Czechs and Slovaks.

The Czech Americans. Stephanie Sakson-Ford. New York: Chelsea House Publishers, 1989.
- Well-researched book, one of dozens in this series, tracing the origins and development of Czech society in the US. Full of great old photos.

Economics and Business
Embedded Politics: Industrial Networks and Institutional Change in Postcommunism. Gerald A. McDermott. Ann Arbor: University of Michigan Press, 2003.
- Delves into the complex political-economic relationships of the Communist era and the changes since.

Managing Radical Organizational Change. Karen L. Newman and Stanley D. Nollen.
- Thousand Oaks: Sage Publications, 1998. Studies the changing organisational dynamics of Czech corporations in the 1990s, with case studies of the successes and failures of six Czech companies.

Art, Architecture, and Culture
A Guide to Czech and Slovak Glass. Diane E. Foulds. Prague: European Community Imports, Ltd., 1993.
- The complete story of glass and crystal manufacturing in the Czech and Slovak Republics, encompassing thorough explanations of what glass and crystal are and how they are made, the illustrations history of their production, and a shopping and shipping guide to all major glass-making towns and institutions.

Czechoslovakia. Erhard Gorys. London: Pallas Athene, 1991.
- Amazing in-depth study of the architectural history of the entire country—the very best guide to every castle, chateau, church, cathedral, tower and wall of interest in the country.

The Czech Republic: Music in the Web of Life. Jana Marhounová. Prague: Empatie Publishers, 1993.
- Encompasses Czech music and its role in society, based on interviews with prominent Czech musicians, including pianist Rudolf Firkušný and composer Petr Eben.

Prague: Eleven Centuries of Architecture, a Historical Guide Jaroslava Staňková; Jiří Štursa; and Svatopluk Voděra. Prague: PAV Publishers, 1992.
- The single best guide to every building of any architectural interest in Prague, including many that are no longer standing. A fascinating, thorough study.

Prague and Art Nouveau. Marie Vitochová; Jindřich Kejr; and Jíří Všetacka. Prague: V ráji Publishing House, 1995.
- Beautifully photographed guide to the Art-nouveau style in Prague.

Best Czech Recipes. Harald Salfellner. Prague: Vitalis, 2003
- Recipes for all those variations of pork, cabbage and dumplings.

Travel
The Rough Guide: Czech and Slovak Republics. London: Rough Guides. 2005.

Lonely Planet: Czech and Slovak Republics. Melbourne: Lonely Planet Publications, 2003.

Cadogan Guides: Prague, London: Cadogan Guides. 2002.

ABOUT THE AUTHOR

Tim Nollen hails from Washington, DC. After earning a degree in philosophy from Georgetown University, he moved to Prague in 1992, and spent the first two years there following the common English-teaching route, meanwhile pursuing his musical interests by studying at both the Prague Conservatory (piano) and at Charles University (musicology). He then worked at a Czech-American real estate firm for several years where he learnt some of the intricacies of cross-cultural communication through balancing the demands of an international clientele with the internal logic of the Czech market. At the same time he became a regular contributor to *The Prague Post* travel section, and worked on numerous travel guidebooks.

Tim has written extensively on destinations in Europe, particularly central and eastern Europe, for publications such as *The Rough Guide, Lonely Planet*, and *Thomas Cook*. His works on the Czech Republic alone have appeared in several books and articles, and he has also contributed to publications on places from Spain to Lithuania to West Virginia.

Fully embracing the odd twists to his career path, Tim returned to Georgetown for an MBA degree. He subsequently entered the world of finance as a research analyst, where he intends to stay put. He currently lives in New York, but maintains strong ties to the Czech Republic and visits frequently. He still aims to settle down one day in a wood-frame cottage somewhere in Bohemia.

INDEX

Titles in the CULTURESHOCK! series:

Argentina	Hong Kong	Paris
Australia	Hungary	Philippines
Austria	India	Portugal
Bahrain	Indonesia	San Francisco
Barcelona	Iran	Saudi Arabia
Beijing	Ireland	Scotland
Belgium	Israel	Sri Lanka
Bolivia	Italy	Shanghai
Borneo	Jakarta	Singapore
Brazil	Japan	South Africa
Britain	Korea	Spain
Cambodia	Laos	Sweden
Canada	London	Switzerland
Chicago	Malaysia	Syria
Chile	Mauritius	Taiwan
China	Mexico	Thailand
Costa Rica	Morocco	Tokyo
Cuba	Moscow	Turkey
Czech Republic	Munich	Ukraine
Denmark	Myanmar	United Arab
Ecuador	Nepal	Emirates
Egypt	Netherlands	USA
Finland	New York	Vancouver
France	New Zealand	Venezuela
Germany	Norway	Vietnam
Greece	Pakistan	

For more information about any of these titles, please contact any of our Marshall Cavendish offices around the world (listed on page ii) or visit our website at:

www.marshallcavendish.com/genref